The Delta Queen *Cookbook*

The *Delta Queen* with American flags (From the collection of The Public Library of Cincinnati and Hamilton County)

Cynthia LeJeune Nobles

The Delta Queen Cookbook

THE HISTORY AND RECIPES OF THE LEGENDARY STEAMBOAT

LOUISIANA STATE UNIVERSITY PRESS ❖ BATON ROUGE

Published by Louisiana State University Press
Copyright © 2012 by Louisiana State University Press
All rights reserved
Manufactured in Canada
First printing

Designer: Barbara Neely Bourgoyne
Typefaces: Arno Pro and Myriad Pro, display; Whitman, text
Printer and binder: Friesens Corporation

Unless otherwise noted, all photographs are by the author.

"Filé Gumbo, Red Beans and Rice" @1995 Pay The Band Music
Music & Lyrics by Rich Campbell
All rights reserved. Used by permission.
(recorded by Cadillac Moon on *Plug Me In*, SNV Records)

Recipes for Banana Pudding, Meringue, Southern Praline Pecan Pie, Sweet Potato Pie, and Unbaked Pie
Crusts (9-inch) were first published in *The Soul of Southern Cooking* (Jackson: University Press of Mississippi,
1989), by Kathy Starr, and are reproduced by permission of the University Press of Mississippi.

Library of Congress Cataloging-in-Publication Data
Nobles, Cynthia LeJeune, 1954–
  The Delta Queen cookbook : the history and recipes of the legendary steamboat / Cynthia LeJeune Nobles.
     p. cm.
  Includes bibliographical references and indexes.
  ISBN 978-0-8071-4537-1 (pbk. : alk. paper) — ISBN 978-0-8071-4538-8 (pdf) — ISBN 978-0-8071-4539-5
(epub) — ISBN 978-0-8071-4540-1 (mobi)
  1. Cooking, American—Southern style. 2. Cooking—Mississippi River Region. 3. Delta Queen
(Steamboat) I. Title.
  TX715.2.S68N63 2012
  641.5975—dc23
                                                                                                2011051512

The paper in this book meets the guidelines for permanence and durability of the Committee on Production
Guidelines for Book Longevity of the Council on Library Resources. ∞

For Howard

Special Thanks to Terry G. Newkirk, CEC, AAC

Red Beans and Rice, recipe on page 99

Filé Gumbo,
Red Beans and Rice

Music and lyrics by Rich Campbell;
recorded by Cadillac Moon

Down in New Orleans you can go for a ride
Up the Mississippi, muddy and wide
Big red paddle wheel will cruise you along
Louisiana cookin' will never steer you wrong

 Delta Queen shines in the moonlight
 Creole chef cure your appetite, serve up

 Filé Gumbo, Red Beans and Rice
 Blackened redfish, crawfish so nice
 Jambalaya, fill your plate twice
 Filé Gumbo, Red Beans and Rice

Creole maids keep the boys blood pumpin'
Steamboat pilots got the ladies' hearts thumpin'
The band kicks in, and then there ain't no excuse
Your hips start shakin' and your limbs all come loose

 Delta Queen shines in the moonlight
 Creole chef cure your appetite, serve up

 Filé Gumbo, Red Beans and Rice
 Blackened redfish, crawfish so nice
 Jambalaya, fill your plate twice
 Filé Gumbo, Red Beans and Rice

Under the Hill at Natchez you'll be throwin' down
Laughing and singing, good times all around
There ain't no party like it from Miami to Nome
You'll promise yourself you're never going home

 Delta Queen shines in the moonlight
 Creole chef cure your appetite, serve up

 Filé Gumbo, Red Beans and Rice
 Blackened redfish, crawfish so nice
 Jambalaya, fill your plate twice
 Filé Gumbo, Red Beans and Rice

Buttermilk Pancakes, recipe on page 51

Contents

Oyster Po-Boy, recipe on page 96

Foreword

WHAT KIND OF FOOD was served to steamboat passengers? Where was it prepared, and how was it cooked? Were the meals as glamorous as legend claims?

Cynthia Nobles answers these questions by drawing on her research about the history, cuisine, and recipes of the best-known American overnight boat of the twentieth century, the iconic *Delta Queen*.

In the formative years of steamboat passenger service on the Mississippi River (the 1820s through 1830s), the boats were still primitive affairs that served as floating dormitories with limited amenities and communal toilets. The galleys (or cookhouses, as they were called then) were cramped and often in dank, unlighted hulls. The fare was basic and generally poor, on a par with meals served at the typical boardinghouse of the time. And it is said that passengers sometimes had to help provision their boat by hunting along the riverbanks.

A British traveler named Mrs. Frances Trollope details the table etiquette (or lack of it) found on steamboats of this period in her *Domestic Manners of the Americans* (1832): "The total want of all the usual courtesies of the table, the voracious rapidity with which the viands were seized and devoured; . . . the frightful manner of feeding with their knives, till the whole blade seemed to enter the mouth; and the still more frightful manner of cleaning the teeth afterward with a pocket knife . . . the dinner hour was to be any thing rather than an hour of enjoyment."

Food service had changed dramatically by the mid-1800s when steamboat captains, who were often the boats' owners, got the message that "groaning boards," gargantuan buffets, attracted passengers. By the time grand meals were the trend, boats were larger and faster, and they featured private rooms and dining tables—no more communal table. The increased space on the boats allowed for chickens, cows, and pigs to be carried on board and butchered in spaces unseen by passengers. (The last butcher shop on an inland riverboat was carried on the *Delta Queen* until 1968, as was the last bakery.)

It was difficult to keep fruits and vegetables fresh on nineteenth-century steamboats, so those needs were met by purchasing fresh produce at freight and passenger stops at towns, farms, and plantations. The *Delta Queen* continued this practice through 1968, and bought melons, fruit, and vegetables at U.S. government locks, where lock personnel often maintained on-site gardens.

This abundant dining was a companion to overall sumptuous accommodations. In 1883, in his immortal *Life on the Mississippi*, Mark Twain wrote, "The steamboats were finer than anything on shore. Compared with superior dwelling-houses and first-class hotels in the [Mississippi] Valley, they were indubitably magnificent, they were palaces."

It was my good fortune to work on board the *Delta Queen* when she was still operated by the Greene family. Until the late 1960s, these icons of Cincinnati steamboating were well known for keeping their old retainers on board as long as possible. I was also lucky to work with outstanding cooks such as George Peters and Charley Clay, the latter a veteran of the famous Lee Line out of Memphis, as well as waiters Claude Fry, Mack David, and Mose Englin, who hailed from the *Tom Greene, Chris Greene,* and *Queen City.* I could not hear enough about their adventures, and I could not eat enough of their good food.

Serving variously as mate, pilot, and master, I was from 1965 to 1968 general manager under the tutelage of Letha C. Greene, president of Greene Line Steamers, and all the while doubling in brass as co-captain of their only boat, the *Delta Queen.* After I retired from the New Orleans excursion steamer *Natchez* in 1991, my wanderlust sent me back upriver to pilot or command the *Delta Queen* and her progeny, *Mississippi Queen* and *American Queen.*

In these pages, Cynthia Nobles has thoroughly captured the gastronomic essence of the legendary *Delta Queen* when the boat was both the grand old lady and the best-known vessel on the Mississippi River and its tributaries. Nobles's research is, to me, quite amazing, even going back to the *Delta Queen*'s U.S. Navy service in San Francisco harbor during World War II. All this brought back memories, some of which made me realize that a chance to repeat my life's work would be welcomed with no hesitation and few changes.

CAPTAIN CLARKE C. "DOC" HAWLEY
New Orleans, 2009

The Delta Queen *Cookbook*

Introduction

FOR MOST YEARS from 1927 through 2008, the fabled stern-wheel steamboat *Delta Queen* paddled up and down America's inland waters as a luxury hotel that delighted passengers with unparalleled views, snug accommodations, rousing entertainment, and hearty, down-home food. The *Queen's* historical enchantment—it was, after all, the world's longest-running authentic overnight wooden steamer—was the main draw. But most passengers also looked forward to sitting down to whatever was cooking in the galley (or cookhouse, as the kitchen was called on early riverboats). And whether it was fried chicken, creole gumbo, simple pancakes, or a complex crawfish *en croûte*, the *Delta Queen's* food almost always received high marks. Sometimes, of course, experiments with food trends fell flat, and the magic of sailing on a legend made the occasional tough cut of beef seem tender. But many dishes were stellar and could have easily stood up to what was served on the swankiest ocean liners.

The most remarkable thing about the *Delta Queen's* food, however, is that it was served over the span of eighty-two years. This record of longevity would be amazing even for land-based restaurants. Instead, it was accomplished in a moving galley that was stiflingly small, and one that did not have access to needed ingredients at a moment's notice. As with steamboats of old, it was not uncommon for a *Delta Queen* cook to slip ashore and try to find needed supplies. But in spite of this logistical challenge, the Orleans Room, the boat's only dining room, served meals promptly. Soups were hot and salads were well chilled. Linens were starched, servers were in uniform, and after the advent of the computer, most meals were accompanied by printed menus.

On each trip, menus changed daily, and deciding what went on them involved input from many sources. The overall vision of what was served was always molded by the paddleboat's owner. From the sophisticated California Transportation Company to the unyielding U.S. Navy, and from the folksy Greene family to the string of trendy corporations that followed, the home office always set the template for the food's style. Galley details and actual menu creation fell on the shoulders of chief stewards in the early years, and later these duties went to corporate or executive chefs.

Another huge influence on the *Delta Queen's* food story was her passengers, with an extraordinary number of them repeaters. While other inland riverboats have average repeats between 25 and 30 percent, at times the *Delta Queen* enjoyed an astonishing 70 percent in returning passengers. This rate sometimes reached 100 percent, with many who had taken twenty-five, fifty, or even more than one hundred trips. A typical passenger list would include the occasional honeymooners, middle-aged professionals, and families with children. But the overwhelming majority belonged in a category that Letha C. Greene, a former owner of the boat and author of *Long Live the Delta Queen* (1973), describes as mostly "past the halfway mark of life or even into advanced age." Surprisingly, most of this "well-seasoned" group hailed from the West Coast, Florida, and the Northeast, not from towns along the Mississippi River. Not surprisingly, they expected top-notch service and food. They certainly could afford it, and they were not shy about letting a waiter, chef, or maître d' know if the galley had failed.

The boat, like the cookhouse, was small—only 285 feet long and 58 feet wide—and held just 174 overnight passengers in 88 staterooms, her size downright minuscule compared with today's mega–cruise ships. But despite her compact size, the *Delta Queen* entertained presidents, movie stars, and jazz-era tycoons. She bobbed along the Pacific and Gulf coasts on a historic trip from Sacramento, California, to New Orleans through the Panama Canal. She then spent the biggest part of her life sailing the Western Rivers System, a water highway made up of the unforgiving Mississippi River and the Ohio and Missouri rivers and their tributaries. Through it all, the *Delta Queen's* cuisine intertwined with the cultures of the ports she visited and the nationwide culinary fads that came and went, this blending of regional foods a throwback to the exciting time when America was clamoring for rides on "fire boats," the first form of mechanical travel.

American passenger steamboats almost always offered food service. But before you have steamboat cuisine, you must first have a steamboat. Early attempts at steamboats date back to at least sixteenth-century Spain, with significant advances made in eighteenth-century France. In the United States, most grade-schoolers learn that the "father of steam navigation" was Robert Fulton. However, the first U.S. patent for a steamboat actually went to Isaac Briggs and William Longstreet of Savannah, Georgia, on February 1, 1788, some nineteen years before the introduction of Fulton's *Clermont.* Also preceding Fulton, Robert John Fitch and James Rumsey had battled it out for yet another U.S. patent for a steamboat (Fitch won it in 1791). Fulton is celebrated because his *Clermont* was the first *commercially successful* passenger steamboat, having made a 150-mile trip with passengers from New York City to Albany, New York, on August 17, 1807.

Fueled by dry pine wood and an engine made in England, the *Clermont* puffed along at five miles per hour (inland rivers use mph, not knots). More than a nifty new way to travel, however, this trip was significant in that it triggered an all-out transportation revolution. Faster transportation meant a faster way to get perishable food from one place to another, and in this respect, the *Clermont* deserves tremendous culinary recognition.

Fortunately, the *Clermont* also left a hint of how its cookhouse managed meals. This circa 1807 newspaper advertisement lays down rules for onboard dining on the boat's Hudson River route:

> All the passengers are to pay at the rate of $1.00 for every twenty miles, and half a dollar for every meal they may take . . . Passengers will breakfast before they come aboard . . . Dinner will be served up exactly at 1 o'clock; tea, with meats, which is also supper, at 8 o'clock in the evening; and breakfast at 9 o'clock in the morning. No one has a claim on the steward for victuals at any other time.

The era of the Mississippi steamboat began when another Fulton-influenced design, the *New Orleans,* left Pittsburgh in the fall of 1811 and smoked its way down the Ohio and Mississippi rivers to its namesake city, arriving in January 1812. The captain on this first Mississippi River steamboat trip was Nicholas Roosevelt, great-granduncle of President Theodore Roosevelt. He was accompanied by his pregnant wife, Lydia; the couple's young daughter, Rose; and their pet Newfoundland, Tiger. Among the crew were a cook, a waiter, and two servants. At a stop in Louisville, Kentucky, Lydia gave birth to a son, Henry. We also know that while in Louisville, the Roosevelts hosted a dinner for new friends aboard the *New Orleans* at tables in the forward cabin. Unfortunately, we do not know what was on that early dinner party menu.

Improvements to those first boats came fast as inventors tackled problems associated with maneuvering both deep and shallow water, on unruly rivers. Sunken trees and boat wrecks, known as snags, were particularly dangerous. Henry Shreve, a Pennsylvania flatboatman, receives the most credit for making the snag problem less hazardous. In 1816, Shreve's *Washington* wowed the steamboat world with its shallow flat bottom and a widened and lengthened deck. The engine sat on a main deck topped by another deck, and everything was crowned with a pilot's cabin—the design closely associated with today's vision of tiered steamboats.

Another huge improvement came in 1816 when the *Chancellor Livingston* started using coal. By 1824, fifteen steamboats were sailing on U.S. inland waters, and it was at this time that America started utilizing this cost-effective way of shipping produce and goods. This new form of transportation offered so much promise that New York governor DeWitt Clinton convinced the public to fund the Erie Canal, an artery that in 1825 became the most important trade route between the American West and Atlantic seaports. The reliability of steamers along this convenient waterway spurred the growth of agriculture in New York and Pennsylvania, a development that drastically lowered food prices, with the cost of staples such as flour dropping by as much as 75 percent.

The first steamer in the American West was the *Beaver*, a side-wheeler that chugged along the Columbia River in 1835. The discovery of gold in 1848 stimulated the use of steamboats in California, with miners and their supplies winding their way up the Sacramento River to goldfields. Like those in California, early Western Rivers System steamers were mostly packets, boats with regular schedules that carried mail, commodities, and passengers. Sharing few of the frills with the likes of the *Delta Queen*, these boats were instrumental in streamlining inland immigration, including the horrific forced resettling of Native American populations.

For westbound settlers, the steamboat meant that scouts did not have to risk ambush by traveling over unfamiliar terrain; now whole families were able to reach their destinations together. But while much safer, a trip on an early steamboat did not guarantee arrival in good health. These early journeys usually involved nights sleeping with livestock on cramped decks. Disease was rampant, fires were a constant threat, and boilers exploded regularly. To accommodate these recurrent tragedies, steamboats carried ample supplies of coffins.

Even with Shreve's improved design, early steamboats had an average life span of just five years. This grim statistic improved when safer tubular boilers were introduced in 1830. In 1840, Isaac Newton (the New York steamboat magnate, not the Sir Isaac of gravity fame) introduced a new fuel, anthracite coal, which cut fuel expenses in half. Newton is also credited with popularizing the "floating palace" when he lengthened two of his boats by sixty feet each—the *Isaac Newton* to 338 feet and the *New World* to a colossal 385 feet. In addition, he constructed double tiers of staterooms, introduced gas-lighted grand saloons, and surrounded the ships with galleries—all of which planted a seed for the change to luxury travel. But even though steamboats were getting more glamorous and did not explode as often, they were still vulnerable to snags. In 1842, engineer James Eads became wealthy after inventing a submersible diving bell that allowed him to safely salvage steamboat accidents.

Around 1849, steamboating was in its heyday, its popularity aided by a surge of settlers attracted to the opening of the Minnesota Territory and vast swaths of untouched farmland. Farther south, cotton was fueling an economic explosion, and plantation owners not only transported their crops aboard steamboats but also bought expensive furniture, imported food, and slaves directly from these floating department stores. During this time, an estimated eleven thousand steamboats clogged America's canals and rivers, and they carried every imaginable commodity as well as families and the stereotypical slicked-down gamblers, banjo players, and ladies of opportunity.

Steamboats were considered the height of luxury travel, but their cookhouses still operated under primitive conditions. Typical passenger boats stopped often "to wood" and to pick up coal for both the boat's boilers and the cook's cast-iron stove. Water for washing and drinking was generally hauled up in buckets directly from rivers, and produce came from farms along rivers and canals. Fresh meat and milk, however, were stored below deck and transported in the form of live cows, hogs, ducks, and turkeys, this menagerie of farm animals assuring that steaks and cream would not spoil in sweltering heat.

Lack of refrigeration was an ongoing problem for nineteenth-century steamboat cooks. This is mildly surprising considering that even before the invention of steamboats, Boston-area ice barons were shipping their product on brigs to customers as far south as Cuba. This "frozen gold," however, was almost exclusively saved for sale to onshore customers. When finally made available for steamboat cookhouse use, mostly after the 1890s, ice was served only to first-class passengers. Meats and produce seldom were put on ice, although dairy products sometimes merited refrigeration. In 1842, John Gorrie created the first crude refrigerator, but his sometimes toxic invention did not catch on in homes, or on steamboats, until the 1930s, when Thomas Midgley introduced Freon.

Even though early steamboats usually had access to fresh food, the quality of meals served to passengers depended on the class of passage. For the upper classes, servants accompanied masters and, later, employers on the upper decks in private staterooms, and they often cooked for them onboard. Another option for the wealthy was the first-class dining room, often called a dining saloon, with its largely African American wait staff and menus with multiple courses. Meals were not included in the price for steerage passengers, customers who slept in small cabins filled top to bottom with berths. Deck passengers, the even lower class, slept and ate alongside the cargo on the main deck. Both of the economically priced classes either paid for food separately or brought their own. Some boats offered stoves to deck passengers, and others even allowed the lower classes to dine with the crew.

In addition to improving transportation, the steamboat must also be recognized for its part in diversifying the way America ate. Before steamboats, the oat farmers of Minnesota knew very little about the grits lovers in Mississippi, and the gumbo eaters in Louisiana were the stuff of myth. That all changed with the advent of the steamboat, a true culinary melting pot and a nexus where ladies traded recipes, dining rooms served unfamiliar foods, and adventurous passengers eagerly tried out unheard-of restaurants at shore stops. Land-based grocers, too, became more cosmopolitan as steamboats allowed northern cities to more economically ship items such as cheese, flour, beans, pickles, and vinegar to the South, while southerners shipped sugar, molasses, coffee, and rice up north. And although steamboat cooks are not generally credited with inventing memorable dishes, through their travels they helped popularize such foods as pecan pie, ice cream, angel food cake, and fried chicken. When all this intermingling is added up, the steamboat deserves high acclaim for significantly upgrading America's culinary habits.

Despite the steamer's relative efficiency, the age of the steamboat did not last long. In 1856, the first railroad bridge spanned the Mississippi River, and this new, quick mode of transportation quickly cooled off steamboat mania. Then the Civil War started in 1861, and blockades all but put an end to the steamboat. After the war, steamboat travel did resume, but the industry's arch rival, the train, was now attracting the lion's share of business. This competition forced a new way of thinking that ultimately targeted the well-to-do. In the late 1800s, many of the remaining steamers outfitted themselves luxuriously with cushy parlors, gilt furnishings, thick carpets, and barbershops. Dining rooms were set with real china and crystal, and orchestras and bands kept the upper crust waltzing and two-stepping until dawn. Trains remained popular for the majority, especially those on tight schedules and budgets, but the steamboat was considered the ultimate party venue.

In this golden age of opulence, the grandest steamboat was the *J. M. White*. Built in 1878 for the Greenville and New Orleans Packet Company, this "Mistress of the Mississippi" was an elegant 320 feet long and 91 feet wide. A bona fide floating palace decorated in the steamboat gothic style, she flaunted overstuffed furniture, chandeliers, skylights, ornate mirrors, and a silver watercooler. The *White*'s main cabin dining room boasted sterling utensils and monogrammed linen napkins, while the china bore hand-painted images of the boat, the décor in total rivaling that of the grandest hotels of Europe. Unfortunately, the *White* went up in flames after only eight years of service, but she did leave a legacy of splendor that was hard to match.

Whenever high society traveled on late nineteenth-century Mississippi River steamboats, they were waited on by African American stewards, and food was cooked by African American cooks, many of whom had learned skills on the Pullman cars of the railway system. And although wages were comparatively low, tips were good, the work was steady, and the jobs carried a certain prestige. Then there was the bonus of the adventure of travel. For all these reasons, once black porters, waiters, cooks, and maids landed jobs on steamboats, they tended to stay, and this trend carried on well into the twentieth century.

On the most fashionable boats, meals were served in the grand saloon on a single long table. Breakfast started around 7:30 A.M. The main meal, "Dinner," was served anywhere between noon and 2:00 P.M. and went on for at least three hours, as did the evening "Supper," which some steamers also referred to as afternoon tea. All meals lavished on the eager public an experience as fine or finer than in any restaurant. This dining grandeur is typified by an 1865 breakfast menu from a side-wheeler built in Cincinnati, the *C. T. Dumont,* which offered five seafoods, lamb, beef, veal, blue-winged teal, chicken, and a large assortment of eggs, potatoes, bread, and fruit. The *Robert E. Lee,* a "New Orleans and Vicksburg Steamer," sailed from 1866 to 1882 and offered her passengers four choices of beefsteak along with dishes such as mutton chops, brains, stewed kidney, "jambolaya," fricassee of tripe, codfish balls, chocolate, nine types of bread including Sally Lunn, green and black tea, and "Havana Coffee"—all this, again, just the breakfast "Bill of Fare." By today's standards, these menus are outlandishly extravagant. But it is important to remember that this was the heart of the Victorian era, a time when asparagus deserved its own fork and cucumber merited its own spoon. It should not be surprising, therefore, that the number of courses at a gourmet meal, like the flatware of the time, was pretentious.

Despite the floating palaces' gallant effort to sell decadence, trains and eventually newfangled automobiles were cutting sharply into the steamboat market day by day. By the 1920s, travel by steamboat was almost totally finished. This drastic fall from favor makes the *Delta Queen* even more remarkable. In 1925, at the end of the steamboat era and in the middle of Prohibition, the California Transportation Company decided to build two steam-driven floating hotel/nightclubs, the *Delta Queen* and her twin, the *Delta King.* Geared to the overnight luxury trade between Sacramento and San Francisco, both boats also carried freight and automobiles. For a while, they were sensational hits. Then the stock market crashed, and the boats eventually went out of business in California. But with that daring beginning, the *Delta Queen* started amassing a spectacular lifetime's worth of memories, not only through her adventures but also through her food.

The following pages could have been formatted merely as a cookbook; the *Delta Queen*'s chefs certainly left behind enough recipes to fill a large volume. But the fare served on the *Queen* was always part of a larger story about the clash between steamboat culture and popular culture, and this never-ending battle was reflected on the boat's menus. All chapters, therefore, begin with snippets of the boat's fascinating history and end with authentic *Delta Queen* recipes from newspapers, promotional materials, and

Delta Queen chefs and guest chefs. All dishes were at one time cooked on the boat. Some recipes are dated, but since they were extremely popular in their era, they are included to give a better understanding of the boat's total food history.

Drink recipes are all courtesy of former *Delta Queen* bartender Brandon Gipson, and most recipes for dishes not attributed to a specific chef are adapted from the archives of Terry Newkirk, a former *Delta Queen* chef. Recipes originally written to serve twenty or more have been downsized and tested for home kitchens. Former passengers will instantly recognize their favorites. And for readers not lucky enough to have traveled overnight on the *Delta Queen,* this book will give you a taste of the charm that made this icon of Americana so historically and culinarily unique.

1 The California Connection

THE FIRST YEARS OF SERVICE

ALTHOUGH CELEBRATED FOR her many years plying the Mississippi River and its tributaries, the *Delta Queen* actually started her career on California's Sacramento River. It all began in the high-flying year of 1925, a time when music was still influenced by jazz pioneers such as Fate Marable, Fats Pichon, and Louis Armstrong. A decade earlier, greats such as these had set the entertainment world on fire with performances on Streckfus excursions. (An excursion is a short trip on a steamboat with no overnight stay). The fleet of elegant musical side-wheelers was owned by Captain John Streckfus, and his boats bopped up and down the Mississippi River between New Orleans and Saint Paul and on the Ohio River to Pittsburgh, and offered fine dining as well as dancing. Now, during the mid-1920s, jazz was still hot and a dance party on a steamboat was still considered the "bee's knees."

On the financial front, commodities were relatively cheap and food prices were declining. The nation's urban centers were immersed in consumerism, and most Americans felt that easy access to money would never end. The California Transportation Company (C.T. Co.) was confident in the economy too. In fact, the company was so optimistic that it bet that businessmen, vacationers, families, and legislators would support not one but two new palatial steamboats on the "Delta Route," the convergence of the Sacramento and San Joaquin rivers. It did not matter that Prohibition was crippling the restaurant industry, that automobiles were more and more common, and that trains were sucking up freight and long-distance passenger business. Lobbyists traveling between California's capital city of Sacramento and San Francisco wanted luxury, and the C.T. Co. was ready to provide it on the increasingly passé yet romantic steamboat.

California author Stan Garvey chronicled the authoritative early history of the C.T. Co.'s two boats in his *King & Queen of the River* (1995), and he writes that the impetus behind the ambitious project was Captain A. E. Anderson, the company's president. According to Garvey, Anderson argued that something modern would attract more passengers, and that larger cargo holds would draw more freight. At the time, two of the company's stern-wheelers, the *Fort Sutter* and the *Capital City,* were servicing the overnight Delta Route. Plush in their own right, the two older boats were turning a profit and offering high-end service, prompting a few skeptics, including the company's highly respected port engineer, Jim Burns, to advise against the expensive and seemingly unnecessary outlay. New-steamboat fever, however, had taken hold of Anderson. So in spite of their more-than-adequate riverboat stock, the company's board of directors ordered construction of what would be the two most luxurious steamboats of the time: the *Delta King,* designated as the company's flagship, and the identical *Delta Queen,* both boats named after the waterway where they would sail.

The bid for the two boats' hulls went to the William Denny and Sons Shipyard of Dumbarton, Scotland. The *Delta King*'s was ordered on April 1, 1924, and the *Delta Queen*'s on May 11 of the same year. Fabricated of galvanized steel, the hulls were a first for riverboats in California. When completed, the parts of both the hulls and the frames were numbered, then disassembled and shipped to Stockton, California. There, at the California Navigation and Improvement Company (CNI) Shipyard, the *Delta Queen*'s keel was laid on May 18, 1925. Construction was guided by the talented and now compliant Jim Burns.

The *Delta Queen* under construction, 1925–1926 (From the collection of The Public Library of Cincinnati and Hamilton County)

I watched the cooks in the cookhouse, and by the big ranges they kept large cans to save the rich drippings for gravy and other recipes.

—JOHN BURNS (son of Jim Burns) to R. Dale Flick on the California histories of the *Delta King* and *Delta Queen*

It took only five months to piece the hulls together, but complete assembly of the superstructures crawled along over two years. When finished, the four-deck-high *Delta King* and *Delta Queen* each weighed in at 1,837 gross tons, measuring 285 feet long overall with a 58-foot beam and only a 7½-foot draft. Both had a sturdy internal truss system that reinforced their hulls, and six athwartships bulkheads divided each of the paddleboats' seven watertight compartments.

Four of the compartments held operating machinery, engines, and boilers. Both the *Delta King* and the *Delta Queen* were outfitted with wheel shafts and cranks sent from Denny's Shipyard. The well-known San Francisco naval architecture firm of Charles H. Evans Company designed the engines from rough castings molded by both Denny's and the Krupp Foundry of Germany. Burning bunker C oil, the *Delta Queen*'s main engine was designed as a horizontal, double-acting, compound steam-powered (225 PSI) engine, and was built with two cylinders: a 26-inch-diameter high-pressure cylinder, and a 52½-inch-diameter low-pressure cylinder. She was provided with a California (variable) cutoff and Western Rivers–style lever-operated valve gear, the latter the same as what was used before the Civil War. The boiler room in the center of the hold housed the *Queen*'s two Foster Marine boilers, equipment that was bought as World War I surplus and, remarkably, was still operational in 2008.

Two compartments (one forward and one aft of the boiler room) held the crew's quarters, and the final compartment held the cookhouse, complete with a dumbwaiter that traveled two decks up to the Saloon Deck.

The superstructure of the *Delta Queen* comprises four decks. The Freight Deck (later called the Main Deck) held up to four hundred tons of cargo and the engine. This deck was open forward, allowing up to forty automobiles to park, while fifteen could park on the outside decks. The Saloon Deck (later called the Salon Deck and then the Cabin Deck) held the dining saloon along with a smoking lounge, lobby, social hall, and staterooms. The Observation Deck (also called the Boat Deck and then the Texas Deck) had a lounge and cabins; and the uppermost level, originally called the Texas Deck (later called the Sun Deck), housed officers and had more passenger cabins. A

Speaking tube in the engine room

forward-sitting pilothouse, complete with wooden wheel, and a single stack topped it all. Scoffing at expense, Anderson equipped both boats with water-cooled air-conditioning. Many staterooms were also equipped with inside baths, a luxury new to California.

By today's standards, navigational communication on the boat was primitive. Clanging bells sent messages to the crew. A speaking tube ran from the engine room to the pilothouse, and the steam whistle was a crucial guiding tool. The *Delta Queen*'s whistle is a one-pipe, three-chime steam Lunkenheimer, and its distinctive moans and croaks were indispensable for navigating along the San Joaquin River. Both the *Delta King* and the *Delta Queen* sailed at night, a dangerous task on its own, and especially treacherous when fog rolled in. During these times of virtual blindness, the noise from the *Delta Queen*'s famous throaty whistle would bounce off bluffs, hillsides, and the sides of barns. And just by judging the amount of time it took for the echo to bounce back, a pilot could actually tell the boat's location.

A blast from the *Delta Queen*'s whistle always turns heads, but unarguably the boat's trademark is its massive 59-ton stern-wheel paddle, a whopping twenty-nine feet in diameter and eighteen feet long, and the vessel's only means of propulsion. The wheel, turned by Pitman arms, averages eighteen turns per minute, and while in California was covered with a wood and steel paddle box.

Aesthetically, the *Delta King* and *Delta Queen* stunned the riverboat world with Tiffany-style windows, grand staircases, and brass railings. Crystal chandeliers sparkled on ceilings, and parlors featured overstuffed furniture, grand pianos, and imported tapestries. The stylish aura was highlighted by acres of wood paneling and trims of oak, teak, mahogany, and Oregon cedar, along with Freight Deck floors made of rare ironwood from Siam—all fine hardwoods that, although spectacular, would later prompt the Coast Guard to question the boat's fire resistance. Completed at a cost of $875,000 each, the twins *Delta King* and *Delta Queen* were easily the most expensive steam-wheelers built to date. After they were trimmed and decorated, their respective costs soared to $1 million, the unheard-of expenditure earning them the title of "million-dollar boats."

SAILING IN STYLE

To much hoopla, the *Delta Queen* and the *Delta King* were both christened on May 20, 1927, and on June 2, the *Delta Queen* made her maiden voyage from San Francisco to

The *Delta Queen* at San Francisco (Photograph courtesy San Francisco Maritime National Historical Park)

Sacramento, with the *Delta King* plying the opposite route. Early passenger fares cost $1.80 one way and $3.00 round trip, with the price of cabins and meals not included. Following the Delta Route, the boats departed at 6:30 P.M. from San Francisco's Pier No. 3 and Sacramento's M Street Wharf. They passed each other around midnight somewhere close to Rio Vista, and landed at 5:30 A.M. Accommodating up to 234 passengers each, the boats offered the option of sleeping in the men's dormitory for fifty cents or in any of the 117 double-occupancy staterooms or suites that featured call buttons for all-night room service. Visitors at either port had access to their cabins all day while the boats were docked.

A dance orchestra provided music Saturday and Sunday nights, and dinner and breakfast were sold daily. But many passengers were attracted to something more thrilling than dancing and fine dining. Although Prohibition was in full swing, a 1928 *Delta King* menu prominently displays that a bar was located off the smoking room. In a nod to California's substantial Mexican population, this bar served tamales and enchiladas. But it also sold "Beverages" such as Old Scotch Brew, Budweiser, Schlitz, Buffalo Brew, Rainier ("Light, Dark and Malt"), and Golden Glow Brew, all low-alcohol near beers

that were legal and could easily be spiked with something strong. Crew members recount that a blind eye was turned to whatever alcohol happened to find its way on board both the *Delta King* and the *Delta Queen*. This indiscretion, along with the excitement and romance of a steamboat ride, made the boats instantly successful with everyone from honeymooners to wide-eyed teenagers, and even to the occasional movie star and Vanderbilt.

Unlike the boats' laid-back bars, their restaurants were sophisticated operations. The soft notes of the steward's gong chimes announced dinner, served from 6:30 to 8:30 P.M., and breakfast, from 6:00 to 9:00 A.M. Waiters sported white jackets. The dining room was breathtaking with fresh flowers, starched white tablecloths, mahogany chairs upholstered in brown morocco leather, English oak paneling, and checkerboard tile floors made of Goodrich sheet rubber. Three of the room's walls were made of glass, the openness making the space a prime location for river watching, the elegance impressing even the most jaded millionaire.

Although the boats were considered the height of luxury, meals were relatively inexpensive. A 1928 menu shows that the "Plate Dinner" was a paltry fifty cents, a real bargain, especially considering that more than one hundred years earlier, a meal on

The fifth [hull] compartment in order houses the galley and cold storage rooms, the dish washing equipment, the brine tanks for the refrigerating system, and two dining rooms for the crew. The galley has ample room and is equipped with plenty of utensils to take care of the hotel upstairs. A hydraulic elevator is installed to take care of supplies being brought in or taken out, and there is adequate dumb-waiter service to the pantry above. The famous Ingle oil-burning range is used.

—From "King and Queen of the Delta," *Pacific Marine Review*, July 1927

Fulton's *Clermont* had commanded the same price. The tab, however, soon jumped to seventy-five cents, but was still considered extremely low. Although the *Queen* ran at passenger capacity the first few years, the real money was made with freight. As with the majority of steamers, passenger revenue was a bonus.

SHORT-LIVED FUN

Only two years after the *Queen's* and *King's* smooth start, the stock market crashed and the Great Depression began. In this devastating business climate, river freight commerce all but vanished and was made worse by the rise of truck farming and the dissemination of produce from isolated farms by means of refrigerated wheeled vehicles and railcars. Although truck farming had been commercially viable in the Northeast since at least 1900, decades later in the partially connected West, a steamboat was still a dependable way to transport fruits and vegetables. Steamboat enthusiast R. Dale Flick recounts that much of the freight the *Queen* and *King* carried in their early California years was produce, with some of it finding its way onboard through "brush landings" or "potato landings" (unscheduled stops at farms). At first there was no limit on volume for this cargo. But with some customers netting the two steamers as little as $1.25, the C.T. Co. was forced to establish minimums for produce, an action that spurred disgruntled farmers to turn to increasingly reliable land transportation.

A greater obstacle, understandably, was the Great Depression. At the time, many lower-class American families were eating just two meals a day while, for others, basics such as fresh produce and meats were considered treats. The formerly well-off, a large part of the two steamboats' clientele, suffered a double shock; not only did this class have to forgo porterhouse for chuck, but they also had to let go of their cooks and servants. It is against this humbling backdrop that the *Delta Queen* and *Delta King* tried

MENU

STEAMER DELTA QUEEN
W. L. Cooley, Captain   L. Files, Steward

—————Table d'Hote Dinner $1.00—————

Hors D'Oeuvres
Anchovies on Toast   Imported Salami
Fruit Cocktail

SOUP
Scotch Barley   Bouillon in Cup

SALAD
Lettuce and Tomatoes, Mayonnaise

FISH
Fillet of Boston Cod

ENTREES
Choice of One
Fresh Pig's Knuckles, Braised Red Cabbage
Chicken Patties a la Reine
Roast Leg of Lamb, Mint Jelly
Small Club Steak and Mushrooms
Grilled Calves Liver with Bacon

VEGETABLES
Fresh Asparagus   String Beans
Boiled or Mashed Potatoes

DESSERT
Strawberry Shortcake   Cocoanut Pudding
Assorted Pies
Strawberry Ice Cream, Small Cakes
Cafe Noir   French Rolls
Tea, Coffee, Milk or Iced Tea
BEER (Eastern) 25¢ (Western) 20¢
Additional per bottle
Child's Dinner Portion 50¢
ARTICLES NOT ON THIS BILL A LA CARTE PRICES

1930s *Delta Queen* menu
(From the collection of
Mary Sward Charlton)

to promote extravagance. Not surprisingly, they failed. And with revenues drastically down, in 1932 the California Transportation Company formed an operating service with the Sacramento Navigation Company and the Fay Transportation Company, the new consortium called The River Lines. In this, the *Queen*'s fifth year of service, fares dropped from $1.80 to $1.50 one way and from $3.00 to $1.95 round trip. A room cost as little as $1.00, and a passenger could sleep in a chair or on a bench for free.

Laura Yorg remembers paying those inexpensive prices when she rode both boats between 1934 and 1935, when she was only eleven or twelve. She would hop on board at midnight during a freight stop near her home at Rio Vista, California. She would settle into a chair, read books, and then fall asleep until she reached San Francisco, where she met her married sister. Yorg never ate in the dining room, but she remembers Saturday nights and the ladies in their elegant thin-strapped cocktail dresses, the well-tailored young waiters, the dining room's sparkling crystal, and the overall relaxed atmosphere.

During this time, grocers were already offering now-familiar staples such as Kool-Aid, Jell-O, and Velveeta cheese. The *Queen*'s depression-era menus, however, show no hint of the use of convenience or processed food, or even an attempt to downsize in the feeble economy. On the contrary, in this period when food was still a measure of a steamboat's prestige, menus were relatively lavish.

A period "À La Carte Menu" on these "floating hotels deluxe" lists upscale choices such as an array of fish cooked to order, plus beef, mutton, pork, lamb, chicken, and desserts that include cheeses. A five-course "Table d'Hôte" meal featured mouthwatering items such as Scotch broth, halibut, braised oxtail jardinière, creamed spinach, apple pie, bread and butter, and tea. Garvey's *King & Queen of the River* includes a 1933 *Delta King* menu that offers salmon, prime rib, leg of mutton, small French carrots, and homemade pies. At the same time, the *Delta Queen* was serving four dishes featuring oysters. None of these menus was reflective of a crippling recession.

The *Delta Queen*'s cooks performed their craft on a "famous Ingle oil-burning range" made of cast iron. Two helpers assisted the chef, and eight stewards served meals in the dining room. Some accounts state that the *Delta Queen* often carried a complement of

June 26, 1938, race on the Sacramento River at Freeport, California, between *Delta Queen* (*left*) and *Port of Stockton* (formerly *Capital City*) (Photograph courtesy San Francisco Maritime National Historical Park)

fourteen waiters, all Filipinos. In the 1920s, California was relying heavily on Mexican workers, so much so that employers feared quotas would be imposed. To head off a possible labor shortage, companies started recruiting low-skilled labor from the Philippines. Since most employment was in low-wage jobs under harsh conditions, organized labor gave little opposition. By 1930, three hundred thousand Filipinos were working in the fields, homes, restaurants, and boats of the Golden State, with many of them finding employment on the *Delta King* and the *Delta Queen*.

BAD TIMES GET WORSE

Wasting no time after Prohibition, both boats started offering eastern and western beer. A later "Beverage List" shows that martinis were only 25 cents, a bottle of claret cost $1.00, and a good burgundy cost a measly $1.25. But although the end of Prohibition gave passengers the luxury of drinking alcohol in the open, it also spurred competition in the form of land-based nightclubs, and these now-legal bars cut drastically into the *King*'s and *Queen*'s profits.

The boats' financial misery intensified in 1934 when dockworkers went on strike, and worsened further in 1935 when government-mandated sprinklers put the boats out of service for months. With revenues deep in the dumps, that same year the C.T. Co. filed for bankruptcy.

By 1936, Californians were increasingly tightening their belts instead of cruising on luxury boats, and most of those who had to travel over inland waters preferred driving on the newly opened San Francisco–Oakland Bay Bridge or the new Golden Gate Bridge. This competition could not be beat, and shutting down the two boats was inevitable. But the *Queen* and *King* were given short reprieves with the opening of the 1939 Golden Gate International Exposition on Treasure Island in San Francisco Bay, when the two boats were recruited to ferry a welcome explosion of passengers to the site. As part of the prefair festivities, on June 26, 1938, the *Delta Queen* even competed against the *Port of Stockton* in California's first steamboat race in fifty years (the *Queen* lost by a nose).

During this period, land-based restaurants were mainly offering "American food," this in reaction to a widespread national crusade to force immigrants to assimilate. The *Queen*'s International Exposition menus followed this gastronomic style and offered a wealth of traditional regional choices, with breakfast items featuring not only then-trendy citrus fruit, dried cereals, and eggs, but also hearty fare such as club steak with french-fried potatoes and lamb chops.

The price of an International Exposition "Table d'Hôte" dinner was $1.00, only twenty-five cents more than a set menu had cost six years earlier. And these modestly priced menus not only offered the expected prime rib of beef and chicken, but also listed upscale items such as canapé of caviar, French sardines, and celery Victor, the popular early twentieth-century salad made famous by San Francisco's St. Francis Hotel. Their offerings also reflected the bounty of California, with regional specialties such as avocado salad, asparagus, artichokes, Sacramento River pears, and California wines, plus popular menu items of the era such as shrimp cocktail and pear and cottage cheese salad. Curiously, this and early menus also list chicken gumbo, a dish that, at the time, was almost unheard-of outside of the Deep South, and one that may have also been copied from the St. Francis Hotel.

In spite of the two boats' pizzazz and strong International Exposition bookings, the growing avalanche of negative events and competition won out. The end of the fair signaled the end of the *Delta King* and the *Delta Queen* as commercial steamers in California, and on September 29, 1940, the two boats made their last trips.

CAVIAR MOUSSE

Yield: 10 canapes

Although Russia has always been renowned for its high-quality beluga caviar, in the late 1800s U.S. sturgeon caught in lakes from California to Minnesota to New Jersey actually provided most of the world's edible fish roe. Overfishing caused American caviar to almost completely disappear by the early 1900s, when the Caspian Sea became the most important source. Today, improved harvesting practices are protecting the world's wild caviar-producing fish, and aquafarms are increasingly meeting demands for the luxury item.

4 ounces caviar (preferably red lumpfish), divided

3 tablespoons chopped fresh parsley, divided

2 tablespoons minced onion, divided

1 cup sour cream

¼ teaspoon black pepper

1½ teaspoons unflavored gelatin

2 tablespoons water

½ cup heavy cream, whipped

Vegetable oil for greasing dish

½ cucumber, thinly sliced

10 slices melba toast

Reserve 2 tablespoons of caviar, 1 tablespoon parsley, and 1 tablespoon onion for garnish.

In a nonmetallic bowl, combine remaining caviar, parsley, and onion with sour cream and pepper. Blend well.

Sprinkle gelatin over water in a small saucepan. Heat and stir over low heat until gelatin dissolves. Remove from heat and combine with caviar mixture. Fold in whipped cream.

Lightly oil a 1½- to 2-quart crockery soufflé dish. Pour mixture into dish, cover, and refrigerate for 8 to 10 hours or overnight. To unmold, run a sharp knife around edge, then dip pan in warm water no longer than 10 seconds. Invert onto a glass plate. Garnish with reserved caviar, parsley, and onion and cucumber slices. Serve with melba toast.

Citrus and Watercress Salad with Chili Dressing

CITRUS and WATERCRESS SALAD

Yield: 4 servings

24 walnut halves

1 head Bibb or butter lettuce

1 bunch watercress, stems removed

8 grapefruit sections (reserve 1 tablespoon juice for dressing)

8 orange sections (reserve 1 tablespoon juice for dressing)

Chili Dressing (*recipe follows*)

Toast walnut halves in a 350°F oven for 8 to 10 minutes, checking frequently. Coarsely chop toasted nuts. Tear lettuce and watercress into bite-size pieces. Arrange greens attractively on salad plates. Crown with grapefruit and orange sections. Drizzle with chili dressing. Garnish with walnuts.

CHILI DRESSING

Yield: about ½ cup

2 tablespoons reserved citrus juice

2 tablespoons bottled chili sauce

2 tablespoons red wine vinegar

4 teaspoons olive oil

Combine all ingredients and mix well. Cover and refrigerate until ready to serve.

HONEY SAUCE for FRUIT

Yield: about 2 cups sauce | Recipe courtesy of Sir Robin Hixson

⅓ cup honey

⅓ cup sugar

⅓ cup vinegar

1 teaspoon celery seed

1 teaspoon dry mustard

1 teaspoon paprika

1 teaspoon lemon juice (optional)

1 cup vegetable oil

In a blender, combine honey, sugar, vinegar, celery seed, mustard, paprika, and lemon juice. Process to blend. Drip oil very, very slowly into mixture with blender running and continue processing until all ingredients are well blended.

Serve over your choice of fresh fruit that has been cut into bite-size pieces.

CHICKEN and ANDOUILLE GUMBO

Yield: 6 entrée or 10 appetizer servings

*Even during the boat's
early California years,
gumbo was served on
the* Delta Queen.

*This version uses the pork specialty andouille, a heavily smoked sausage that gives the dish a
bold, authentic Cajun flavor.*

1 cup chopped onion

1 green onion, chopped

¾ cup chopped celery

2 tablespoons vegetable oil

1 bay leaf, crushed

½ teaspoon granulated garlic

½ teaspoon paprika

½ teaspoon white pepper

¼ teaspoon dried oregano

¼ teaspoon black pepper

⅛ teaspoon cayenne

2 quarts chicken stock

½ cup dark roux (*see page 24*)

½ pound andouille sausage, parboiled and
    cut into ⅜-inch slices

3 large chicken breast halves, cooked and
    chopped into ½-inch dice

Cooked white rice

Fresh parsley (for garnish)

In a large Dutch oven, sauté onion, green onion, and celery in oil briefly. Add bay leaf,
garlic, paprika, white pepper, oregano, black pepper, and cayenne. Cook until vegetables
are soft.

Add stock and bring to a boil. Reduce heat and simmer about 15 minutes, skimming foam
from top if necessary.

Add roux and blend. Simmer 1 hour, skimming top if necessary.

Add andouille. Return to a simmer and cook 30 minutes. Add chicken. Bring to a boil,
then reduce heat to a simmer. Cook 10 minutes, skimming top if necessary.

Serve with rice. Garnish with parsley.

Chicken and Andouille Gumbo

ROUX

Roux, in all its differing shades, was an ingredient in many Delta Queen dishes. Restaurants that use large amounts of the thickener commonly make big batches in the oven, as did the chefs on the Delta Queen. The following is the boat's base recipe:

ROUX (commercial recipe)

> 60 percent butter, melted
> 40 percent all-purpose flour
> (or, 6 parts butter to 4 parts flour)

Fold butter and flour together in a roasting pan. Bake at 325°F for 30 minutes. The roux should be a light gold color. Bake longer for a darker roux.

The following traditional method of preparing roux is usually preferred by home cooks. A thick-bottomed pot is essential, as is the patience to stir until the roux reaches the right color. Unused roux keeps for several weeks in the refrigerator.

ROUX (home recipe)

Yield: about 1¾ cups

> ¾ cup butter or vegetable oil
> 1 cup all-purpose flour

Place butter or oil in a heavy-bottomed skillet and heat over medium heat. Add flour and stir constantly over the entire skillet bottom. (Watch closely so that the roux does not burn. If black specks do appear, discard and start over.)

When cooked over medium heat, roux should reach its proper color according to the following timetable:

> white roux: 2 minutes
> blond roux: 4–5 minutes
> brown roux: 8–10 minutes
> dark brown roux: 10–15 minutes

When roux is done, immediately transfer from the skillet to a metal bowl. Cool before using. (Adding hot roux to hot liquid causes splatters and separation.)

MOCK TURTLE SOUP

Yield: 4 to 6 servings | Recipe courtesy of Chef Howie Velie

CHEF'S NOTE

"If you can't find oxtails, use coarsely ground or roughly chopped beef (a shoulder or leg cut). Cook until very tender for the best flavor. The original dish was made with all turtle meat. I prefer it with buffalo or coarsely ground beef, but oxtail is more refined. The garnish is traditional, and it is nice to add a drop of sherry tableside."

2 tablespoons olive oil
1 tablespoon butter
1 large onion, finely chopped
2 pounds meaty oxtails (*see Chef's Note*)
4 garlic cloves (3 whole, 1 mashed)
2 tablespoons chopped fresh parsley
   (plus additional for garnish)
1 whole bay leaf
½ teaspoon cayenne
¼ teaspoon ground allspice

¼ teaspoon dried thyme
1 tablespoon flour
3 cups chicken stock
3 cups hot water
1 cup chopped peeled tomatoes
½ thin-skinned lemon, chopped
   (rind and all)
Salt and pepper
2 hard-boiled eggs, coarsely chopped
Sherry

Heat oil and butter in a large kettle. Add onion and sauté until brown. Add oxtails and brown slightly. Add garlic, parsley, bay leaf, cayenne, allspice, and thyme. Add flour and cook, stirring constantly, until mixture bubbles, adding more butter and oil if needed. Add stock and hot water, and bring to a boil. Add tomatoes, lemon, salt, and pepper. Simmer 2 hours.

Remove bay leaf and oxtails from soup and cut meat and marrow from the bones. Discard the bones, and add meat and marrow to soup.

When ready to serve, stir eggs into the soup. Ladle soup into bowls, stir a teaspoon of sherry into each serving, and top with parsley. Put a cruet of sherry on the table, for atmosphere if nothing else.

MARINATED PORK TENDERLOIN

Yield: 3 servings | Recipe courtesy of Chef Terry Newkirk

1 pork tenderloin (12 ounces), trimmed

1 recipe Marinade for Pork Tenderloin
 (*recipe follows*)

Vegetable oil for frying

½ cup all-purpose flour

¼ teaspoon Cajun Seasoning (*recipe follows*)

2 tablespoons butter

1 small apple, peeled, cored, and cut into
 ¼-inch slices

¼ cup raisins

1 recipe Calvados Sauce (*recipe follows*)

Combine pork and marinade in a nonreactive bowl (glass or stainless steel) or in a zippered, leakproof plastic bag. Cover bowl or seal bag and refrigerate 8 to 10 hours or overnight.

Remove pork from marinade and slice into 9 even pieces. Discard marinade. Pound pork with a meat tenderizer until slices are thin, about ⅓ inch thick.

Pour ¼ inch oil into a skillet and heat over medium-high heat. In a medium bowl, combine flour and Cajun seasoning. Dredge pork in seasoned flour and pan-fry in hot oil until both sides are golden brown. Place pork slices on a warm platter and cover. Drain oil from skillet but leave brown bits in pan for Calvados sauce.

Melt butter in a small skillet over medium heat. Add apple slices and sauté until soft and edges begin to turn brown, about 2 minutes. Add raisins and heat through. Remove from heat.

Place 3 pork slices on each dinner plate and top with apples and raisins. Spoon Calvados sauce over all.

MARINADE for PORK TENDERLOIN

Yield: about 1½ cups | Recipe courtesy of Chef Terry Newkirk

½ cup white wine

¼ cup apple cider

¼ cup vegetable oil

2 tablespoons honey

1 tablespoon chopped fresh garlic

1 tablespoon chopped shallots

1 tablespoon sherry

¼ teaspoon dried basil

¼ teaspoon dried oregano

¼ teaspoon dried thyme

Combine all ingredients and mix well.

CAJUN SEASONING

Yield: about ⅔ cup

Like roux, Cajun seasoning appears as an ingredient in many Delta Queen *recipes.*

3 tablespoons dried thyme

2 tablespoons paprika

2 tablespoons salt

4 teaspoons dried oregano

2 teaspoons granulated garlic

2 teaspoons onion powder

2 teaspoons black pepper

2 teaspoons white pepper

1 teaspoon cayenne

Combine all ingredients and mix well. Store in an airtight container.

CALVADOS SAUCE

Yield: about ¾ cup | Recipe courtesy of Chef Terry Newkirk

2 tablespoons chopped shallots

1 tablespoon butter

⅔ cup chicken demi-glace or chicken stock

¼ cup Calvados

⅓ cup heavy cream

Place shallots and butter in the same skillet in which the pork was fried. Cook over medium heat for 30 seconds, scraping up brown bits from the bottom of the skillet. Remove skillet from heat and stir in demi-glace and Calvados. Return to heat and cook until liquid is reduced by half. Add cream and stir until sauce thickens and is heated through. Strain and serve.

DEMI-GLACE:

available in specialty food shops and some supermarkets

STRAWBERRY SHORTCAKE

Yield: 6 servings

2 pints fresh strawberries, rinsed and
    hulled
¼ cup plus 2 tablespoons sugar
1 cup heavy whipping cream

½ teaspoon vanilla extract
3 fresh biscuits (3 inches each), sliced
    in half (*see page 174*)
6 whole strawberries (for garnish)

Twenty-four hours before serving, cut strawberries into teaspoon-size pieces. Combine cut berries and ¼ cup sugar in a medium bowl. Cover and refrigerate.

In a medium bowl that has been chilled, combine cream, vanilla, and remaining 2 tablespoons sugar. Beat until stiff peaks form.

Place a half biscuit in each of 6 deep dishes or bowls. Spoon berries and juice over biscuits. Top with whipped cream. Garnish each serving with a fresh strawberry.

SEASONAL FRESH BERRIES in PASTRY CUP with FRESH LEMON CREAM

Yield: 6 to 8 servings | Recipe courtesy of Chef Paul Wayland-Smith

2 cups fresh strawberries, hulled
and quartered

1 cup fresh blackberries

1 cup fresh blueberries

1 cup fresh raspberries

6 to 8 pastry shells or phyllo dough shells
(the size of muffin cups, baked)

Fresh Lemon Cream (*recipe follows*)

Place a mixture of berries in pastry shells and top with a dollop of fresh lemon cream. Serve on chilled salad plates.

FRESH LEMON CREAM

Yield: about 1 cup | Recipe courtesy of Chef Paul Wayland-Smith

¾ cup heavy whipping cream

1 tablespoon sugar

1 teaspoon lemon extract

2 tablespoons sour cream

In a medium bowl that has been chilled, whip cream, sugar, and lemon extract until mixture thickens slightly. Fold in sour cream.

2 Mess Hall Days

THE *QUEEN* JOINS THE NAVY

BY 1940 THE GERMANS and Italians were thoroughly terrorizing Europe and North Africa. On the other side of the world, the Japanese were engaged in China, Korea, and Manchuria, and direct U.S. military involvement in all of these conflicts was growing closer every day. Few therefore balked when President Franklin D. Roosevelt issued an order declaring a limited national emergency, the edict establishing the *Delta Queen* and the *Delta King* as receiving ships for naval reservists.

The *Queen* began her "hitch" on October 16, 1940, and took on the First, Second, and Third Divisions of the San Francisco Naval Reserve at what is now called Yerba Buena Island, situated in San Francisco Bay. A few weeks later, the *Delta King* steamed to duty at Tiburon, located in Marin County across the bay from San Francisco. That Thanksgiving and Christmas, homesick reservists found comfort on board the boats in the form of Middle America–influenced feasts of turkey, ham, cornbread dressing, and pie. Aside from the accompanying cigarettes and cigars, the menus presented to the diners would still be popular today.

The River Lines and the government ended up negotiating two six-month leases for the boats. After that relatively uneventful prewar year expired, the consortium sold both the *Queen* and the *King* to Isbrandsten Steamship Company, a New York firm that had plans for their refurbishment and future service on the Mississippi and Ohio rivers. In no time, the boats were boarded up and made ready for their trip east. Plans were halted abruptly, however, with the horrific events of December 7, 1941.

After the bombing of Pearl Harbor, the navy called both boats back to duty. Immediately the government paid off Isbrandsten and, to absolutely no fanfare, the former royal pair were now proclaimed yard harbor boats. The *King* was named YHB-6, and

Instead of the discreetly muffled notes of the steward's gong, their three passenger decks are echoing to the shrill piping of the bosun's whistle.

—*New York Times* reporting on the *Delta King* and the *Delta Queen*, June 8, 1941

the *Queen* YHB-7. Both were painted battleship gray, and they were transformed into hospital transports for the Pearl Harbor wounded.

One week later, on December 15, the *Delta Queen* received her first complement of wounded navy and marine personnel from the Hawaiian Islands. By 1943, both boats were shuttling military personnel between Treasure Island, Alameda Naval Air Station, Fort Mason, and San Francisco. A year later, they were reclassified to reflect their transport duties; the *King* was renamed YFB-55 (yard ferry boat), and the *Queen* YFB-56. Technically the boats were "in service" and not officially commissioned, so they were never given the title USS.

With their shallow drafts, the boats were perfect for the waters of the Bay area—and their numerous staterooms were ideal for desperately needed military lodging. Initially these living quarters remained unchanged from the boats' luxury liner days. Starched napkins and Filipino waiters even greeted navy cook-striker Joe Cornyn on his first day on the *Delta Queen*. (The term *striker* refers to a seaman who performs authorized on-the-job training that will result in higher pay.) Cornyn laughs that the *Queen* had been brought into service so quickly that no one had time to make the proper personnel changes. But the mistake was quickly remedied, and Cornyn's white-tablecloth service lasted for only one meal.

Author and historian Branwell Fanning served in the navy on the *Delta Queen* beginning in 1945, and he documents life aboard the boat in his lighthearted *Wartime Adventures of the Delta Queen* (1976). Among numerous and entertaining details about daily routines, dirty jobs, and a booze-drinking dog named Chigger, Seaman First Class Fanning records that in 1943, the *Delta Queen* received a much-needed machinery overhaul. During the course of the *Queen*'s service, the navy also replaced the high-pressure piston, refabricated the entire bow, and meticulously kept her painted—expensive repairs Fanning believes saved the *Queen* from ruin.

Fanning also remembers that by that time he came on board, near the war's end, the cabins were locked to enlisted personnel, and that sailors were assigned to standard navy pipe berths on what he refers to as the Salon Deck, the level known as the Saloon Deck in the boat's earlier excursion days. Water tenders and machinists were quartered portside, while seamen and cooks stayed starboard. The former dining room on the Salon Deck was turned into the crew's lounge, and the grand staircase area became the officers' wardroom and dining room; the crew's dining room was in the galley in the hold.

Cornyn remembers that the navy upgraded both the *Queen*'s and the *King*'s galleys to military standards. Each paddleboat's cooking space was equipped with a walk-in refrigerator, a grill, and two ovens. Soups and vegetables to serve one hundred were cooked in "coppers," gigantic steam-jacketed kettles that held up to thirty gallons. Cornyn also recalls that at this time, both boats were using cast-iron Ray Burner ranges, but it is not certain if this was the trade name of the burners or of the stove.

Throughout the war, growing numbers of America's military and bomb-stricken allies all needed to be fed, and supplying these priority groups prompted Secretary of Agriculture Claude Wickard to worry about food shortages. Civilians, he concluded, needed to make sacrifices. To coalesce support, Wickard coined the slogan, "Food will win the war and write the peace." The resulting and much written-about "Meatless Tuesdays," "Trumanburgers," ration books, and victory gardens did not, however, seem to adversely affect the dining habits of the *Delta Queen* troops.

It is true that in between scarce shipments of fresh food, military personnel in far reaches were forced to eat powdered, dried, and canned food along with the newly invented K-rations. But those with easy access to supplies often ate better than they had at home. Joe Cornyn spent most of his hitch cooking on the *Delta King*, but he did complete the first part of his duty on the *Queen*. In his view, the chow on board both boats was exceptionally good. He remembers that favorite dishes included steaks (served once every two weeks), chops, chicken, and baked beans. In sunshine-rich California, produce (especially carrots) was plentiful and was supplied to the *Delta Queen* by both boats and trucks.

Although the galley had access to a wealth of foodstuffs, Cornyn says the navy did not encourage creativity. Consequently, during her military years, the *Delta Queen* offered dishes that were prepared exclusively from the latest edition of *The Cook Book of the United States Navy*. Menu preparations followed navy guidelines that revolved meals around seasons. Cornyn offers the following as typical:

NAVY WINTER MENU

Breakfast—prunes, oatmeal, milk, grilled sausages, home-fried potatoes, whole wheat bread, butter, coffee

Dinner—navy bean soup, fried pork chops with gravy, hominy spoon bread, apple coleslaw salad, lemon cream layer cake, bread, butter, coffee

Supper—meatloaf, tomato sauce, baked potato, buttered carrots, peach half, sugar cookies, bread, butter, milk

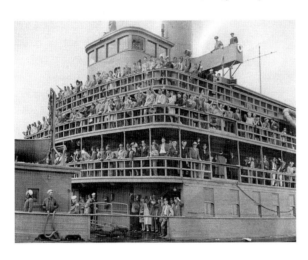

Twelfth Naval District gives Shriners a ride on the *Delta Queen,* July 26, 1946. (Photograph courtesy San Francisco Maritime National Historical Park)

And did Cornyn ever cook up that infamous "something" on a shingle? He says he remembers serving chipped beef on toast once a week. To Cornyn's dismay, most of the crew did not like it, in his view due to its reputation and not because of its taste.

At the end of the war, Branwell Fanning wrote a letter to his parents and relayed his own kitchen adventure, his words giving a clue about why a real cook, like Cornyn, might think the boat's food was exceptionally tasty: "Our cooks were discharged, so Smitty [Fanning's friend], a couple of other guys, and I took over the galley chores. You sure eat better this way!"

During World War II, the U.S. Navy had turned the regal boats into lowly workhorses, and instead of serving caviar and champagne, their galleys had become cafeterias. On the upside, however, their time in the service had given the two boats life extensions. On April 25, 1945, during the founding conference of the United Nations, the *Delta Queen* had even been given the honor of riding fifty-one delegates on a sightseeing tour of San Francisco Bay. But the hope for more sailing time ended in 1946. That year, on April 17, the *Delta King* was taken off the navy records, and the *Queen* followed suit on August 28. Soon after, both steamers were mothballed to the "ghost fleet" of decommissioned navy ships at Suisun Bay, California.

Cornyn recalls that the following recipes were crew favorites, dishes that are sure to bring back memories to many World War II veterans. He points out that on the *Delta Queen*, pot roast and stew were "dinner items" while goulash, chili, and chop suey were always "supper items"; dinner was at noon and supper at 5 P.M.

NAVY BEAN SOUP

Yield: 8 servings

3 tablespoons bacon drippings	½ teaspoon white pepper
1 carrot, medium dice	½ teaspoon dried marjoram
1 rib celery, medium dice	½ teaspoon dried oregano
1 clove garlic, minced	¼ teaspoon dried basil
1 large onion, medium dice	2 quarts ham stock
½ teaspoon granulated garlic	1 pound dried navy beans
½ teaspoon black pepper	1 can diced tomatoes (14.5 ounces), undrained

Heat bacon drippings in a soup pot. Add carrot, celery, garlic, onion, and all seasonings and herbs. Sauté until onion is transparent.

Add stock and bring to a boil. Add beans and tomatoes. Reduce heat and simmer until beans are tender and creamy, about 3 hours. Skim foam from top as necessary. Adjust seasoning.

MACARONI and CORN AU GRATIN with BACON

Yield: 6 to 8 servings

Original recipe found in the 1944 edition of *The Cook Book of the United States Navy*.

1 cup milk

2 tablespoons vegetable oil or melted butter (*see Notes*)

2 tablespoons flour

½ teaspoon salt

¼ teaspoon dry mustard

¼ teaspoon paprika

Dash of pepper

½ cup chopped cheese (American or Cheddar)

6 cups water

¼ teaspoon salt

1 cup uncooked macaroni or spaghetti

2½ cups canned cream-style or whole-kernel corn (*see Notes*)

6 slices bacon

Preheat oven to 350°F. Grease a 9" × 9" baking pan.

Bring milk to a boil in a medium saucepan. In a small bowl, combine butter, flour, salt, mustard, paprika, and pepper. Blend until ingredients form a smooth paste. Add to hot milk and cook, stirring constantly, until mixture thickens. Remove pan from heat and add cheese. Stir until cheese melts.

Combine water and salt in a large pot and bring to a boil. Add macaroni and cook according to package directions.

Drain macaroni and combine with cheese sauce and corn. Transfer macaroni mixture to prepared pan and bake for 25 minutes.

While macaroni is baking, broil bacon until slices begin to curl. Place bacon on top of macaroni during the last 5 minutes of baking.

NOTES:

All original recipes from the U.S. Navy cookbook called for beef fat or "fat" instead of vegetable oil or butter.

If using whole-kernel corn, drain corn and use liquid in cheese sauce in place of milk. If liquid does not measure 1 cup, add milk to make up the difference.

Pot Roast of Beef (Braised Beef) with Savory Brown Gravy

POT ROAST of BEEF (BRAISED BEEF)

Yield: 8 servings

Original recipe found in the 1944 edition of *The Cook Book of the United States Navy.*

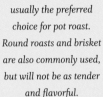

Although this recipe does not specify the cut of beef, chuck roast is usually the preferred choice for pot roast. Round roasts and brisket are also commonly used, but will not be as tender and flavorful.

2 tablespoons vegetable oil	½ cup beef stock or water
4½ pounds bone-in beef (or 3 pounds boneless beef)	¾ teaspoon salt
½ onion, chopped	½ teaspoon pepper
	Savory Brown Gravy (*recipe follows*)

Heat oil in a large Dutch oven over medium-high heat. Add beef and cook until meat is browned on all sides, turning frequently.

Add onion, stock, salt, and pepper. (Onion may be sautéed until brown before adding to pot.)

Cover tightly and simmer for 3 hours or until meat is tender. (Roast can also be baked at 300°F.) Turn meat two or three times while cooking. Add more liquid in small amounts as needed.

Reserve ¼ cup drippings for gravy. To serve, slice roast across the grain into ⅛-inch slices. Top with savory brown gravy.

SAVORY BROWN GRAVY

Yield: about 2 cups

¼ cup reserved meat drippings	½ teaspoon salt
¼ cup flour	¼ teaspoon pepper
2 cups meat stock	

Heat meat drippings in a skillet over medium heat. Add flour and blend well. Cook, stirring constantly, until flour is browned.

Add stock slowly, stirring constantly. Cook until gravy is thick and smooth. Season with salt and pepper.

BEEF STEW

Yield: 8 servings

Original recipe found in the 1944 edition of *The Cook Book of the United States Navy.*

4 pounds bone-in beef (or 2½ pounds
   boneless beef)

½ cup plus 2 tablespoons flour, divided

½ teaspoon salt

¼ teaspoon pepper

2 tablespoons vegetable oil

4 cups beef stock or water

2 tablespoons tomato paste

3 potatoes, peeled and cubed

2 carrots, sliced or cubed

2 ribs celery, diced

1 small onion, cut into 8 pieces

1 cup peas (fresh or frozen)

Salt and pepper

Cut meat into 1- to 2-inch cubes.

Mix together ½ cup of the flour, salt, and pepper. Dredge meat in seasoned flour. Heat oil in a Dutch oven over medium-high heat. Cook meat in hot oil until browned, stirring constantly.

Add stock and tomato paste, cover, and simmer 1½ to 2 hours or until meat is tender.

Add potatoes, carrots, celery, and onion. Cover and cook 40 to 45 minutes.

Cook peas in small amount of water for 10 to 15 minutes. Drain and reserve for garnish.

Drain liquid from Dutch oven into a saucepan. Blend together remaining 2 tablespoons flour and 1½ tablespoons cold water to make a smooth paste. Add flour mixture to broth and bring to a boil, stirring constantly. Season with salt and pepper.

Pour thickened broth over meat and vegetables and heat through. Garnish with peas.

BEEF GOULASH

Yield: 8 to 10 servings

Original recipe found in the 1944 edition of *The Cook Book of the United States Navy.*

4½ pounds bone-in beef (or 3 pounds boneless beef)

2 tablespoons beef or bacon drippings

1½ cups chopped or sliced onions

2 cans tomatoes (14.5 ounces each; see Note)

1 clove garlic, minced

1½ teaspoons salt

1 teaspoon paprika

Flour for thickening gravy

Hot cooked rice

Cut meat into 1-inch cubes.

Heat drippings in a Dutch oven over medium-high heat. Add onions and sauté until clear. Add meat and cook until browned.

Add tomatoes, garlic, salt, and paprika. Cover pan tightly and simmer about 3 hours or until beef is tender. Add more liquid as needed.

Drain broth from meat into a saucepan. Stir in enough flour to thicken slightly, and boil for 2 minutes over medium heat.

Combine gravy and meat, and reheat. Serve with rice.

NOTE:

Four cups of stock or water may be used in place of the tomatoes.

BEEF CHILI CON CARNE

Yield: 6 to 8 servings

Original recipe found in the 1944 edition of *The Cook Book of the United States Navy.*

4½ pounds bone-in beef (or 3 pounds
   boneless beef)
2 tablespoons vegetable oil (*see Note*)
1 clove garlic, crushed
3 cups beef stock
2 tablespoons chili powder

1 teaspoon salt
¼ teaspoon cayenne
1 can small red chili beans (15 ounces),
   drained
1 can tomatoes (14.5 ounces)

Grind meat or cut into ½-inch cubes.

Heat fat in a Dutch oven over medium heat. Add garlic and sauté until yellow. Increase heat to medium-high. Add meat and cook until browned.

Add enough stock to cover meat. Stir in chili powder, salt, and cayenne.

Cover pan tightly and simmer 2 hours or until meat is tender. Add remainder of stock as needed to keep meat covered.

Chop two-thirds of the beans with a food chopper. Add chopped beans, whole beans, and tomatoes to meat. Bring to a boil. Serve immediately.

Beef Chili Con Carne

PORK CHOP SUEY

Yield: 6 servings

Original recipe found in the 1944 edition of *The Cook Book of the United States Navy.*

Food historians disagree on whether this dish is a totally American invention or actually had roots in Taishan in southwest China. It is certain, however, that chop suey became popular overnight in America when Chinese ambassador Li Hung Chang visited New York in 1896.

2½ pounds bone-in pork cuts (or
    1½ pounds boneless pork)
2 tablespoons vegetable oil
1 cup meat stock or water
1 teaspoon salt
¼ teaspoon pepper
2 ribs celery, cut in strips

1 onion, thinly sliced
2 tablespoons cornstarch
1 can bean sprouts (14.5 ounces),
    reserve liquid
2 tablespoons soy sauce
Cooked white rice

Cut pork into cubes or 1" × ½" × ¼" strips. Heat oil in a large skillet over medium-high heat. Cook pork in hot oil until browned on all sides. Add stock, salt, and pepper. Reduce heat and simmer 30 minutes.

Add celery and onion, and continue cooking 30 minutes.

Make a smooth paste of cornstarch and ¼ cup liquid from bean sprouts.

Drain hot broth from meat and vegetables into a bowl. Add cornstarch mixture and stir to blend.

Return broth to skillet along with drained bean sprouts and soy sauce. Cook until ingredients are well blended and sauce thickens.

Serve over rice.

CHERRY ROLL

Yield: 8 servings

2 cups flour

1 teaspoon salt

2 tablespoons plus ⅔ cup sugar

1 tablespoon baking powder

⅓ cup vegetable shortening

⅔ cup whole milk

2 cans pitted red tart cherries
(water-packed, 14.5 ounces each)

¼ teaspoon cinnamon

Cherry Sauce (*recipe follows*)

Preheat oven to 375°F. In a medium bowl, blend together flour, salt, 2 tablespoons sugar, and baking powder. Cut in shortening. Stir in milk.

Transfer to a hard surface and knead lightly, about 30 seconds. Roll dough on a floured surface to a 15" × 10" rectangle.

Drain cherries, reserving juice for sauce. Combine remaining ⅔ cup sugar and cinnamon. Spread cherries over dough. Sprinkle with sugar mixture.

Starting at one long end, roll up jelly-roll style. Pinch seam and ends to seal. Line a rimmed cookie sheet with parchment paper and place cherry roll in the center.

Bake 30 minutes. Remove to a rack and cool at least ½ hour. To serve, cut into slices and top with Cherry Sauce.

CHERRY SAUCE

Yield: 1¼ cups

½ cup sugar

2 tablespoons cornstarch

Pinch of salt

Reserved cherry juice and water
to equal 1½ cups

¼ teaspoon grated nutmeg

1 tablespoon butter

½ teaspoon grated lemon rind

1 teaspoon lemon juice

In a small saucepan combine sugar, cornstarch, salt, nutmeg, and cherry juice.

Stir over medium heat until mixture reaches a boil. Lower heat and cook until thickened, about 5 minutes, stirring constantly.

Stir in butter, lemon rind, and lemon juice. Reheat to boiling and serve.

3 Hello Cincinnati

A NEW HOME IN AMERICA'S HEARTLAND

HEAVY WITH CASH yet eager to find a bargain, Captain Tom Greene was sniffing around at the Maritime Commission's surplus auction in Suisun Bay on a fall day in 1946. He and his wife, Letha, had just made a train ride from Cincinnati to California, and there they met up with an old friend, river engineer George Wise. Soon Greene found what he was seeking, and he anxiously started inspecting the decks, boilers, and cabins of the mothballed and drab gray steamboats *Delta King* and *Delta Queen*. Instead of hunting for steam, Captain Greene could have shopped for a cheaper boat that ran on diesel, the growing trend in engines. But he did not yet trust diesel's dependability. He had grown up with and knew steam, and this was the reason Greene had his eye on the California *Queens*.

Captain Fred Way Jr., a licensed steamboat pilot and close friend of Captain Greene's, was also an accomplished writer, and he penned a book called *The Saga of the Delta Queen* (1951), a chronicle of the *Queen*'s departure from California. Way's book recounts that Tom Greene was the son of Captain Gordon C. Greene, a former flatboatman who, in 1890, founded Greene Line Steamers, a Cincinnati-based inland packet steamboat dynasty. During World War II, stressed-out pleasure seekers got away from it all by escaping on excursions on the company's only luxury passenger boat, the *Gordon C. Greene*, and the brisk business had filled up Tom's bank account. By 1946, with the war over and the economy on the brink of exploding, Captain Greene dreamed of owning something more sumptuous. At the time, the smallish *Gordon C. Greene* was barely standing up to the wind and waves of a new route on the Mississippi River, and this inadequacy bolstered his argument for a boat that was bigger and therefore safer.

At the end of the Maritime Commission's auction, the Southeast Asia Importing and Exporting Company outbid Greene's offer of $26,350 for the *King*, but on December 17, 1946, the government accepted Greene's bid of $46,250 for the *Delta Queen*. Tom was ecstatic; according to Way, the shrewd captain knew "a winner" when he saw one. But now he faced a huge and unique problem—how would he transport his flat-bottomed, freshwater prize down the Pacific Ocean and to America's heartland?

The *Delta Queen* and the *Gordon C. Greene* (From the collection of The Public Library of Cincinnati and Hamilton County)

PADDLING THROUGH THE PANAMA CANAL

The monumental task of relocating the boat went to Way, who, along with Charles Dietz, a steamboat engineer, and William Horn, a ship carpenter, went to California with instructions to figure out how to deliver the *Delta Queen* to New Orleans. Impossible as the mission seemed, Way recalls that the ordeal became much easier after he lucked up on Les Fulton, a "graduate of Sacramento steamboating," a boatman who, through lineage with early Mississippi captains that had gone west, fully knew river steamers.

Together the men devised a plan to sail the *Queen* down the Pacific Ocean, through the Panama Canal, and up the Gulf of Mexico to New Orleans. By now a media sensation, the *Queen* began her odyssey at the Fulton Shipyard in Antioch, California, some forty miles northeast of San Francisco. Way writes that workers there encased the boat's first two decks in fifty thousand board feet of Oregon fir, the siding to protect the boat's framework from the battering ocean. A second layer of wood was secured vertically to the height of the main deck. Tar paper was inserted between the layers, and a bow house was removed from the forecastle and replaced with a "cow catcher," a V-shaped falsework meant to take the heaviest blows of a head-on sea. The paddle box did remain, but the dismantled paddle wheel was stored in the deck room. Now ready for the trip, the *Delta Queen*, at least to Way, looked like a huge piano box.

While at Fulton Shipyard preparing for the trip, Horn bought a used two-burner stove that was much less than perfect. Every time Way tried to heat it up, he found that "a quarter turn on our oil stove and it became a blow-torch vomiting tear gas; a quarter-turn too little and it was out." In spite of the cantankerous stove, one day Way and Fulton invited the aging designer of the *King* and *Queen*, Jim Burns, for lunch, and the three ate their meal in a makeshift dining room, a stateroom on what they called the Lifeboat Deck (now the Texas Deck). The room was later numbered room 215. In all

Above left: Captain Fred Way and *Delta Queen* construction supervisor Jim Burns, 1947 (From the collection of The Public Library of Cincinnati and Hamilton County)

Above right: Tug *Osage* tows the *Delta Queen* to the Panama Canal, Antioch, California, April 19, 1947. (From the collection of The Public Library of Cincinnati and Hamilton County)

likelihood, this was the first entertaining done on the *Delta Queen* as a member of the Greene Line Steamers.

Way paid the Portland (Oregon) Tug and Barge Company $33,000 to furnish a tug and crew to deliver the *Delta Queen* to New Orleans. According to Way's book, before he could leave, the captain found himself in the middle of a union dispute. With deadlines looming and the Pacific storm season knocking on the door, Way judiciously decided to dismiss the crew he had already assembled. He then signed on union labor, including a cook who was "a rotund, small, pasty-faced person with a hacking cough" and who complained that he did not have enough beans.

On April 19, 1947, Captain Steve King, skipper of the diesel-powered tugboat *Osage*, hooked to the *Delta Queen*. Following instructions from Tom Greene, Way did not go on the trip. Instead, the *Delta Queen* was captained by Fred Geller. At 6:10 A.M., the mooring lines were cast off the tug and, making headlines around the country, the *Delta Queen* moved out into the San Joaquin Channel, first pulled by the stern and then, after running aground, towed by the bow.

Way documented that drinking water for the trip was held in fifteen fifty-gallon drums lashed in what he calls the deck room, while water for washing was stored in spare lifeboats. And aside from beans, it is not clear what the whining cook served the crew. It is certain that there was no refrigerator, and according to Way, the crew's biggest hardship was the lack of fresh foods such as butter, milk, green vegetables, and fresh meat. Still, whatever did end up on the table surely tasted better than what was stored in the large gray cans of emergency rations, provisions that were likely left over from the *Queen's* time in the navy.

Anyone hungry enough could dine on a seven-ounce portion of pemmican, dried beef mixed with suet that was processed to keep for a year. The 1896 *Manual for Army Cooks* gives a good historical overview of pemmican, a traditional Native American dish that is popular with wilderness lovers:

> Pemmican.
>
> Meat, without fat, cut in thin slices, dried in the sun, pounded, then mixed with melted fat, and sometimes dried fruit, and compressed into cakes, or in bags. It contains much nutriment in small compass, and is of great use in long voyages.
>
> Pemmican may be made of the lean portions of venison, buffalo, beef, etc., and may be cooked the same as sausage, or eaten simply as dried beef. A little salt added would make it more palatable to the civilized taste.

Other emergency food items included malted milk, C-ration biscuits, and chocolate, all of it certainly more appealing than the "entrée."

Lloyd's of London insured the trip, and fortunately no claim had to be made. Even though she bobbed like a fishing cork for the entire month-long trip, the *Delta Queen* made it to the mouth of the Mississippi River virtually unscathed. On Monday, May 19, at 2:30 P.M., she docked at Avondale Marine Ways in Harvey, Louisiana, across the Mississippi River from the city of New Orleans, where, for the first time, Captain Tom Greene met Captain Geller. Upon close inspection of the boat, Fred Way noted that, except for a few crustings of salt, the *Queen* truly was in top condition. The rocking back and forth for 5,378 statute miles, however, had not been easy on the crew; evidence of seasickness in staterooms proved they had taken a beating.

FROM CLUNKER TO LUXURY CRUISER

Fred Way writes further that in New Orleans he signed on as the *Delta Queen's* captain and stayed on board for two months while the boat was docked for uncrating. During this time, while her paddle wheel and machinery were being reinstalled, the quality of the *Queen's* cuisine increased considerably. Charlie Dietz from Cincinnati rejoined Way, and he brought along his wife, Hazel, a "red-headed and voluble" woman who "lost little time taking over the culinary department." Now, for the first time since Greene Line Steamers purchased the *Delta Queen*, the crew looked forward to dinner.

Way's crew was an ever-growing hodgepodge of experienced carpenters and firemen, along with assorted wealthy curiosity seekers from Cincinnati who were hell-bent on taking the first ride on the first stern-wheel steamboat that had sailed through the Panama Canal. The final crew for the historical trip up the Mississippi River also included three male cooks. The Coast Guard gave the *Delta Queen* approval to sail up to Pittsburgh on July 16, 1947. And sporting her California-style forward-sitting pilothouse and single smokestack (instead of the traditional two smokestacks seen on Western Rivers steamers), she set off.

On July 27, with the *Delta Queen*'s jackstaff waving flags from the United States, Mexico, Guatemala, El Salvador, Honduras, Nicaragua, Costa Rica, and Panama, the boat sailed into Cincinnati. On August 10, 1947, the boat arrived at the Dravo repair yard

Freight deck (later the Orleans Dining Room), Neville Island, Pennsylvania, 1947 (From the collection of The Public Library of Cincinnati and Hamilton County)

Foggy shore stop on the Ohio River (Photo courtesy Howard Nobles)

on Neville Island, Pennsylvania. Garvey's *King & Queen of the River* states that the *Delta Queen* remained there for a record six months while workers insulated and relocated water pipes, replaced the water-cooled air-conditioning, enlarged the fuel bunkers, made promenade space from the two forward decks, added two front parlors, and shortened the smokestack so the boat could safely glide under bridges. The interior woods were refurbished, and the grand staircase was shined and polished. The Freight Deck's original ironwood floor remained intact, but the area was transformed into a dining room, later named the Orleans Room, and was completed with a new tin ceiling. One of the most welcome improvements was the boat's color change; when the battleship gray paint was removed, the *Delta Queen* received a gleaming new coat of steamboat white.

On June 30, 1948, with her staterooms filled to capacity, the *Delta Queen* made a second inaugural trip, this one from Cincinnati to Muscle Shoals, Alabama. No longer an excursion, the boat was now an overnight cruiser, and from then on, the cost of meals was included in trip fare.

LEAVIN' DAY

When the *Delta Queen* first started cruising from Cincinnati, the relatively high cost of printing meant that waiters were required to rattle off menu items from memory. Printed menus appeared only during special events or at a captain's dinner, and a menu from that first trip could not be found. A passenger from that time does, however, remember the boat's first formal meal and recalls that diners were served fried chicken, mashed potatoes, a green salad, and ice cream.

The cook had fired up the old cast-iron stove and had obviously taken a page from the cookhouse of the *Gordon C. Greene,* whose menus were influenced by the American South. Undoubtedly, few southern foods are more recognizable or craved than fried chicken. For many years, well into the 1970s, this much-loved entrée was typically part of the *Delta Queen*'s first-night fare. Unlike most meats, fried chicken travels well, and was popular on steamboats before refrigeration. Naturally all cooks had their own way of preparing the dish. And through 2008, almost every *Delta Queen* cook served it at least once on a trip, if not on "leavin' day" then for picnics. But no matter who fried the bird or how often it was served, few passengers ever tired of its savory crunch.

BEIGNETS

Yield: 28 beignets | Recipe by Chef Herbert C. Cade Jr.

The beignet (pronounced bin-YAY) is a puffy square of fried and sugared dough, and while it is "hole-less," it is the official Louisiana State Doughnut. This French-inspired treat is traditionally served alongside a hot mug of café au lait (coffee and chicory with milk), and was a frequent breakfast item on the Delta Queen. The traditional round doughnut, with a center hole, was supposedly invented by a hungry sea captain who designed the fried ring of sweet bread dough to fit over the spoke of his steering wheel.

1 package active dry yeast	1 teaspoon salt
¼ cup warm water (110°F)	¾ teaspoon vanilla extract
4 large eggs, at room temperature	4 cups all-purpose flour
½ cup (1 stick) butter, at room temperature	Vegetable oil for frying
⅓ cup granulated sugar	Confectioners' sugar for dusting

In the bowl of a standing mixer, sprinkle yeast over warm water and stir until softened. Add eggs, butter, granulated sugar, salt, and vanilla. Beat with the paddle attachment on medium speed for 30 seconds. Reduce mixer speed to low and incorporate flour. Raise speed to medium and mix until smooth and elastic, about 2 minutes. Dough will be soft.

Form dough into a ball and place in a clean bowl. Press plastic wrap onto exposed surface of dough. Refrigerate for at least 2 hours or overnight.

Turn dough out onto a lightly floured hard surface and roll into an 8" × 16" rectangle. With a sharp knife or pizza cutter, cut dough into 2-inch squares. Cover lightly with a cloth. Let stand 30 minutes.

In a large, heavy-bottomed skillet, heat 1 inch of oil to 350°F. Flatten each piece of dough slightly and drop carefully into the hot oil. Fry beignets approximately 1 minute per side, turning once, until both sides are light golden brown. Drain on a wire rack. While hot, dust liberally with confectioners' sugar.

BUTTERMILK PANCAKES

Yield: 12 5-inch pancakes | Recipe courtesy of Chef Herbert C. Cade Jr.

1 cup all-purpose flour

1 tablespoon sugar

2 teaspoons baking powder

½ teaspoon baking soda

½ teaspoon salt

¾ cup buttermilk

1 large egg

2 tablespoons unsalted butter, melted

Vegetable oil for frying

Combine flour, sugar, baking powder, baking soda, and salt. Sift into a medium bowl.

In a separate bowl, beat together buttermilk, egg, and butter. Add to dry ingredients and mix just until combined.

Lightly coat a griddle or skillet with oil and heat to 375°F (medium heat). Ladle or spoon batter (¼ cup per pancake) onto griddle. When bubbles cover the entire top of the pancake, flip and cook until the other side is brown. Remove pancake from griddle and keep warm while cooking the other pancakes.

CREAM of TOMATO SOUP

Yield: 4 servings

2 tablespoons bacon drippings

½ cup finely diced carrot

⅓ cup finely diced celery

⅓ cup finely diced onion

¼ cup fresh parsley leaves

1 bay leaf, crushed

1 whole clove

1 clove garlic, minced

½ teaspoon whole black peppercorns

2 tablespoons all-purpose flour

2½ cups chicken stock

1 can diced tomatoes (15 ounces)

1 can tomato puree (15 ounces)

⅔ cup heavy cream

⅔ cup half-and-half

Salt

Chopped fresh parsley (for garnish)

Heat bacon drippings in a large saucepot. Add carrot, celery, onion, parsley, bay leaf, clove, garlic, and peppercorns. Sauté until onion is transparent.

Add flour and stir to blend well. Cook for 3 to 4 minutes. Do not brown.

Add stock and blend well. Add tomatoes (with juice) and tomato puree. Bring to a simmer and cook 1 hour, uncovered, stirring occasionally. Mixture will be thick.

Press through a strainer. Return to saucepot and add cream and half-and-half. Bring to a simmer. Season with salt. Adjust seasoning and consistency. Garnish with parsley.

LIGHTHOUSE SALAD

Yield: 4 servings

2 medium red apples, cored and diced

2 ribs celery, finely diced

¼ cup raisins

½ cup chopped walnuts, divided

2 tablespoons mayonnaise

2 tablespoons sour cream

2 tablespoons sweetened
    whipped cream

In a medium bowl, combine apples, celery, raisins, and ¼ cup walnuts. Add mayonnaise, sour cream, and whipped cream. Fold together. Garnish with remaining walnuts when serving.

Cream of Tomato Soup

*Some southerners
still believe that
a collard green nailed
above a door chases
away evil spirits,
and that a collard leaf
pressed against the
forehead cures headaches.*

FLASH SAUTÉED COLLARDS

Yield: 4 servings | Recipe courtesy of Chef Howie Velie

The quintessential southern green, the collard is a mild type of kale and a member of the cabbage family. African slaves are credited with introducing the traditional way of preparing collards, simmered with smoked pork, and they taught other southerners to drink the remaining nutritious "pot likker."

2½ pounds fresh collards, rinsed
and stemmed

2 tablespoons olive oil

2 cloves garlic, thinly sliced

Salt and pepper

Roll collards as if you were making a cigar. Slice into very thin ribbons (this is called a chiffonade). Set aside.

Heat a skillet over high heat. Add enough olive oil to coat the pan, then add collards, garlic, salt, and pepper. Cook and stir about 2 minutes, or until collards are bright green. Serve immediately.

STRAWBERRY PIE

Yield: 1 9-inch pie

5 cups whole fresh strawberries

1 cup plus 1 tablespoon sugar, divided

3 tablespoons cornstarch

½ cup water

1 tablespoon lemon juice

1 9-inch pie shell, baked and cooled

1 cup heavy whipping cream

Wash and hull berries. Mash 1 cup of the softest berries and place in a medium saucepan. Set whole berries aside.

In a small bowl, mix 1 cup of the sugar, cornstarch, and water; stir to blend. Add sugar mixture to mashed berries and cook over medium heat, stirring constantly, until mixture is thick and translucent, about 3 minutes. Stir in lemon juice. Remove pan from heat and cool.

Combine reserved whole berries with cooked mixture, then pour into pie shell. Cover lightly and refrigerate at least 6 hours.

When ready to serve, whip cream with remaining 1 tablespoon sugar. Top each slice of pie with whipped cream.

SOUTHERN-STYLE FRIED CHICKEN

Yield: 4 servings

Southern cooks might be surprised to learn that the cream gravy they have always served over fried chicken is actually a French-style velouté sauce.

4 skinless chicken breast halves (8 ounces each), or 1 whole chicken (3 to 3½ pounds), cut into serving pieces
Shortening for frying
½ cup buttermilk

2 large eggs, beaten
1½ cups flour
1½ teaspoons salt
1 teaspoon black pepper
Chicken Velouté (*recipe follows*)

Rinse chicken and pat dry with paper towels. Place shortening in a large cast-iron skillet and heat to 350°F. Melted shortening should be ½ inch deep.

In a shallow bowl, whip together buttermilk and eggs. In another shallow bowl, combine flour, salt, and pepper. Dip chicken pieces in egg mixture, then dredge in seasoned flour. Carefully place about half of the chicken pieces in hot shortening. (The temperature of the shortening will drop when you add the chicken; try to maintain a temperature of 325°F.) Fry chicken until golden brown on all sides or until each piece reaches an internal temperature of 160°F, turning the chicken several times to prevent burned spots. This will take about 10 minutes for skinless breasts and 20 minutes for pieces with skin and bones. Drain cooked chicken on a rack, then keep warm in a 200°F oven while frying remaining chicken. Serve with chicken velouté.

CHICKEN VELOUTÉ

Yield: 2 cups

1 cup chicken stock
2 tablespoons pan drippings (from frying chicken)
2 tablespoons flour

1 cup heavy cream
½ teaspoon chicken base
¼ teaspoon black pepper

Pour stock into a saucepan, cover, and bring to a simmer. Heat pan drippings in the same skillet used to fry the chicken. Add flour to drippings and blend. Cook over medium heat, stirring constantly, for 1 to 2 minutes. Add stock to skillet; cook and stir until mixture thickens. Stir in cream, chicken base, and pepper. Simmer until desired consistency is reached. Strain into a serving bowl.

Southern-Style Fried Chicken

4   At Home with the Greenes

CAPTAIN TOM GREENE himself was a stickler for good food, and reportedly the area of the *Delta Queen* he most enjoyed modernizing was a "dream" serving pantry, kitchen, and dishwashing area down in the hold. In 1953, Fred Way wrote an article for *Ships and the Sea* magazine, and in it he recalls that Tom Greene "dominated" the culinary department by setting the menus, personally creating specialties of the house, and overseeing the serving. Dale Flick vividly recalls that in Greene's early years with the boat, steaks were served precisely to order. Salads were always crisp, and rice and raisin pudding and bread pudding were "to roll over for," this perfection all at the direction of the paddle-boat's food-savvy owner.

Captain Tom also had a hand in decorating another special room on the *Delta Queen*, this one for his mother, the legendary Captain Mary Becker Greene, one of the few licensed female boat pilots of her day. Mary was the widow of Captain Gordon C. Greene, and she had secured her pilot's license in 1896 and earned a master's credential a year later, becoming the first woman to accomplish both feats. After her husband's death in 1927, she and her sons Tom and Chris took ownership of Greene Line Steamers. By the time Tom bought the *Delta Queen*, Chris had already passed away and the aging Captain Mary was more into cruising than piloting. Sadly, she died aboard the *Delta Queen* only a year later, on April 22, 1949.

Those who knew Captain Mary still like to quote her often-repeated philosophy that she would do whatever it took to make a passenger content, and that complete satisfaction was achieved when a passenger felt they were with family. To both Captain Mary and Captain Tom, the *Gordon C. Greene* and the *Delta Queen* were more than mere businesses; they were floating homes. Like a doting grandmother and engaging uncle, the

Captain Tom and Mrs. Letha
Greene, Neville Island,
Pennsylvania, September 13,
1947 (From the collection of
The Public Library of Cincinnati
and Hamilton County)

two therefore showered their passengers with attentive service. They hired musicians who played folksy music. They engaged in sparkling conversation, made sure everyone had a rocking chair, and, not the least of all, they served honest, solid meals.

In 1950, in the midst of the excitement of running a new boat and while everyone was still grieving Captain Mary, tragedy struck again when Tom Greene died of a heart attack. His passing left his widow, Letha, the owner of five steamboats. Letha was heartbroken over her husband's death. And as the mother of four small children, she could have taken the easy way out and sold her interest in Greene Line Steamers. Instead, she learned more about the business. In no time, she took over management of the company as its president, thus keeping Cincinnati as the *Delta Queen*'s home base and giving the boat another extension on her sailing life.

INFLUENCES ON THE POSTWAR COOKHOUSE

The late 1940s through the 1950s was a prosperous time in the United States, with returning servicemen building and snatching up houses. Wives, many of whom had worked during the war, were encouraged to stay home and prepare healthy meals for their families. To help them along, television, a rapidly expanding form of entertainment, offered local cooking demonstrations. The first network cooking show featured James Beard, the "Dean of American Cuisine," whose "I Love to Eat" show ran in 1946 and 1947. The show featured "all-American" foods such as beef, pork, chicken, and eggs, and shied away from the growing infatuation with prepackaged goods such as cake mixes and frozen vegetables.

At the time, the *Delta Queen*'s galley also cooked virtually everything from scratch. But dining room menus were heavy with southern-style choices, and therefore only partially reflected what was considered standard American fare. Also they rarely included ethnic dishes historically popular at the boat's own home port.

Cincinnati's food tradition, like that of most cities, was shaped by its immigrants. The city was founded by the Scots and English, and in 1828, seventeen years after the first steamboat chugged past Cincinnati, English author Mrs. Frances Trollope made a visit. Trollope noted that, at least with men, drinking seemed preferable to eating:

. . . rarely they dine in society, except in taverns and boarding houses. Then they eat with the greatest possible rapidity, and in total silence; I have heard it said by American ladies, that the hours of greatest enjoyment to the gentlemen were those in which a glass of gin cocktail, or egging, receives its highest relish from the absence of all restraint whatever; and when there were no ladies to trouble them.

Hot foods hot . . .
cold foods cold.

—Captain Tom Greene

Mrs. Trollope further chastised the city for having "no butchers, fishmongers, or indeed any shops for eatables, except bakeries." She also felt that residents consumed too much corn and pork. But she did compliment the quality of some grocery items by saying that, aside from "miserable" fruits, the city's markets offered excellent beef, poultry, eggs, and vegetables.

When English writer Charles Dickens visited Cincinnati in 1842, he seemed impressed with local merchants and the city's architecture. But like Mrs. Trollope, he was appalled by the region's primitive table manners, and recorded that while dining on an Ohio River steamboat, "I never in my life did see such listless, heavy dullness as brooded over these meals . . . such a mass of animated indigestion in respect of all that was genial, jovial, frank, social, or hearty, never, sure, was brought together elsewhere since the world began."

Although there seemed to be few epicures in open public, by the time of Dickens's visit, Cincinnati was home to America's largest inland port, averaging some 3,000 steamboats docking each year, and reaching a height of 8,000 in 1852. The Ohio River and the Miami and Erie Canal had made Cincinnati a main waypoint for miners and western settlers, and for northern and western goods bound for southern plantations. The "Queen City of the West" was also the base for a major steamboat-building industry. Agriculture, too, played a vital role in expansion, with farmers hauling produce in for shipment south to New Orleans. Livestock was herded in and butchered and processed. Hogs were lead to packing plants through the streets, and until 1861 Cincinnati was dubbed "Porkopolis" for its dubious distinction as the pork-packing capital of the world. River commerce, along with steamboat construction, made 1850s Cincinnati the fastest growing city in the country.

Fashionable restaurants did follow in the wake of Cincinnati's steamrolling success. Many were considered world-class, but they largely catered to simple American tastes. In 1850 the elegant Burnet House Hotel opened, and although it offered many impressive imported wines, food menus listed mainly boiled and roasted meats and relatively pedestrian sides such as beets, cabbage, and turnips. Another noteworthy dining establishment was the flamboyant Grand Café in the Hotel Sinton. Opened in 1907, the hotel was celebrated for its glamorous arches and frescoes inspired by Versailles. But even

though the Grand Café's menus featured numerous authentic French preparations, its two most requested dishes were Sinton Noodle Soup and Chicken à la King, the latter created either in London or, most likely, in the United States.

After World War II, Cincinnati flaunted a wealth of posh restaurants. And, in this city largely descended from Europeans, pastry lovers were flocking to the city's Virginia Bakery for German *Bundkuchen* (an almond-topped bundt cake). German sausage shops were selling regional specialties like goetta, a fried breakfast patty of ground meat, steel-cut oats, and seasoning. Cincinnati Chili, a Greek-inspired dish of chili with optional spaghetti, cheese, onion, and beans, had been a favorite since before the war. And for dessert, there was always Graeter's ice cream, the chain established in 1870; it is still producing ice cream that many enthusiasts consider the world's best. For 1950s-era home dining, all-American barbecue and casseroles were popular, and in kitchens throughout the city, old-country favorites such as stuffed cabbage, dumplings, *hamantaschen* (Jewish cookies), and ravioli were still staples.

Although Cincinnati has a rich food history, many culinary researchers focus not on restaurants but instead on the city's historical love of beer. Bringing their affinity for lager, Germans began settling in Cincinnati in large numbers in the 1830s. Soon after, anti-German sentiment played a large part in starting a never-ending temperance

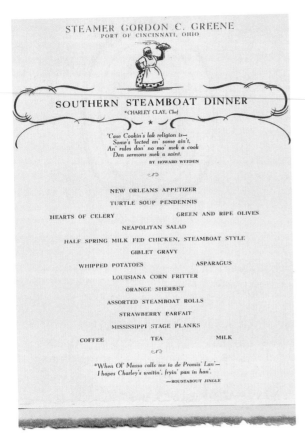

STEAMER GORDON C. GREENE
PORT OF CINCINNATI, OHIO

SOUTHERN STEAMBOAT DINNER
*CHARLEY CLAY, Chef

'Case Cookin's lak religion is—
Some's 'lected an' some ain't.
An' rules don' no mo' mek a cook
Den sermons mek a saint.
BY HOWARD WEEDEN

NEW ORLEANS APPETIZER

TURTLE SOUP PENDENNIS

HEARTS OF CELERY   GREEN AND RIPE OLIVES

NEAPOLITAN SALAD

HALF SPRING MILK FED CHICKEN, STEAMBOAT STYLE

GIBLET GRAVY

WHIPPED POTATOES   ASPARAGUS

LOUISIANA CORN FRITTER

ORANGE SHERBET

ASSORTED STEAMBOAT ROLLS

STRAWBERRY PARFAIT

MISSISSIPPI STAGE PLANKS

COFFEE   TEA   MILK

*When Ol' Massa calls me to de Promis' Lan'—
I hopes Charley's waitin', fryin' pan in han'.
—ROUSTABOUT JINGLE

Undated *Gordon C. Greene* menu (Courtesy Jeffery L. Spear, Riverview Antiques, Marietta, Ohio)

movement. Even with all the anti-beer rancor, in 1860 Cincinnati was home to 36 breweries. According to historian Timothy Holian, in 1890 Cincinnatians drank more beer per capita than anyone else in the United States, and by 1893 residents were averaging 50 gallons per person per year. Consequently, in contrast with the city's restaurant history, much has been written about Cincinnati's legendary saloons and beer gardens and the devastating effects of Prohibition.

While Captain Mary was alive, alcohol was not sold on the *Delta Queen*. Captain Greene had been a staunch supporter of the Women's Christian Temperance Union, and although liquor was sneaked on board unchallenged, she would not sell any of it, not even Cincinnati's beloved beer. Beef and pork, perennial Cincinnati favorites, almost always appeared on menus in some form. And ice cream, a staple with Cincinnatians, was usually available. But instead of adopting the city's ethnic-regional dishes for other menu items, the boat's cooks, like those on the *Gordon C. Greene*, looked across the Ohio River for inspiration. During the entire time both boats were owned by Greene Line Steamers, the company proudly advertised that they followed the tradition of "fine steamboatin' eating," this meaning that menus were a mixture of the countrified fare of the South and the sophisticated French Creole cooking of New Orleans.

Captain Fred Way was able to boast that on the *Gordon C. Greene*, his pal Tom "put on banquets for meals," and from interviews it is known that the same "top-rated food" was also served on the *Delta Queen*. A few surviving and rare printed *Gordon C. Greene* menus tell that these "feasts" included many southern-influenced items such as gumbo, corn fritters, and a "New Orleans Appetizer—Turtle Soup Pendennis." A recipe for Pendennis Turtle Soup appears in *The Southern Cook Book of Fine Old Recipes* (1935) and claims that it is "the soup that made Kentucky famous." This recipe is extremely similar to the roux, egg, and sherry-tinged recipe for Turtle Soup that is served today in New Orleans restaurants and at Louisville's Pendennis Club. It is also like the turtle soup the *Delta Queen* served until 2008. According to food historian Lynne Olver, the legendary soup likely received its name at the Pendennis Club. This social organization was named after Victorian author and food lover William Makepeace Thackeray's autobiographical

A trip on a Greene Line Steamer means being the guest of Captain Mary and Captain Tom, always pleasant, always gay, with a yarn about every important spot, and one gets rest the like of which is unobtainable anywhere else in the world.

—G. Andrews Espy in *Bulletin of the Historical and Philosophical Society of Ohio*, 1948

Pendennis character, who languished in England some thirty years before Kentucky's Pendennis Club was established in 1881.

The *Gordon C. Greene* menus also feature Mississippi Stage Planks, the rectangular gingerbread cookie named for the Mississippi River and the steamboat stage plank, or gangplank, the movable walkway connecting a boat to the shore. Stage plank recipes are extremely similar to those for ginger cakes and hard gingerbread found in early American cookbooks such as *The Good Housekeeper* (1839) and *New England Economical Housekeeper* (1845). An early recipe for "Stage Planks, or Gingerbread without Butter or Eggs, *Estomac Mulâtre* (mulatto's stomach)" appears in the 1901 edition of New Orleans's *Picayune Creole Cook Book*. The book uses racially insensitive terms to explain that this "ginger cake" was sold in the streets of New Orleans by "the old darkies" to "those of their own race and to little white children." According to the recipe, the treat earned the name "mulatto's stomach" because supposedly only a mulatto could digest it.

Like many cookbooks of the late 1940s, the *Gordon C. Greene* menus paid little regard to racial sensitivity. In particular, they featured jingles that today would be considered extremely disparaging to African Americans. But aside from appalling rhymes and a preference for southern-inspired food, the menus also reveal that the *Gordon C. Greene* and the *Delta Queen* offered relatively few dishes. In comparison, large ocean liners of the time were still following the template of the old floating palaces and listed eye-popping numbers of menu selections. But on the Mississippi River, where overnight steam travel was dying, the dining rooms of the Greene Family boats were more pragmatic.

The *Gordon C. Greene* and the *Delta Queen* ran simultaneously out of Cincinnati from 1949 to 1952, and it is safe to assume that during the time they sailed together, the two boats shared not only the same food philosophy but also the same food vendors. An ordering list from the *Gordon C. Greene* shows that a typical trip started off with a pantry full of basics such as fresh fruit and vegetables, olives, prunes, sugar, parsley, spices, dry cereals, chicken, sausage, calf's liver, and veal. A few items not typically found in today's homes but that were popular then included lard, Postum (a caffeine-free beverage

In Louisville and Natchez and the plantations along the River Road, many of the best of the public cooks by 1850 were black and male and so well trained that those of them who took over the galleys of the luxury steamboats plying the Mississippi and Ohio were masters of the intricacies of haute cuisine. Aboard the shining white, gold-trimmed sternwheelers and sidewheelers, these chefs created plantation meals for passengers from all over the country and many parts of the world. Among voyagers dining under chandeliers swaying to the boat's motion they spread the enthusiasm for food of the Vieux Carré and Greek revival mansions.

—Evan Jones, *American Food: The Gastronomic Story* (1981)

mix), and sago (a cornstarch-like thickener) along with calf's head, frog saddles, smoked tongue, and sweetbreads. Some of today's restaurants, however, might consider the latter few items chic; in fact, frog legs were still popular on the *Delta Queen* in 2008.

THE AFRICAN AMERICAN IMPACT

A 1950 *Delta Queen* brochure advertised that "the ship's dining room will offer Southern cuisine, prepared by Southern chefs to whom cooking is a natural art." Virtually all of these Dixie-trained cooks were African American males, some from Cincinnati and many others hailing from river towns that dot the Mississippi River from New Orleans up to Memphis. African American men have a long history of working on Western Rivers steamboats. During antebellum days, slaves accompanied traveling masters. Bond servants were allowed to work on riverboats on a contract basis, and runaway slaves sometimes blended in with black crews and sailed their way to freedom.

Although there was the rare black captain, free blacks generally wound up as firemen and porters, finding it easy to hire on to those jobs. Many were also hired as cooks, and through their work in steamboat cookhouses they are credited with popularizing New Orleans and plantation-style cuisine. After the Civil War, many African Americans stopped working on boats to accept more prestigious positions as porters or dining-car waiters on the railway system's swanky Pullman sleeper cars. When the Pullman Company ceased its sleeper operations and liquidated its assets in 1968, many out-of-work employees sought domestic employment on riverboats.

Working wonders from memory rather than "receipts," recipes, African Americans were recognized in early twentieth-century cookbooks as having "magical" cooking talents. In reality, they had learned their skills from food-wise ancestors who had worked in plantation kitchens and, later, in private homes and restaurants. And although it is rumored that in the 1950s one *Delta Queen* steward occasionally took a peek at the boat's old reliable *Navy Cook Book*, on the whole, the galley's cooks prepared food the same way as their pre–Civil War steamboat predecessors, from know-how. Through the 1970s, hardly any of the *Delta Queen*'s cooks had formal training, having instead learned their trade by cooking for white employers. And they reportedly had little need for written recipes. They were also at home in any kitchen. Many of these cooks worked on steamboats for a season and then spent time in restaurants on land, especially in food-crazy New Orleans. They then moved back to the boats again, this hopscotching enriching their already expansive culinary repertoires.

It is also noteworthy that the *Delta Queen*'s meals were prepared by cooks who had to perform job duties while maneuvering around Jim Crow laws. As on most riverboats, this meant that after black cooks prepared meals for passengers, they cooked and ate their food separately. And at mealtime through the 1950s and early '60s, it was not uncommon to find black crew members congregating on what they considered their front porch, the bow of the *Delta Queen*'s Main Deck. In the morning, before work, they would sing haunting spirituals, play the banjo, read scriptures, and "pat Juba," the tapping and clapping dance that had survived from the days of slavery. At night, they would gather on deck and sing again. Desegregation finally took root on the *Delta Queen* in the late 1960s. But before then, black and white crew members worked on the same boat yet lived in entirely separate worlds.

WORKING THROUGH TOUGH TIMES AGAIN

During the mid-1950s, the lure of modern transportation was making it increasingly difficult for steamboats to compete for freight. Eventually things became so bad that Letha Greene was forced to sell four of the five boats she had inherited—the *Evergreene*, *Chris Greene*, *Tom Greene*, and the company's beloved *Gordon C. Greene*. But Letha kept the *Delta Queen*, and through her determination the boat was given another reprieve. Financial problems persisted, however, and in 1958, California businessman Richard Simonton assumed $70,000 of debt and became majority stockholder of Greene Line Steamers. Letha Greene remained as president, while E. Jay Quinby, a friend and business associate of Simonton's, became chairman of the board.

First visit to Pittsburgh, June 11, 1958 (From the collection of The Public Library of Cincinnati and Hamilton County)

Through all the behind-the-scenes economic turmoil, the quality of the *Delta Queen's* food continued to receive rave reviews, but the boat's traditional and limited menus surprised the unprepared. In 1958, renowned New York food critic Clementine Paddleford took a trip on the *Queen* and freely admitted that "disappointment came at dinner the first evening out." Before embarking on her trip, Paddleford had spent too much time salivating over groaning board menus from steamboating's golden age, and she was mildly shocked at such modest choices as ham, mustard greens, and cornbread. But in her article in *This Week* magazine (August 31, 1958), she did praise the way the food tasted. And she was able to wrangle a few recipes out of chef Floyd Matthews, a busy cook who rattled off ingredients and instructions to Paddleford "right out of his head."

HUSH PUPPIES

Yield: 30 hush puppies

Recipe given to Clementine Paddleford by Chef Floyd Matthews; cited here courtesy of the Kansas State University Clementine Paddleford Collection, Richard L. D. and Marjorie J. Morse Department of Special Collections

Vegetable oil for deep-frying
2 cups white cornmeal
1 tablespoon flour
1 teaspoon baking powder
1 teaspoon salt

½ teaspoon baking soda
1 cup buttermilk
1 egg, beaten
1 clove garlic, minced

Heat oil to 375°F in a deep-fryer or deep skillet.

In a mixing bowl, combine cornmeal, flour, baking powder, salt, and baking soda. Add buttermilk, egg, and garlic; mix well. Carefully drop batter by tablespoonfuls into hot oil (a few at a time) and fry until golden brown, about 2 to 3 minutes. Drain. Serve hot.

CORNBREAD

Yield: 6 to 8 servings

Recipe given to Clementine Paddleford by Chef Floyd Matthews; cited here courtesy of the Kansas State University Clementine Paddleford Collection, Richard L. D. and Marjorie J. Morse Department of Special Collections

¾ cup sifted flour
2 tablespoons sugar
2 teaspoons baking powder
1 teaspoon salt

1½ cups yellow cornmeal
1¼ cups milk
2 eggs, beaten
¼ cup shortening, melted

Preheat oven to 425°F. Grease and flour a 9-inch square pan.

Combine flour, sugar, baking powder, and salt. Sift together into a mixing bowl. Add cornmeal and mix. In a small bowl, combine milk and eggs. Add to flour mixture and blend. Stir in shortening. Pour batter into prepared pan and bake for 25 to 30 minutes.

TURTLE SOUP

Yield: 8 cups | Adapted from a recipe by Chef Herbert C. Cade, Jr.

For stock:

1 pound turtle meat

2 tablespoons olive oil

2 cloves garlic, chopped

1 cup chopped onion

1 stalk celery, chopped

2 cloves garlic, chopped

1 carrot, chopped

1 whole bay leaf

1 teaspoon salt

½ teaspoon black peppercorns

Pat turtle meat dry. Heat olive oil in a heavy-bottomed stock pot and brown turtle well on all sides. Add remaining ingredients to pot. Cover with water by 2 inches. Cover and simmer until meat is very tender, about 45 minutes, skimming surface as necessary. Remove bay leaf. Reserving liquid, remove meat and dice into ¼-inch cubes. Strain reserved stock and set aside.

For soup:

1 stick plus 3 tablespoons butter

½ cup flour

1 cup onion, finely chopped

1 medium bell pepper, seeded and finely chopped

1 stalk celery, finely chopped

1 carrot, grated

½ teaspoon dried thyme

1 clove garlic, minced

1 whole bay leaf

1 teaspoon salt

½ teaspoon freshly ground black pepper

2 cups beef stock

2 teaspoons tomato paste

Juice from ½ lemon

Reserved turtle stock

½ cup sherry

2 hard-boiled eggs, finely chopped

2 tablespoons minced parsley

Make a roux by melting 1 stick butter in a heavy-bottomed saucepan, then stirring in flour. Stir constantly over medium heat until dark brown. To prevent further browning, carefully remove roux from saucepan and transfer to a small cold pot until ready to use.

In a large saucepan, melt 3 tablespoons butter. Add onion, bell pepper, celery, and carrot and sweat over medium-low heat for 15 minutes, stirring occasionally. Add

thyme, garlic, bay leaf, salt, and black pepper and cook 10 minutes longer. Stir in beef stock, tomato paste, lemon juice, reserved turtle stock, and roux and simmer 30 minutes. Add reserved turtle meat and half of chopped eggs. Bring to a boil. Lower heat and simmer 5 minutes. Remove from heat and remove bay leaf. Stir in sherry and divide soup between individual bowls. Mix remaining egg with parsley for garnish.

OYSTER STEW DULAC

Yield: 6 cups, 4 to 6 appetizer servings

6 tablespoons butter, divided

1 rib celery, chopped

½ cup chopped onion

¼ teaspoon dried basil

¼ teaspoon dried oregano

¼ teaspoon dried thyme

1 bottle clam juice (8 ounces)

1 cup seafood stock

⅓ cup light roux (*see page 24*)

½ cup heavy cream

1 cup whole milk, scalded

1 pint oysters (do not drain)

Chopped fresh parsley (for garnish)

Melt 2 tablespoons of the butter in a large pot. Add celery, onion, basil, oregano, and thyme; sauté until onion is transparent.

Add clam juice and stock. Bring to a boil, then reduce heat to a simmer. Add roux and whip well. Add remaining 4 tablespoons butter and cream. Boil briskly for 1 minute.

Remove from heat and add hot milk. Adjust seasoning.

Just before serving, poach oysters in their liquor for 2 minutes. Add oysters and poaching liquid to soup. Serve soup very hot, garnished with parsley.

FROG LEGS MEUNIÈRE

Yield: 4 servings | Recipe courtesy Chef Terry Newkirk

Widely known as a specialty of French cuisine, frog legs are also popular in the American South. This delicacy is especially loved in south Louisiana, where sportsmen hunt at night with a spotlight and "gig" frogs with a pronged spear.

Vegetable oil for deep-frying
4 pairs frog legs
1 cup all-purpose flour
½ teaspoon salt
½ teaspoon white pepper
1 cup buttermilk

1 cup Zatarain's Fish-Fri (seasoned cornmeal)
Meunière Sauce (*recipe follows*)
Chopped fresh parsley and lemon wedges (for garnish)

Heat oil to 365°F in a deep-fryer or deep skillet.

Rinse frog legs and pat dry with paper towels. In a shallow bowl, mix flour, salt, and pepper. Dredge frog legs in seasoned flour. Dip in buttermilk. Coat with seasoned cornmeal.

Carefully place frog legs in hot oil and deep-fry to a golden brown, about 5 to 7 minutes. Serve each portion on a pool of meunière sauce. Garnish with parsley and a lemon wedge.

MEUNIÈRE SAUCE

Yield: about ¾ cup | Recipe courtesy Chef Terry Newkirk

In French, the word meunière *literally means "miller's wife," and in cooking it refers to something dredged in flour. Traditionally, a meunière sauce is made from pan drippings, which should contain browned butter.*

5 tablespoons butter, divided
1 tablespoon minced shallots
2 tablespoons fresh lemon juice

½ cup demi-glace
⅓ cup heavy cream
1 teaspoon minced fresh parsley

Melt 1 tablespoon of the butter in a medium saucepan over medium-high heat. Add shallots and sauté briefly. Add lemon juice and simmer until liquid is reduced by half.

Add demi-glace and bring to a boil. Cook until mixture is reduced by one third. Add remaining 4 tablespoons butter and cream; simmer until thick. Strain, then stir in parsley.

Stage Planks

STAGE PLANKS

Yield: 16 cookies

These spicy molasses cookies were a popular nineteenth-century New Orleans street food. For years, grocery stores throughout the United States have been selling them prepackaged, and often topped with white or pink icing.

3–3½ cups all-purpose flour

1 tablespoon ground ginger

1 teaspoon cinnamon

½ teaspoon ground cloves

1 teaspoon baking soda

1 cup buttermilk

¼ teaspoon salt

¾ cup molasses

¼ cup sugar

6 tablespoons unsalted butter, softened

Preheat oven to 375°F. Line 2 cookie sheets with parchment paper and set aside. In a medium bowl, sift together 3 cups flour, ginger, cinnamon, cloves, baking soda, and salt. Set aside. In bowl of a standing mixer, add molasses, sugar, and butter. Mix on medium-high speed until color turns lighter, about 2 minutes. On low mixer speed, alternate flour and buttermilk with butter mixture. Raise speed to medium and mix 30 seconds. Dough should be stiff enough to roll out. If not, mix in up to ½ cup more flour to reach proper consistency.

On a hard floured surface, roll dough to a 10" × 16" rectangle. Slice down the middle horizontally, then vertically at 2-inch intervals to make 16 cookies. Place individual pieces at least 1 inch apart on prepared cookie sheets. Bake until tops are firm, about 15 minutes. Remove from oven and cool completely in pans.

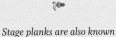

Stage planks are also known as Louisiana gingerbread, gingerbread tiles, mule bellies, and estomac mulâtre (mulatto's stomach).

BLACKBERRY COBBLER

Yield: 4 to 5 servings

Recipe given to Clementine Paddleford by Chef Floyd Matthews; cited here courtesy of the Kansas State University Clementine Paddleford Collection, Richard L. D. and Marjorie J. Morse Department of Special Collections

2 cans blackberries (8.75 ounces each)	Pastry dough (*see page 115*)
½ cup sugar	1 egg white, slightly beaten
1 tablespoon butter or margarine	Sugar (for garnish)

Preheat oven to 400°F.

Combine blackberries, sugar, and butter in a saucepan. Heat until butter melts, stirring gently. Transfer berries to an 8-inch square pan.

Place dough on a floured surface and roll into a square slightly smaller than the pan. Place dough on top of berries. Cut steam vents in the dough, then brush with egg white and sprinkle with sugar. Bake for 25 to 30 minutes.

PO-BOY PUDDING

Yield: 8 servings

Recipe given to Clementine Paddleford by Chef Floyd Matthews; cited here courtesy of the Kansas State University Clementine Paddleford Collection, Richard L. D. and Marjorie J. Morse Department of Special Collections

14 slices white bread	½ cup (1 stick) butter or margarine,
1 cup seedless raisins	softened
1 bag shredded coconut (4 ounces)	6 eggs, beaten
1 cup sugar	1 can evaporated milk (14.5 ounces)

Preheat oven to 400°F. Grease a 13" × 9" × 2" pan.

Cut bread into 1-inch pieces and place in prepared pan. Sprinkle raisins over bread, then sprinkle coconut over raisins. Cream sugar and butter. Add eggs and blend. Stir in milk. Pour mixture evenly over ingredients in pan. Bake 20 minutes. Serve warm with lemon sauce (recipe not provided).

5 "Play Your Music"

BY 1960, GREENE LINE STEAMERS had paid off its mortgage on the *Delta Queen*, and the boat was operating at full capacity. The uptick was aided by E. Jay Quinby, who was luring passengers aboard with a thirty-two-note steam calliope, a "steam piano" that makes music by forcing steam through whistles. Historically, calliopes were used by circuses and steamboats to let towns know that they were nearing. Calliopes can be heard up to five miles away, and they make distinctive and loud calling cards.

The *Delta Queen*'s calliope dates from 1897, and Quinby bought it from a Connecticut circus buff named Ellsworth W. "Slim" Somers, who most likely had rescued it from the sunken showboat *Water Queen*. Travis Vasconcelos, a *Delta Queen* historian and calliope enthusiast, has researched the antique and recalls that at first Letha Greene was against the purchase. She was afraid a calliope's heady noise would keep the crew awake and might appear unsophisticated to folks in cities such as Pittsburgh, Cincinnati, and St. Louis. But Quinby won out, and immediately he mounted the calliope's whistles at the stern on the roof of the Sun Deck. The steam came through pipes from the boiler and was controlled by the keyboard beneath the calliope's steam whistles. At night, the calliope's steam would gush out in an eerie rainbow of color, dubbed the "aurora effect." The secret to the display was a bank of hidden colored lights, but wide-eyed passengers were always told that it came from colored Jell-O. Adding to the hokum, any passenger plucky enough to give the keyboard a whirl and produce at least five recognizable notes was awarded a certificate emblazoned with the banner "Vox Calliopus."

Ever the showman, Quinby would dress in a Prince Albert coat and top hat and hand out vintage-style promotional brochures to townsfolk after the boat landed. At shore stops or when the boat was departing, he belted out old favorites such as "Camptown Races" or

Above left: Passenger on deck next to steamboat bell (From the collection of The Public Library of Cincinnati and Hamilton County)

Above right: Colorful steam from the calliope creating the "aurora effect."

"Waitin' for the *Robert E. Lee*." When the music started, crowds gathered at docks. Automobiles stopped on riverbanks, and it was not uncommon for the calliope to cause traffic jams. And when the calliope was not playing and the *Queen* was quietly slipping through narrow stretches of the Ohio, Tennessee, or Cumberland rivers, children from shore could often be heard yelling with all their might, "Play your music! Play your music!"

BETTY BLAKE

In 1962, Letha Greene felt the need to more strongly promote the *Delta Queen,* so she hired the energetic Betty Blake, the daughter of a long-standing Kentucky senator and a "fireball" who knew how to make the most of the media and finagle her way around Washington D.C. Equally comfortable in mink and a hardhat, Blake "bewitched" travel agents, travel editors, and talk-show hosts, and made an immediate splash by revitalizing the tradition of steamboat racing. She also made a big impact on the *Queen's* cuisine in 1969, when she played an instrumental role in replacing strictly fresh produce and meats with more cost-conscious institutionalized food.

COOKING FROM SCRATCH

Captain Clarke C. "Doc" Hawley, a calliope maestro himself, nostalgically recalls that not all of the boat's groceries came from designated vendors. Hawley says that in the 1950s and '60s, it was common for the *Queen* to pull up to any of the locks on the upper Mississippi and Ohio rivers to buy produce. The lockmasters of the time grew vegetable

BY COMPUTER . . . Dinner table seating will be arranged by a computer, matching up couples with the kind of mutual interests that guarantee sparkling conversation. (If you're basically scared of automation, you can play it safe and sit with your dull old friends.)

—From the brochure "Dance on the *Delta Queen* with the Cincinnati Symphony," 1967–68, courtesy Cincinnati Historical Society Library at the Cincinnati Museum Center

The *Delta Queen* in St. Louis (From the collection of The Public Library of Cincinnati and Hamilton County)

gardens, and they gladly sold the riverboats items such as tomatoes, squash, and pole beans. The crew also bought sweet melons from Evansville, Indiana, and in New Orleans they snatched up French pastry. Paducah, Kentucky, was a place for more fresh produce, along with the local haymarket's Tennessee River catfish, which was fried up whole, minus the head, for Friday lunch.

With the galley still staffed exclusively by African American cooks, a typical early- to mid-1960s crew meal favored dishes such as smothered greens, cornbread, and fried cornmeal mush, foods that later gained notoriety as soul food. Gumbo was always a favorite, as was yaka mein, a crew specialty that was cooked on turtle soup night. Yaka

MENU ABOARD THE

Steamboat
DELTA QUEEN.

Monday July 15,1968

LUNCHEON

FRESH VEGETABLE SOUP
GRILLED HAMBURGER DELUXE
POTATO CHIPS
TUNA FISH SALAD PLATE
CREAMY COLE SLAW
FRUIT JELLO

COFFEE   TEA   MILK

DINNER

CHILLED APPLE JUICE
RELISH TRAY
BEAN SPROUT SALAD
BROILED LAMB CHOPS-MINT JELLY
GRILLED CALVES LIVER WITH ONIONS
BAKED POTATO
BUTTERED YELLOW SQUASH
HONEY AND SPICE CAKE

COFFEE   TEA   MILK

Lunch and dinner menu,
July 15, 1968

mein was made with a salty, spicy broth brimming with noodles, leftover ground turtle (instead of the traditional ground beef), chopped green onions, and boiled egg. Dubbed "Old Sober," the curious concoction reportedly cures hangovers. One story says that the dish found its way to New Orleans through African American soldiers who had served in the Korean War, but it is more likely that the dish was first introduced by Chinese railroad workers in the late 1800s.

While the cooks and crew enjoyed food that was common in the rural Deep South, a dinner menu from 1968 shows that passengers dined on fare that was more "All-American":

Chilled Pineapple Juice
Tossed Green Salad

Roast Sirloin of Beef
With Mushroom and Wine Sauce

or

Broiled Rainbow Trout
Au Gratin Potatoes

Apple Brown Betty

Coffee, Tea, Milk, Sanka, Postum

It is worth noting that this from-scratch menu was cooked up during a time when convenience items such as preportioned meats and frozen vegetables were quickly becoming the foundations of much restaurant cooking. Most home pantries were stocked with such shortcuts as potato flakes, canned vegetables, Pop-Tarts, and Tang, the "space age" orange drink, and the diet-conscious were seeking out newly minted products by Lean Cuisine and Weight Watchers. On the other end of the gastronomic spectrum, Julia Child and President John F. Kennedy's White House were dazzling Americans with French cuisine, while suburban dinner parties were ablaze with fondues or slicing up quiche.

While the *Delta Queen*'s cooks were not totally oblivious to food fads of the 1960s, for the greater part of the decade the boat's butcher shop still hand-sliced bacon, carved up sides of beef and lamb according to use, and cut steaks to order. The cookhouse crew also snapped beans, cored apples, shucked fresh corn, and squeezed oranges for juice. And in this, the era of frozen and reheated pies, the *Delta Queen*'s bakery was turning out handmade rolls, cakes, cookies, and bread pudding.

Every once in a while the New Orleans-bred chefs even fried up a batch of *calas* (cah-LAHZ), spiced rice fritters with origins in preslavery West Africa. Long before the Civil War, female slaves and free women of color sold calas in New Orleans's French Quarter and at the docks. While balancing baskets of the sugar-dusted fried dough on their heads, these "Cala Women" would shout, "Calas, calas. Belles calas! Tout chaud!" ("Calas, calas. Beautiful calas. Very hot!") In the early 1900s, African American women were still peddling calas in New Orleans's streets. The delicacy was rarely served in restaurants, but in homes thrifty housewives with leftover rice also made calas, and they typically served them with syrup for breakfast.

After World War II and the rise of packaged foods, the New Orleanian taste for calas faded. Historians credit food preservationist Poppy Tooker with saving the nostalgic sweet from extinction by giving it attention in cooking classes and persuading chefs to find a place for it on modern New Orleans restaurant menus. There is little evidence that calas were cooked on the *Delta Queen* after the 1960s—the decade of a "new" calliope and reenergized public relations, and the last when the galley cooked mostly from scratch.

Delta Queen List of Pantry Items for a Typical Six-Day Trip, 1965

144 lbs. coffee	2,520 eggs
1,000 lbs. meat including:	125 loaves white bread
120 lbs. bacon	80 loaves rye bread
75 lbs. sausage	120 gallons milk
15 hams	36 lbs. butter chips
15 prime ribs	120 half-pints buttermilk
65 lbs. round of beef	120 quarts coffee cream
225 t-bone steaks	20 lbs. American cheese
95 frying chickens	20 lbs. Swiss cheese
400 pork chops	10 lbs. Nauvoo Blue cheese
75 lbs. fresh brisket	13 cases fresh fruit
75 lbs. flank steak	20 bushels vegetables
225 veal chops	150 gallons ice cream
75 lbs. calf's liver	
75 lbs. corned beef	
6 lbs. pickled beef tongue	

—Courtesy of the Cincinnati Historical Society Library at the Cincinnati Museum Center

Calas are similar to New Orleans's famous sugar-dusted beignets.

CALAS

Yield: 2 dozen

In the 1800s and well into the twentieth century, Creoles enjoyed calas with café noir (black coffee) or café au lait (coffee with milk). Originally made with yeast, the batter adapted well to the modern baking powders that became widely available after the mid-1800s.

⅔ cup unbleached flour

1 tablespoon baking powder

¼ teaspoon salt

3 large eggs

⅓ cup sugar

¼ teaspoon freshly grated nutmeg

½ teaspoon vanilla

2 cups cold cooked rice

Vegetable oil for frying

Confectioners' sugar for dusting

In a medium bowl, sift together flour, baking powder, and salt. Whisk in eggs, sugar, nutmeg, and vanilla. Stir in rice. Refrigerate batter while oil heats.

In a deep fryer or heavy pot, heat 1½ inches oil to 365°F. Drop batter by a rounded tablespoon and fry until golden brown, about 2–3 minutes. (Refrigerate batter between batches.) Remove cooked calas from oil, drain, and liberally sprinkle with confectioners' sugar. Serve hot.

CHILLED ASPARAGUS SALAD
with RASPBERRY VINAIGRETTE

Yield: 10 servings

40 fresh asparagus spears

2½ cups alfalfa sprouts

20 pitted black olives

2 cups Raspberry Vinaigrette

(*recipe follows*)

1 pint fresh raspberries

Steam asparagus spears lightly, then plunge into a bowl of water with ice cubes to stop the cooking. Drain.

Place 4 asparagus spears on each plate in a fanned design. Place ¼ cup alfalfa sprouts at the base of the spears, and garnish with a black olive on each side.

Drizzle raspberry vinaigrette across the tops of the asparagus spears. Place a raspberry in between asparagus spears. Refrigerate until ready to serve. Serve well chilled.

RASPBERRY VINAIGRETTE

Yield: 2 cups

2 tablespoons red wine vinegar

1 egg yolk (*see Note*)

¼ cup fresh raspberries

½ cup vegetable oil

½ cup skim milk

4 tablespoons bottled melba sauce

1½ tablespoons sugar

Combine vinegar and egg yolk in a blender. Process until well blended. Add raspberries and blend. With motor running, slowly add oil. Thin with milk. With motor still running, blend in melba sauce and sugar.

NOTE:

This recipe contains a raw egg yolk. There is a small chance of salmonella poisoning when consuming raw eggs.

BEER and CHEESE SOUP

Yield: 4 to 6 servings | Recipe courtesy of Chef Terry Newkirk

1 tablespoon butter

2 ribs celery, finely diced

1 cup finely diced shallots

1 clove garlic, minced

¼ teaspoon granulated garlic

¼ teaspoon white pepper

Pinch of cayenne

2 cups chicken stock

¼ cup blond roux (*see page 24*)

1¼ cups heavy cream

1 pound sharp Cheddar cheese, grated

1 bottle stale beer (12 ounces)

¾ cup milk, heated

Chopped green onions (for garnish)

Melt butter in large heavy-bottomed pot over medium-high heat. Add celery, shallots, fresh garlic, granulated garlic, pepper, and cayenne. Sauté until vegetables are soft, about 5 minutes.

Add stock and bring to a boil, then reduce heat to a simmer. Add roux and blend well. Cook, whisking constantly, until mixture is smooth and thick.

Blend in cream. Simmer about 5 minutes. Add cheese and beer. Stir well and remove from heat. Add milk and blend well. Adjust seasonings and consistency. Ladle into bowls and garnish with green onions.

VEGETABLE SOUP

Yield: 8 servings

2 tablespoons butter

½ cup diced celery

½ cup diced onion

⅓ cup diced bell pepper

⅓ cup diced carrot

⅛ teaspoon dried basil

⅛ teaspoon crumbled bay leaf

⅛ teaspoon dried oregano

⅛ teaspoon dried thyme

2 cups beef stock

2 cups chicken stock

1 can diced tomatoes (15 ounces), with juice

1 can corn (15 ounces)

1 cup broccoli florets

1 cup cauliflower florets

1 cup frozen green beans

1 cup frozen green peas

1 cup diced yellow squash (medium dice)

Chopped fresh parsley (for garnish)

Melt butter in a medium stockpot. Add celery, onion, bell pepper, carrot, basil, bay leaf, oregano, and thyme. Sauté until onion is transparent. Add beef stock and chicken stock. Bring to a boil, then reduce heat to a simmer and cook about 1 hour.

Add tomatoes, corn, broccoli, cauliflower, beans, peas, and squash and simmer until vegetables are tender, about 10 minutes. Adjust seasoning. Ladle into bowls and garnish with parsley.

YAKA MEIN

Yield: 6 servings

Although the Delta Queen's cooks enjoyed this dish made with leftover turtle, you can use just about any kind of meat. If you don't have leftovers, try boiling a less-tender cut of beef until tender and use the stock for the soup.

1 (8-ounce) package spaghetti

2 quarts beef stock

1 teaspoon Cajun Seasoning (*see page 27*)

2 cups cooked meat (beef, chicken, pork, shrimp, turtle), finely chopped

2 tablespoons soy sauce

3 hard-boiled eggs, peeled and halved lengthwise

1 bunch green onions, finely chopped

Cook spaghetti according to package directions. While spaghetti is cooking, bring stock and Cajun Seasoning to a boil in a large pot. Add meat and simmer 5 minutes. Reserving stock, strain meat out. Set meat aside and keep warm. Bring stock back to a boil and stir in soy sauce. Simmer 1 minute.

To assemble, place drained spaghetti in 6 individual bowls. Divide meat and egg halves over spaghetti. Ladle on broth and sprinkle with green onions.

Yaka Mein

SOUTHERN FRIED CATFISH

Yield: 4 servings

Vegetable oil for frying
1½ to 2 pounds catfish filets
1 cup all-purpose flour
½ teaspoon salt
¼ teaspoon black pepper

¼ teaspoon cayenne
1½ cups buttermilk
2 cups Zatarain's Fish-Fri (seasoned cornmeal)
2 lemons, sliced (for garnish)

Heat oil to 350°F in a deep-fryer. Preheat oven to 350°F.

Rinse fish and pat dry with paper towels.

In a shallow bowl, combine flour, salt, pepper, and cayenne. Pour buttermilk into a separate shallow bowl, and place seasoned cornmeal in a third shallow bowl.

Dredge fish in flour, then in buttermilk, and finally in cornmeal.

Carefully place fish in hot oil (a few pieces at a time) and cook for 3 minutes or until golden brown. Remove from oil and place on a baking sheet. Finish in oven for 5 minutes. Garnish with lemons.

STEAK DIANE

Yield: 5 servings

Popular in American restaurants during the 1950–60s French craze, the dish was often wheeled tableside, doused with cognac, and theatrically flambéed.

1 beef tenderloin (1 pound), trimmed

2 tablespoons butter

1 cup sliced mushrooms

3 tablespoons minced shallots

2 tablespoons chopped fresh parsley

2 tablespoons sherry

1 tablespoon Cognac

2 teaspoons A.1. Steak Sauce

1 teaspoon Dijon mustard

1 teaspoon Worcestershire sauce

Chopped green onions (for garnish)

Cut tenderloin into 5 thin tournedos. Melt butter in a skillet over high heat. Add steaks and sauté briskly until medium rare, turning once. Remove steaks from skillet and hold in a warm (200°F) oven.

Combine all remaining ingredients except green onions in the same skillet. Sauté about 3 minutes, stirring often. To serve, arrange steaks overlapping on a serving platter and top with sauce. Garnish with green onions.

The sauce for this steak dish was named for Diana, the Roman goddess of the hunt, and was likely created in Europe in the late nineteenth century.

APPLE BROWN BETTY

Yield: 6 servings | Recipe courtesy of Chef Terry Newkirk

1 cup dark brown sugar

1 teaspoon ground cinnamon

½ teaspoon ground nutmeg

2 tablespoons apple juice

1 tablespoon lemon juice

1½ cups graham cracker crumbs

1 can apple pie filling (21 ounces)

2 tablespoons butter, melted

Vanilla ice cream

Preheat oven to 350°F. Lightly oil the bottom and sides of an 8-inch square baking pan.

In a medium bowl, mix brown sugar, cinnamon, nutmeg, apple juice, and lemon juice.

Layer one-third of the graham cracker crumbs in prepared pan. Top with half of the pie filling and then half of the brown sugar mixture. Layer another one-third of the graham cracker crumbs, then the remainder of the pie filling, and then the remainder of the brown sugar mixture. Top with remaining crumbs. Drizzle butter over all and bake for 30 to 40 minutes or until brown. Serve warm with ice cream.

An American creation from colonial times, this recipe was first published in the 1864 Yale Literary Magazine as "brown Betty." No one is sure if betty refers to the term as used for some English puddings, or if it comes from an inspired cook named Betty.

STEAMBOAT PUDDING

Yield: 6 servings

2 cups whole milk

3 ounces sweet chocolate, grated

¼ cup sugar

4 egg yolks

¾ cup whipping cream

1 teaspoon vanilla extract

6 fresh strawberries (for garnish)

In a medium saucepan, combine milk, chocolate, and sugar. Cook and stir over low heat until chocolate melts and milk is barely simmering.

Beat egg yolks in a medium bowl. Blend one-third of the chocolate mixture into egg yolks, then add egg yolk mixture to remaining chocolate mixture in pan. Cook and stir over low heat until mixture thickens slightly. Remove from heat and cool.

In a medium bowl that has been chilled, beat cream until stiff peaks form. Blend in vanilla. Fold chocolate mixture into the whipped cream. Use a pastry bag to pipe the pudding into tall glasses, or spoon into dessert cups. Top with strawberries.

Steamboat Pudding

6 The Frenzied Seventies

PERIL, PROMOTIONS, AND A NEW SISTER

THE *DELTA QUEEN*'S ORIGINAL builders spared no expense when they outfitted the boat with rich oak, cedar, mahogany, teak, and, of course, that rare Siamese ironwood floor. Handsome as these hardwoods were, however, to the U.S. Coast Guard and some members of the U.S. Congress they were a catastrophe waiting to happen.

The paddleboat's legislative troubles began in November 1965 when the American cruise liner *Yarmouth Castle* caught fire between Miami and Nassau, The Bahamas, killing ninety passengers, mostly Americans. This tragedy, coupled with the death of 125 passengers two years earlier when the Greek ship *Laconia* caught fire in the North Atlantic, prompted Congress in 1966 to pass Public Law 89-777, known as the Safety at Sea Act. Requiring compliance with the International Convention for Safety of Life at Sea (called SOLAS), the new regulation did not allow wooden ships to carry more than fifty overnight passengers. The law included both oceangoing ships and boats on inland rivers, and it affected all vessels with wooden superstructures, including steamers such as the *Delta Queen*.

Letha Greene immediately panicked. At the time, she was barely making a profit, and completely rebuilding the *Delta Queen* to meet SOLAS guidelines was both impractical and financially impossible. Dropping her passenger limit down to fifty from her then-full complement of 188 would not have generated enough operating income, and it appeared that the new law was destined to shut the *Delta Queen* down for good. Greene turned to majority stockholder Richard Simonton for help, and in May 1966 he responded by sending his sharp point man Bill Muster to save the day. After Muster and cohort E. Jay Quinby spent much time maneuvering and schmoozing anyone with influence who would listen, their efforts were rewarded that same year when the *Queen* was

Captain Ernest Wagner, long-ago captain of the Delta Queen, *was nicknamed Big Gravy. Some of the cooks and a clerk on the* Delta Queen *had such nicknames as Fats, Ham, Beans, Texas Tender, Big Rabbit and Little Rabbit.*

—Covington [Kentucky] resident Virginia Bennett in *Steam Cuisine* (1999)

granted a two-year exemption with an order to be refit and made fire-resistant with new paint and machinery. Another exemption in 1968 extended the boat's life to November 2, 1970. But since there were no plans to bring the boat up to modern construction standards by replacing the wooden superstructure, Congress's mandate to shut the boat down at the end of 1970 still stood.

In 1968, Muster was named president of Greene Line Steamers. Betty Blake was promoted to vice president, and Letha Greene retired. For the first time since the company's inception, a Greene family member was not running Greene Line Steamers. As the new bosses took over, they realized that their employees might soon be out of jobs. The company needed a new boat, and for that they needed money, and lots of it, and that kind of cash was not going to fall out of the sky. Or was it?

SKULLDUGGERY AND SPIES

With hope fading, in 1969 the plight of the *Delta Queen* caught the eye of G. F. Steedman Hinckley. The philanthropist and preservationist, who also happened to be chairman of a charter airline named Overseas National Airways (ONA), purchased Greene Line Steamers that year, and he also made a promise to build a new all-steel paddle wheeler.

Right away, ONA offered crew members reciprocal travel agreements with other airlines, and they were able to fly anywhere at deeply reduced rates. This perk was greatly appreciated. But the new owner's generosity, along with the home office's obvious abundance of cash, also added fuel to gossip that was gaining steam below decks.

The scuttlebutt was that ONA was actually owned by the CIA and that the corporation was a smokescreen for military airplanes that were transporting troops to Vietnam under civilian cover. Some even speculated that Hinckley was a CIA agent and that the *Delta Queen* was a front for government money-laundering. None of these cloak-and-dagger rumors were ever proved. But they did take on heightened legitimacy in 1976 when Doc Hawley was captain of the *Natchez* and was working with White House representatives on crew clearance for a charter trip for President Gerald Ford. Hawley recalls jokingly telling a government agent that he hoped he would not have a problem passing their background check. Without missing a beat, the agent told the shocked captain that both he and his first mate Captain Robert Hammett already had clean CIA files. He also said that the two rivermen's clearance documents had been gathered years earlier, when the pair was working on the *Delta Queen* and the boat was owned by ONA.

Food: You may be assured that only the best food will be served, in ample quantities, as we cannot afford to do otherwise. Many of your people may be prospects for future trips on the steamer, and the Delta Queen *is always remembered for its excellent and plentiful cuisine.*

—From a Greene Line Steamers booklet titled *Charter Services Policy,* by Betty Blake

---

FIGHTING FOR THE *QUEEN*

Although Hinckley never did declare to anyone associated with Greene Line Steamers that he was a spy, he certainly did affirm to Muster and Blake that he would build a replacement for the seemingly doomed *Delta Queen.* But boats take years to build, so as he took ownership of the company, Hinckley also crossed his fingers in hopes that Congress would allow the *Delta Queen* to continue running in the interim.

U.S. Representative Edward Garmatz of Maryland, chairman of the House Committee on Merchant Marine and Fisheries, would have none of it. Although the *Delta Queen* did have an iron hull and supports, her wooden superstructure violated the law. And it did not matter that no Greene Line boat had ever had a fire-related fatality—or that the *Queen* had all the required safety features, that she had passed all safety inspections with flying colors, and that she was always within minutes of shore. Garmatz had made up his mind, and in 1970 he quashed a total of twenty-five bills that would have extended the *Queen's* exemption.

Undaunted, Muster and Blake started national letter-writing campaigns and petitions that set off an avalanche of support. The *Delta Queen's* precarious situation was covered by all major national television news stations. Stories appeared in newspapers in almost every state, including the front page of the *New York Times.* Locals up and down the Mississippi and Ohio rivers held rallies and bake sales. A little-known rock band called Carp released a record titled "Save the *Delta Queen*." Johnny Cash honored the boat on his *Johnny Cash Show* with the song "Salute to the *Delta Queen*," and in June 1970, the *Delta Queen* was listed on the National Register of Historic Places. But none of this swayed Garmatz. With all hopes exhausted, on October 12, 1970, the *Delta Queen* left Cincinnati for St. Paul, Minnesota, and then on October 20, she left St. Paul for a final two-week "Farewell Forever" run to New Orleans.

The trip was a combination wake, family reunion, party, and food festival. Captain Ernie Wagner, who had worked nonstop to extend the exemption, commanded the somber crew. All along the way, in towns such as La Crosse (Wisconsin), Clinton (Iowa), Nauvoo (Illinois), Memphis (Tennessee), and Natchez (Mississippi), throngs lined the riverbanks and waved signs, shed tears, and wished the grand old lady well. On November 2, at the Bienville Street Dock in New Orleans (the boat's final shore stop), entertainment director Vic Tooker played taps.

But the game was not over. In a behind-the-scenes move, a benevolent Congress sidestepped the furious Garmatz, passing the Elmer M. Grade bill (HR 6114) to reimburse a federal employee and attaching to that bill legislation that gave the *Delta Queen* another extension. President Richard M. Nixon signed the extension on December 31, 1970. Once again, the *Delta Queen* found new life.

On April 29, 1971, after an expensive winter layup, the *Delta Queen* was surrounded by music, cheering, and a small-boat escort as she docked triumphantly at her old home in Cincinnati. As part of a never-ending quest to make the boat indispensable, in September that same year the *Delta Queen* was declared a U.S. post office, and in October she made her inaugural U.S. mail trip with much-publicized stops in such places as La Crosse, St. Paul, Muscatine (Iowa, where the president of the chamber of commerce presented two bushels of Muscatine sweet potatoes to Captain Ernie Wagner), St. Louis, Hannibal (Missouri), Memphis, Vicksburg, Natchez, and New Orleans. In addition to prestige, the distinction of housing a post office gave the boat an advantage at locks: The *Delta Queen* got to jump ahead of every boat except federal watercraft because she had on board a U.S. post office with her own postmark.

A COMPANION *QUEEN*

Still trying to head off the potentially disastrous whims of Congress, in January 1973, Muster let out a contract to Jeffboat, Inc., of Jeffersonville, Indiana, for the gigantic *Mississippi Queen*. That same year, Greene Line Steamers changed its name to the more identifiable Delta Queen Steamboat Company, and the *Delta Queen* underwent a massive overhaul. Also in 1973, with Garmatz no longer in Congress, the *Delta Queen* received another SOLAS extension, this one without coercion and good for five years.

Muster resigned as president in January 1974, and the *Mississippi Queen*, the "largest steamboat in the world," was launched the following November. The new boat was christened in Louisville, Kentucky, on April 20, 1975, and took on her first passengers in July. For twenty years, the stalwart *Delta Queen* had been America's only paddle wheeler. But now she was joined by a boat made of steel, a true floating palace that had state-of-the-art everything, including a swimming pool, a sauna, a theater, and a salon.

The 382-foot-long *Mississippi Queen,* which held 422 passengers, was completed for $27 million, and the jaw-dropping cost, coupled with a few airplane accidents, left owner Overseas National Airways in financial straits. Once again, the *Delta Queen* flirted with fading into oblivion. But a rescue miraculously came again, this time from the Coca-Cola Bottling Company of New York, which bought the Delta Queen Steamboat Company in April 1976.

GETTING WITH THE TIMES

During the period the boat was owned by Overseas National Airways and managed by Muster and Blake, a few important food-related changes took place. In 1969, the old Observation Room at the top of the Grand Staircase was renovated and renamed the Texas Bar (later called the Texas Lounge). And the cookhouse, by now commonly known as the galley, was moved up from the hold and onto the Main Deck, and equipped with many new appliances, including a safe electric stove. New, however, did not necessarily mean better. Although everything in the galley was shiny and clean, the bakery and butcher shop were gone and, worse yet, the work space was reduced by about half. Fortunately, the dining room was large enough to accommodate overlapping seatings; the new galley was so small that cooks did not have room to prepare a multicourse meal for the entire boat at one time.

Another change was the use of institutionalized food. Ironically, just at the time California's Alice Waters was starting to champion a back-to-the-farm movement, *Delta Queen* chefs were doing away with time-consuming fresh foods and were loading their freezers with pre-prepared vegetables, breads, meats, and desserts. But it

The *Delta Queen* and *Mississippi Queen* on base plate (Photograph courtesy David Dewey)

GALA CHAMPAGNE TOAST

Captains Dinner

MISSISSIPPI STEAMBOAT STYLE

Assorted Relish Tray
Louisiana Shrimp Cocktail   Hearts of Lettuce
Entree Selection
Roast Prime Rib of Beef au jus
or
Filet of Dover Sole
Special   Spears
Steamboat Potatoes   of Green Asparagus
Pecan Pie or Creme de Menthe Parfait

1970s menu (Courtesy of Captain Bob Reynolds)

would be hard to fault the boat's management for this move. Throughout the 1970s, even the highest of high-end restaurants secretly admitted that much of what they served had been processed or frozen. Waters and France's Paul Bocuse, and later Louisiana's Cajun cooking king, Paul Prudhomme, changed all that and shamed restaurants into taking a hard look at the quality of the food they churned out. But before then, in those years of seeking shortcuts, most restaurants chose a healthy bottom line over food quality.

A few more breaks with the past occurred in both the boat and galley crews about this time. Likely attracted by the intense publicity of the 1970 SOLAS campaign, many *Delta Queen* job applicants were now hip young adults. The news media had turned the boat into a cause, and instead of saving whales or trees, a number of the socially active were now on the *Delta Queen* washing dishes and greasing engine parts. One other big change was that employees now belonged to a workers' union, the partnering with organized labor yet another step made to appease the adherents of SOLAS.

Even with the galley serving up mostly institutionalized food, passengers in the late 1970s still had the opportunity to dine on vintage choices such as catfish and shrimp creole. In the Texas Lounge they sipped on the boat's renowned mint juleps and Scarlett O'Haras. The first night of sailing was not breaking much with tradition either, almost always featuring a buffet of fried chicken and sides, including corn pudding, mashed potatoes, and green peas, plus the typical 1970s salad of iceberg lettuce, preshredded carrots, and jarred dressing.

In this era before celebrity chefs and food mania, the *Delta Queen*'s cooks knew about portion control, sauces, presentation, and ordering. But, as in most restaurants of the time, they were just considered "cooks," not professional chefs. And although menus from the late 1970s were appealing, they certainly were not cutting edge. Did the food taste good? Yes, but it was not exceptional. Was any food trend extraordinary at that time? Health food was growing in popularity, but it was mostly bland. Salad bars were gaining steam, but they only offered ho-hum items such as iceberg lettuce, bottled dressings, and artificial bacon bits. The now-boring quiche was still around. And so was soul food, the down-home fad that had started in the 1960s, and a style of eating that *Delta Queen* chefs had taken for granted all their lives. Even high-end restaurants of this period were struggling to establish their identity, with many still relying on the previous decade's French-inspired entrées. And when the *Delta Queen* served elegant fare during this time of transition, her galley also turned to traditional favorites.

OYSTER PO-BOY

Yield: 4 servings

Many New Orleans restaurants call their fried oyster po-boys "peacemakers" in honor of a creamed or broiled oyster sandwich popular in the 1800s. The 1901 edition of "The Picayune's Creole Cook Book" records its colorful history: "Every husband, who is detained down town, laughingly carries home an oyster loaf, or Médiatrice, to make 'peace' with his anxiously waiting wife."

24 fresh oysters, shucked and drained	16 slices pickle
Vegetable oil for frying	8 slices tomato
1 cup buttermilk	2 cups shredded lettuce
2½ cups Zatarain's Fish-Fri (seasoned cornmeal)	Ketchup (optional)
4 loaves French bread (6 inches each), sliced in half lengthwise	

Pat oysters dry with paper towels. Heat oil to 325°F for deep-frying. Pour buttermilk into a shallow bowl. Place seasoned cornmeal in another shallow bowl.

Dip oysters in buttermilk and then in cornmeal. Carefully place oysters in hot oil (a few at a time) and deep-fry until golden brown. Remove oysters from oil and drain on a rack.

Place 6 oysters on the bottom half of each loaf of bread and top with pickles, tomatoes, lettuce, ketchup (if desired), and top half of bread.

SCARLETT O'HARA

Yield: 1 drink

2 ounces Southern Comfort	6 ounces cranberry juice
½ teaspoon fresh lime juice	Lime wedge for garnish

In a Collins glass filled with crushed ice, pour Southern Comfort, lime juice, and cranberry juice. Stir well. Garnish with lime wedge.

Scarlett O'Hara

DELTA QUEEN'S ROAST DUCKLING QUARTERS

Yield: 2 to 4 servings | Printed in *The Advocate* (Newark, Ohio), September 3, 1976

1 duckling (4½ to 5 pounds), thawed
    if frozen and quartered
½ teaspoon salt

Hot fluffy rice
Orange–Green Onion Sauce or Regal
    Port Wine Sauce (*recipes follow*)

Preheat oven to 375°F. Rinse duckling quarters in cold water, then drain and pat dry with paper towels. Sprinkle both sides of duckling quarters with salt and place skin side up on a rack in a roasting pan. Roast uncovered until meat on drumstick is very tender and skin is crisp, 1½ to 2 hours. Serve with rice and sauce.

ORANGE–GREEN ONION SAUCE

Yield: 2 cups

¼ cup sugar
2 tablespoons cornstarch
1¼ cups orange juice
1 chicken bouillon cube, crumbled

1 cup fresh orange sections
2 tablespoons sliced green onions
1 tablespoon grated orange rind

Mix sugar and cornstarch in a small saucepan. Stir in orange juice and bouillon cube. Cook over low heat until sauce thickens and becomes clear, stirring constantly. Add orange sections, onions, and orange rind. Cook until heated through. Spoon warm sauce over duckling and rice.

REGAL PORT WINE SAUCE

Yield: about ¾ cup

1 tablespoon sugar
2 teaspoons cornstarch
¾ teaspoon dry mustard

¼ teaspoon ground ginger
½ cup port wine
½ cup currant jelly

Mix sugar, cornstarch, mustard, and ginger in a small saucepan. Blend in wine. Cook over low heat until sauce thickens and becomes clear, stirring constantly. Add jelly and heat until jelly melts. Spoon warm sauce over duckling and rice.

RED BEANS and RICE

Yield: 8 servings

Begin preparation one day before serving.

1 pound dried red kidney beans

3 tablespoons bacon drippings

2 ribs celery, diced

1 large onion, diced

½ cup diced green bell pepper

10 cups ham stock

2 cloves garlic, minced

1 smoked ham hock

1 whole bay leaf

¼ teaspoon black pepper

¼ teaspoon white pepper

Pinch of cayenne

Few dashes of Tabasco sauce

Salt

2 tablespoons vegetable oil

1 pound smoked pork sausage, cut in half lengthwise, then cut into 4-inch pieces

Cooked white rice

Chopped green onions (for garnish)

Place beans in a large bowl and cover with 2 inches of water. Cover and soak (unrefrigerated) for 8 to 10 hours or overnight. Drain.

Heat bacon drippings in a large Dutch oven over medium-high heat. Add celery, onion, and bell pepper. Sauté until onion is transparent. Add stock, garlic, ham hock, bay leaf, peppers, Tabasco, and salt. Simmer, uncovered, stirring occasionally, for 2½ hours or until beans are tender and broth becomes creamy.

Heat vegetable oil in a skillet over medium-high heat. Add sausage and sauté until browned.

Remove bay leaf and serve beans over rice in shallow soup bowls. Top with sausage and green onions.

This New Orleans staple was traditionally cooked on Monday, wash day, because it did not require much attention and housewives could therefore focus on their scrub boards.

Speckled Trout Pecan with Praline Sauce

SPECKLED TROUT PECAN

Yield: 2 servings | Adapted from a recipe by Chef Terry Newkirk

The silvery, dark-spotted speckled trout is popular with sports fishermen along the shores of the Gulf of Mexico and the southern Atlantic Ocean. Mature fish weigh between 1 and 3 pounds and produce firm, white flesh that is excellent sautéed.

¼ cup all-purpose flour

¼ cup finely chopped pecans

¼ teaspoon Cajun seasoning (*see page 27*)

2 tablespoons milk

1 egg, beaten

Vegetable oil for frying

2 speckled trout filets (8 ounces each)

½ cup Praline Sauce (*recipe follows*)

Lemon wedges (for garnish)

In a shallow bowl, combine flour, pecans, and Cajun seasoning. In a separate shallow bowl, beat together milk and egg.

Pour ¼ inch of oil into a large sauté skillet and heat over medium-high heat. Dip fish in milk mixture, then dredge in flour mixture. Carefully place fish in hot oil and sauté until golden brown on both sides.

Spoon ¼ cup warm praline sauce on each dinner plate and top with trout. Garnish with lemon wedges.

PRALINE SAUCE

Yield: ½ cup

3 tablespoons butter

2 tablespoons brown sugar

2 tablespoons praline liqueur

¼ cup heavy cream

Melt butter in a small saucepan. Add brown sugar and stir to blend. Add praline liqueur and cream; mix well. Simmer to reduce to ½ cup.

Speckled trout is also known as a "speck," "spotted weakfish," and "spotted seatrout."

COUNTRY ROAST CHICKEN

Yield: 2 servings

1 whole small chicken (1½ pounds), or
    a poussin or Rock Cornish game hen
1 carrot, coarsely chopped
1 rib celery, coarsely chopped
1 medium onion, coarsely chopped

2 tablespoons vegetable oil, divided
    or unsalted butter, softened
Julienned celery, carrot, and
    bell peppers (for garnish)
Chicken Pan Sauce (*recipe follows*)

Preheat oven to 450°F. Rinse chicken and pat dry with paper towels.

Scatter carrot, celery, and onion in a baking pan. Place chicken on vegetables, and pour a cup of water in the bottom of the pan. Lightly rub the surface of the chicken with 1 tablespoon vegetable oil or butter. Place pan in oven and immediately reduce heat to 325°F. Roast, basting often, until chicken is done, about 20 to 30 minutes.

Remove pan from oven and place chicken on a platter to cool slightly. Reserve pan juices for sauce.

When chicken is cool enough to handle, cut in half lengthwise and remove breastbone to produce 2 semiboneless chicken halves.

Heat remaining oil over medium-high heat in a small skillet and briefly sauté garnish vegetables. Top room-temperature chicken halves with sautéed vegetables and chicken pan sauce.

CHICKEN PAN SAUCE

Yield: 2 cups

1 cup reserved pan juices from
    Country Roast Chicken
1 cup chicken stock

½ cup blond roux (*see page 24*)
½ cup heavy cream

Strain pan juices and discard vegetables. Combine pan juices and stock in a saucepot. Boil on high heat until reduced in half, about 10 minutes.

Add roux and whip. Simmer, whipping constantly, until mixture is smooth and creamy.

Add cream and simmer 10 minutes. Adjust taste and consistency.

BANANAS FOSTER

Yield: 6 servings

6 tablespoons butter

1½ cups brown sugar

1 teaspoon ground cinnamon

6 green-tipped bananas, peeled and sliced
    lengthwise, then cut in half crosswise

¼ cup banana liqueur

½ cup rum

6 scoops French vanilla ice cream

Melt butter in a large skillet over low heat. Add brown sugar and cinnamon. Cook and stir until sugar dissolves.

Add bananas and banana liqueur. Cook until bananas begin to brown and become slightly soft.

Add rum but do not stir (let rum float on top of the sauce). When rum is hot, carefully ignite. After the flames subside, serve 4 slices of banana and a spoonful of sauce over each scoop of vanilla ice cream.

A 1950s creation of Brennan's Restaurant in New Orleans, this dessert has never gone out of style.

7 Decking Out for a President

THE CARTER FAMILY'S TRIP

CELEBRITIES AND PUBLIC FIGURES were always attracted by the charm of the *Delta Queen*. Helen Hayes, Errol Flynn, James Garner, and *Candid Camera* host Durward Kirby all traipsed her decks, as did entertainers Steve Allen, Jayne Meadows, Marilyn Monroe, Van Johnson, soprano Roberta Peters, historian Shelby Foote, and country singer Tammy Wynette. A few of the many public figures who boarded were Supreme Court Justice William O. Douglas, Chief Justice Earl Warren, President Herbert Hoover, and President Harry S. Truman. As tributes to visits from Lady Bird Johnson and Princess Margaret, their names appear on nameplates on stateroom doors, as does that of the passenger who caused the most on-board excitement, President Jimmy Carter.

In June 1979, President Carter had just successfully concluded the Strategic Arms Limitation Talks II (SALT II) negotiations with Soviet president Leonid Brezhnev and was on Air Force One headed for a short Hawaiian vacation when he received a telephone call from the White House. The Organization of Petroleum Exporting Countries (OPEC) cartel had just announced yet another oil price hike. Gasoline prices were skyrocketing, and long lines were forming at gas pumps. American tempers were out of control, and most of the steamrolling anger was directed at an administration that was facing reelection in 1980. The president's Hawaiian trip would have to be put on hold.

Carter turned back and undertook more than a week of grueling meetings at Camp David, after which he gave the most important speech of his presidency—his infamous "malaise" speech that outlined, among other things, mandatory conservation and standby gasoline rationing. He also vowed to "continue to travel this country, to hear the people of America." Republican senator Howard Baker of Tennessee, the Senate mi-

Doorplate on Jimmy Carter's stateroom

nority leader and a potential rival candidate for the presidency, had taken a trip on the *Delta Queen* the summer before, and he suggested that the president do the same. Carter liked the idea. Reportedly he had always wanted to ride on a steamboat. So on August 9, 1979, the White House announced a combination recreation/campaign trip for the energy proposal, a trip from St. Paul to St. Louis on the *Delta Queen.*

For two frantic weeks, the crew and contract workers spiffed up the *Queen* with new carpets and a communications system. New paint was splashed on everything that stood still. Windows were shined, brass was polished, wood was waxed, and the paddle wheel even got a good scrubbing.

A huge hand-painted sign was raised declaring the *Queen* "Steamboat One," and on August 17, after the Secret Service inspected everything and ran security checks on everyone, Captain Fred Martin welcomed aboard Jimmy Carter along with his wife, Rosalynn, and daughter, Amy. The family was allotted two aft cabins near the paddle wheel on the Sun Deck: Amy was assigned room 338, while President and Mrs. Carter unpacked in stateroom 340, one of two deluxe suites dating from the *Queen's* California period. In 1979, it was not the paddleboat's most palatial room, but it was the easiest to secure.

In spite of the meticulous preparation, not everything went perfectly. One day a 75 mph squall near Fort Madison, Iowa, drove rain through the roof of the Texas Lounge and scattered furniture all over the deck. And while most passengers considered this the trip of a lifetime, not everyone was impressed with the president's jogging habits. The first day, the president and about thirty Secret Service agents started jogging on the Sun Deck at 6 A.M., and their pounding caused complaints. Never mind that the noise was coming from the leader of the Free World; the *Queen's* passengers needed their sleep. Carter's diary shows that he jogged on shore for the rest of the trip.

There were other strains on the administration, too. Before the trip began, the White House levied strict restrictions on photographic coverage—limits that Jody Powell, the president's press secretary, eventually lifted. During the trip, press scrutiny was intense, with some writers blaming every evolving world mishap on the sailing president. And as

Sample *Delta Queen* menus for President Jimmy Carter's visit, 1979 (Courtesy of the Jimmy Carter Library and Museum)

SAMPLE DELTA QUEEN MENUS

BREAKFAST

Juice

Orange   Tomato   Prune   Pineapple
* * * * *
Stewed Prunes   Baked Apple
Grapefruit   Melon
(In Season)
* * * * *
An assortment of Cold Cereals
or
Hot Oatmeal
* * * * *
Eggs
Prepared to your liking
and served with our special fried grits
— Try our Delta Queen Scrambled —
* * * * *
Bacon   Ham   Sausage   Canadian Bacon
* * * * *
Pancakes   French Toast
Danish Pastries   English Muffins
* * * * *
A great cup of coffee

LUNCH

Soup du Jour

Sliced Tomatoes
* * * * *
Southern Baked Chicken and Gravy
Shrimp Salad in Avocado Shell
* * * * *
Mashed Potatoes   Corn O'Brien
* * * * *
Hot Rolls and Butter
* * * * *
Carrot Cake

DINNER

Assorted Relish Tray
* * * * *
Grapefruit Juice   Cream of Carrot Soup
* * * * *
Ceasar Salad
* * * * *
Roast Tenderloin of Beef Sauce Béarnaise
Trout Amandine
* * * * *
Château Potatoes   Mixed Vegetables
* * * * *
Hot Rolls and Butter
* * * * *
Blueberry Pie   Chocolate Pudding

THE CAPTAIN'S DINNER

Garden Relish Tray
Louisiana Shrimp Cocktail
* * * * *
Roast Prime Rib of Beef au jus with Horseradish Sauce
Filet of Lemon Sole Broiled in Butter
* * * * *
Green Peas and Mushrooms
Steamboat Baked Potato with Sour Cream and Chives
* * * * *
Hearts of Lettuce Salad
Choice of Dressing
* * * * *
Pecan Pie
Creme de Menthe Parfait
* * * * *
Coffee   Decaffeinated Coffee
Hot Tea   Iced Tea   Milk

the administration had expected, Carter's political opponents accused him of using the trip for his reelection campaign, but the president was adamant that it was a "working vacation."

The politics of the trip, however, did not seem to faze the folks up and down the Mississippi River as they lined the levees in all kinds of weather and at all hours of the night to witness history. Some even waded into the water to wave. They strung banners across river bridges, gave the president gifts, asked him questions, and shook his hand. At Wabasha, Minnesota, Mrs. Carter celebrated her fifty-second birthday to prayers, anthems, and the melodious calliope. Crowds greeted the family at Alma, Prairie du Chien, and Lock and Dam No. 8 in Wisconsin; in Iowa towns including McGregor, Dubuque, and Davenport; in Hannibal, Missouri, and finally, St. Louis. In all, the *Delta Queen* made forty-seven stops instead of the four originally planned. And whether they approved of his policies or not, just about everyone along the route was excited to see a sitting president stop by their town.

The president's schedule had been exhausting, yet while on board he and his wife did find time to dance to the music of the Riverboat Ramblers. Eleven-year-old Amy played hide-and-seek; Rosalynn did some reading; and the president sipped gin and tonic, attended sessions on riverboat gambling, played the calliope, and went fishing. That week

Early through mid-1980s base plate used on the *Delta Queen* and the *Mississippi Queen* (Photo courtesy David Dewey)

the president certainly did not stop running the country, but by all indications, he did relax.

The chef for the trip was the *Queen*'s longtime cook Robert Jackson. Julie Neil was sous chef, and Adrian Johnson was maître d'. The Carters had a private table in a secure corner, a table the crew swears was never used. Instead, the First Family chose to mingle. At the first night's Sailing Buffet, the Carters even grabbed their plates and waited for fried chicken in line with everyone else. From all reports, they were visible and friendly with other passengers, who in turn were pleasantly surprised that the president himself was so approachable.

The *Queen*'s menus for the week included items such as southern-baked chicken and gravy, shrimp salad in avocado shells, and roast beef. The last night, August 23, was the captain's dinner, and even with a president aboard, the galley did not deviate from its traditional menu:

Garden Relish Tray
Louisiana Shrimp Cocktail

Roast Prime Rib of Beef au Jus with Horseradish Sauce
Filet of Lemon Sole Broiled in Butter

Green Peas and Mushrooms
Steamboat Baked Potato with Sour Cream and Chives
Hearts of Lettuce Salad (choice of dressing)

Pecan Pie
Crème de Menthe Parfait

Coffee, Decaffeinated Coffee, Hot Tea, Iced Tea, Milk

The president's entourage judged the trip a rousing success. The biggest winner, however, was likely the *Delta Queen*. For the whole week, the clamoring press reported on the boat's every move, and the publicity quadrupled booking inquiries. The following year, President Carter lost his reelection bid. But he had already received a great consolation prize—he finally got to take a trip on a real steamboat.

JUMBO SHRIMP COCKTAIL

Yield: 6 servings

1 rib celery, coarsely chopped

½ lemon

¼ cup coarsely chopped onion

1 whole bay leaf

1 tablespoon salt

18 large fresh shrimp, peeled (leave
 tails intact) and deveined

Large bowl of water with ice cubes

Lettuce leaves (Boston, Bibb, or
 green leaf)

6 lemon wedges (for garnish)

6 sprigs fresh parsley (for garnish)

Cocktail Sauce (*recipe follows*)

In a large pot, combine 3 quarts water with celery, lemon, onion, bay leaf, and salt. Boil briskly, uncovered, for 3 minutes. Add shrimp and boil 3 minutes. Using a slotted spoon, remove shrimp from boiling water and place immediately in ice water to stop the cooking. As soon as shrimp are cool, pour off ice water and drain shrimp well.

To serve, arrange lettuce leaves on salad plates. Place 3 shrimp atop lettuce on each plate. Garnish with lemon and parsley. Serve cocktail sauce on the side.

COCKTAIL SAUCE

Yield: about 1¼ cups

1 cup bottled chili sauce

3 tablespoons ketchup

2 tablespoons prepared horseradish

1 tablespoon lemon juice

¼ teaspoon salt

¼ teaspoon Worcestershire sauce

Dash of Tabasco sauce

Combine all ingredients and blend well. Cover and chill. Spoon sauce into 1½-ounce ramekins to serve.

Jumbo Shrimp Cocktail with Cocktail Sauce

CAESAR SALAD

Yield: 6 servings

NOTE:

*This recipe contains
a raw egg yolk.
There is a small chance
of salmonella poisoning
when consuming
raw eggs.*

2 teaspoons white wine vinegar	½ teaspoon Worcestershire sauce
1 anchovy filet	Dash of Tabasco sauce
1 egg yolk (*see Note*)	½ cup olive oil
1 clove garlic, chopped	1 head romaine lettuce, rinsed and drained
1 teaspoon fresh lemon juice	Shaved Romano cheese (for garnish)
½ teaspoon Dijon mustard	Garlic croutons (for garnish)

In blender container, combine vinegar, anchovy, egg yolk, garlic, lemon juice, mustard, Worcestershire, and Tabasco. Process until ingredients are well blended. With blender running, slowly add oil until dressing becomes very thick. If dressing starts to separate, add a few drops of water before adding the remaining oil. Cover and chill.

Tear lettuce into bite-size pieces. Mix with ½ cup dressing. Arrange on salad plates and top with cheese and croutons. Serve immediately.

CREAM of CAULIFLOWER SOUP

Yield: 6 servings

6½ cups chicken stock	¼ cup chopped green onions
1 medium head cauliflower, cut in small pieces	½ cup blond roux (*see page 24*)
3 tablespoons butter	¾ cup milk, scalded
1 cup finely diced onion	¼ cup white wine
¾ cup finely diced green bell pepper	Chopped fresh parsley (for garnish)

Combine stock and cauliflower in a large pot. Cover and boil until cauliflower is tender. Strain, reserving stock.

Melt butter in a soup pot. Add onion, bell pepper, and green onions; sauté until tender. Add reserved stock and roux. Whisk well until roux has completely dissolved in the liquid. Stir in reserved cauliflower.

Add milk and wine. Bring to a boil, then remove from heat. Adjust seasoning and consistency. Garnish with parsley when serving.

SOUTHERN CHICKEN POT PIE

Yield: 4 servings

1 carrot, diced (½-inch pieces)

1 rib celery, diced (½-inch pieces)

½ cup diced yellow onion (½-inch pieces)

¼ cup frozen green peas

2 tablespoons vegetable oil

2 large boneless, skinless chicken breast
    halves, cut into bite-size chunks

2½ cups chicken stock

½ cup diced potatoes

⅓ cup heavy cream

1 tablespoon sherry

Salt and pepper

1 puff pastry sheet (10" × 15"),
    thawed if frozen

Egg wash (1 egg beaten with
    1 tablespoon water)

Chopped fresh parsley (for garnish)

In a heavy saucepot, sauté carrot, celery, onion, and peas in vegetable oil until onion is translucent. Add chicken and cook 2 minutes. Add stock and simmer 15 minutes. Add potatoes and cook until tender. Add cream and cook until mixture thickens slightly. Stir in sherry, salt, and pepper.

Preheat oven to 375°F. Spoon chicken mixture into 4 ovenproof soup plates or ramekins (5- or 6-ounce size). Prepare pie tops by cutting circles of pastry ¼ inch smaller than plates or ramekins. Top chicken mixture with pastry rounds. Brush pastry with egg wash and prick with a fork. Bake until golden brown, 25 to 35 minutes. Garnish with parsley when serving.

GARLIC TOAST

Yield: 1 loaf, 4 to 6 servings

1 16-ounce loaf unsliced French
bread, about 14 inches long
½ cup (1 stick) butter, softened

½ cup grated Parmesan cheese
1 tablespoon granulated garlic

Slice bread in half lengthwise. Butter each half. Sprinkle with cheese and garlic. Toast in a hot (400°F) oven until golden brown. Cut into slices to serve.

SPAGHETTI and MEATBALLS

Yield: 8 servings

2 cloves garlic, chopped
1 rib celery, finely diced
½ cup finely diced yellow onion
½ cup finely diced green bell pepper
1 tablespoon olive oil
1½ pounds ground beef
1 whole egg, beaten
½ cup seasoned bread crumbs
¼ cup grated Parmesan cheese

¼ cup chopped fresh parsley
½ teaspoon dried oregano
¼ teaspoon black pepper
Salt
Marinara Sauce (*recipe follows*)
1 package spaghetti (16 ounces)
Garlic Toast (see *recipe above*)
Grated Parmesan cheese for serving

Preheat oven to 350°F. Sauté garlic, celery, onion, and bell pepper in olive oil until tender. Remove from heat and cool. In a large mixing bowl, combine sautéed vegetables with ground beef, egg, bread crumbs, Parmesan cheese, parsley, oregano, pepper, and salt. Mix well. Form mixture into 8 meatballs and place in a baking pan. Bake for 25 to 30 minutes. Drain meatballs and cover with marinara sauce. Keep warm until ready to serve.

Cook spaghetti according to package directions; drain well. Top each serving of spaghetti with a meatball and sauce. Serve garlic toast and grated Parmesan on the side.

MARINARA SAUCE

Yield: 6 cups

1 cup finely chopped onion

½ cup finely chopped green bell pepper

2 tablespoons olive oil

2 cloves garlic, minced

1 whole bay leaf

½ teaspoon dried basil

½ teaspoon dried oregano

½ teaspoon dried thyme

1 teaspoon ham base (optional)

3 cups tomato sauce

1 can plum tomatoes (28 ounces)

1 can tomato puree (14.5 ounces)

1 teaspoon sugar

¼ teaspoon salt

¼ teaspoon black pepper

¼ teaspoon white pepper

Crushed hot red pepper

Sauté onion and bell pepper in oil until onion is translucent. Add garlic, bay leaf, basil, oregano, thyme, and ham base (if using). Sauté 1 minute. Stir in tomato sauce, tomatoes, tomato puree, sugar, salt, and peppers. Cover and simmer 2 hours. Remove bay leaf. Puree in a blender if a smoother consistency is desired.

Missouri Blackberry Custard Pie

MISSOURI BLACKBERRY CUSTARD PIE

Yield: 1 10-inch pie | Adapted from a recipe by Sir Robin Hixson

1 unbaked pie shell (*recipe follows*)

1 cup sugar

4 eggs

4 tablespoons flour

½ teaspoon vanilla extract

¼ teaspoon salt

⅛ teaspoon almond extract

2½ cups milk, scalded

1½ cups fresh blackberries, rinsed
  and well drained

Freshly grated nutmeg

Prepare pie shell and keep in freezer while making filling.

Preheat oven to 400°F. In a medium bowl, beat together sugar, eggs, flour, vanilla, salt, and almond extract. Add milk and whip gently with a wire whisk until blended.

Place berries in pie shell. Pour custard over berries and sprinkle liberally with nutmeg. Bake 55 to 60 minutes or until a knife inserted in the center comes out clean. Cool 1 hour at room temperature, then chill thoroughly.

PIE SHELL

Yield: 1 10-inch pie shell | Recipe courtesy Sir Robin Hixson

1¼ cups all-purpose flour

¼ teaspoon salt

5 tablespoons shortening

4 tablespoons ice water

Combine flour and salt in a 1-quart bowl. Cut in shortening with an electric mixer until mixture is crumbly. Sprinkle with ice water and mix with your hands until pastry forms a ball. Roll out dough and fit into a 10-inch pie pan. Do *not* prick crust with a fork.

MOCHA PECAN GLAZE

Yield: 6 servings | Adapted from a recipe by Chef Terry Newkirk

NOTE:

*This recipe contains
a raw egg yolk.
There is a small chance
of salmonella poisoning
when consuming
raw eggs.*

6 large scoops vanilla ice cream

1 cup finely chopped pecans

1 teaspoon instant coffee granules

2 tablespoons coffee liqueur

1 egg yolk (*see Note*)

¼ cup sugar

1 cup unsweetened whipped cream

6 thin cookie wafers

Roll scoops of ice cream in chopped pecans. Place on a sheet pan lined with wax paper and keep in freezer until ready to serve.

In a small bowl, dissolve instant coffee granules in coffee liqueur.

In a medium bowl, combine egg yolk and sugar. Beat at medium speed of electric mixer until mixture thickens and a dull sheen appears. Add coffee mixture and continue beating on low speed of mixer for 1 minute. Slowly blend in whipped cream.

To serve, spoon ¼ cup sauce into a serving glass. Top with a pecan-coated ice cream ball and crown with a cookie wafer.

Mocha Pecan Glaze

8 Sailing Out of the Twentieth Century

THE LAST TWO DECADES of the twentieth century started ominously with the *Delta Queen*'s wheel shaft cracking. The mishap occurred in 1980, but fortunately, years earlier, the far-sighted Tom Greene had purchased many of the *Delta King*'s mechanical parts, including the paddleboat's impossible-to-replace wheel shaft. The repair was made, and today the *Delta Queen*'s original wheel shaft is displayed in a yard of the Howard Steamboat Museum in Jeffersonville, Indiana. Back in 1954, parts from the *Delta King* had also saved the *Queen* when a broken piston rod was replaced in the steam engine's high-pressure cylinder. Today, the *Delta King*'s remaining spare parts are stored in a warehouse in New Orleans.

Original *Delta Queen* pilot's wheel, now on display at the Ohio River Museum, Marietta, Ohio

REMEMBERING THE *KING*

For several decades after the navy released her in the late 1940s, the *Delta King,* unlike the *Queen,* did not lead a pampered life. In the years after World War II and until 1953, the *King* was bought and sold several times, but the whole while sat idle at California docks. In 1952, Kitimat Constructors purchased the boat to serve as a barracks for its mining employees in Canada. By 1959, the company no longer needed her, and she was towed back to Stockton, California, where she was eventually sold at public auction to Stockton resident John Kessel.

One bright spot in this otherwise dismal period was the *Delta King*'s role in the 1959 movie *The Adventures of Huckleberry Finn.* But after this brush with fame was over, the *King* spent more than twenty years slowly decaying in different California docks. During that time, lawyers wrangled over rightful ownership, while a string of potential investors proposed various refurbishing schemes, including turning the grand old boat into a motel and nightclub, an entertainment center, a "floating Ghirardelli Square," a Chinese restaurant, and a public monument. None of these ideas panned out. Then for years she underwent a well-intended yet unsuccessful "Save the *King*" campaign. While waiting all that time for someone to rescue her, the *Delta King* sank twice. Finally, in 1984, visionary Californians Walt Harvey and Ed Coyne purchased what was left of the *Delta King* and spent five years and $9.5 million transforming her weathered skeleton into a stationary luxury hotel.

Today, the *Delta King,* like the *Delta Queen,* is listed on the National Register of Historic Places. Permanently moored at Old Sacramento, the striking *King* sports overnight staterooms, conference rooms, wedding and banquet facilities, cocktail lounges, and a theater. The boat's sophisticated Pilothouse Restaurant is located on the third deck. This popular eatery offers "California farm-fresh cuisine" with choices such as organic mixed greens, saffron risotto, free-range chicken, and grass-fed beef. The menu is trendy but elegant, just like it was back in 1927, the golden time when the *Delta King* crossed paths nightly with her twin, the *Delta Queen.*

A NEW OWNER AND HOME

Meanwhile, back in 1980, the Coca-Cola Bottling Company was losing $4 million annually on the Delta Queen Steamboat Company. Anxious to focus only on soft drinks, the corporation spun off stock, giving each holder of Coke stock five shares of the Delta Queen Steamboat Company and essentially making it a separate entity. In 1981, billionaire entrepreneur Sam Zell and his partner, Bob Lurie, bought the company's controlling stock, and it went into private ownership.

Belonging to big-time corporations, however, did not necessarily mean that the *Delta Queen* would have big-league food service. During the beginning of the Zell/Lurie ownership, Iowa travel writer John Field of the *Hamburg Reporter* judged that the food tasted just fine but was "not extravagant," and that breakfast "wasn't much." Field's indictment was not particularly aimed at the chefs. All the corporate juggling had led to high staff turnover on the *Delta Queen*, which in turn caused dining room service to suffer. Adding salt to that sore, the grits and sausage Field ordered for breakfast one morning never did arrive. Apparently a food service company had failed to make a delivery on time.

In the mid-1980s, the *Delta Queen* made substantial menu changes that reflected modern food trends as well as a general improvement of the entire boat. Construction upgrades during the 1983–84 layover included taking apart all the smaller upper and lower berth rooms and combining them into larger rooms, and equipping all staterooms with private toilets and showers. This change resulted in more suites and deluxe accommodations, which lowered passenger capacity from 188 to 174. Also, the high layover costs spurred higher trip prices, and as fares rose, so did passenger expectations for the *Queen*'s cuisine.

On the corporate side, things grew increasingly frenzied when, in 1985, the Delta Queen Steamboat Company moved from Cincinnati to New Orleans. That same year, the courageous woman who had fought so long to save the *Queen*, Letha Greene, passed away. The eighties also witnessed the deaths of two more *Delta Queen* "fighters": Betty Blake in 1983 and Bill Muster in 1989.

WHEN IN NEW ORLEANS . . .

In the pre–Civil War South, steamboats helped make the cotton trade profitable and made travel easier for European immigrants, thereby quickly transforming ramshackle towns such as St. Louis into major cities. Because of the steamboat, Louisville, Memphis, and Vicksburg became even bigger players in the slave trade, and Natchez had more millionaires per capita than any other city in the United States. But none of these cities

Live hogs were sometimes loaded aboard the boats to be slaughtered and freshly cooked, and were washed thoroughly before ascending the gangplank. The water used to wash the hogs was thrown out, of course, and "hog wash" came to mean anything. Passengers ate "high on the hog," and the captain and officers paid handsomely for moving thousands of bales of cotton, "brought home the bacon."

—from *Steam Cuisine,* ed. Kuhl (1999)

were as exotic and glamorous as New Orleans, a former French outpost and hub for pirates that in the nineteenth century grew into one of the most sophisticated cities in the world.

While never a major shipbuilding location, New Orleans was in the mid-1800s the second largest port in the United States and the fourth largest worldwide. Standing at the crossroads of the Mississippi, the Gulf of Mexico, and a web of inland rivers, the French-rooted city became the South's major financial center and the nation's largest slave market. Numerous bars, high-end hotels, and relatively exotic food made New Orleans a natural attraction for plantation owners, seamen, soldiers, wealthy travelers, artists, the curious, and just about anyone who loved to carouse. It was also a major port where immigrants entered the United States before heading north or to the rowdy but promising West, and where, according to writer Col. James R. Creecy, "human beings of all nations and colors" congregated at the levee, a dock covered with globally sourced merchandise.

A major part of the tonnage logged in at New Orleans was food commodities funneled down from the Midwest and West and destined for the international marketplace, including cheese, cider, potatoes, chickens, lard, wheat, flour, pork, bacon, and beef. From Cuba, the Caribbean, and South America came exotic fruits such as pineapples and coconuts, perishables that, along with locally produced sugar, rice, and molasses, could now easily be shipped upriver. During the steamboat era, New Orleans also became a major coffee importer and exporter. According to the Louisiana Department of Culture, Recreation and Tourism, the number of bags imported leapt from 1,438 in 1802 to an astounding 530,000 in 1857, this growth earning the city the nickname of the "Logical Port" for Latin American imports.

Locally, the shallow-drafted steamboat easily traveled to plantations. At docks along narrow rivers and bayous, paddle wheelers efficiently picked up and delivered cotton, sugar, rice, molasses, and slaves. Included were slave cooks who had unknowingly been transforming the bounty of the region into French Creole cooking. This much-celebrated

New World cuisine began not only with French techniques, but also with Native American, Spanish, and African contributions. But, as food writer Susan Tucker notes in *New Orleans Cuisine* (2009), those who cooked Creole considered it French because they intensely identified with France's "monopoly of gastronomy." Tucker elaborates that at the time, chefs in France were setting the pace for international culinary excellence, and that New Orleans cooks copied the style because they lived in a "lingering Francophone world [that] included a vast array of people whose lives revolved around marketing, cooking, and serving food and who [regardless of ethnicity] identified themselves as French." By the time of the 1840s "golden era" of steamboats, slave cooks, both on Louisiana plantations and in New Orleans, had long been cooking with butter, cream, wheat flour, rich stocks, roux, and herbs. With these traditional Gallic ingredients they prepared regional specialties such as étouffée, jambalaya, fricassee, gumbo, and pralines, foods that were served in homes, hotels, cafés, and boardinghouses, and on the menus of northbound steamboats.

A portion of the mountains of food brought in by steamboats stayed in the city, where it was stocked in huge open-air markets, making produce and meats easy and cheap to purchase. This handy cornucopia provisioned everything from homes to brothels, and to stylish hotels such as the St. Louis and the St. Charles—inns as large as small cities themselves, and that had elegant dining rooms and French-trained chefs. The upscale Antoine's, begun in a boardinghouse and still operating today, was established during this period of gastronomic plenty. Coffeehouses, also known as cafés and exchanges, were meeting places that served some food and coffee and lots of imported alcohol, and they thrived. The local appetite was definitely healthy, and food exports were also brisk. But even so, a quantity of food brought in by steamboats was never claimed and ended up left on docks to rot.

Southern steamboat commerce was nonexistent during the first two years of the Civil War, but international trade resumed at the port of New Orleans in 1863. At war's end, the steamboat was still important to trade, and it remained a significant mode of transportation for populating the West. Apparently the steamboat even helped bring refinement to the region. After leaving St. Louis on April 1, 1865, the steamboat *Bertrand* was on the Missouri River, bound for the unruly Montana gold fields, when the boat struck a hidden log twenty miles north of Omaha and sank. A later excavation uncovered not only necessities such as clothing and tools, but also olive oil and mustard from France, bottled tamarinds, brandy, canned fruits, bitters, and brandied cherries, extravagances more closely associated with prewar plantation gentry than with a territory mining camp.

Soon after the Civil War, train tracks were laid throughout the South and the diesel engine was invented. With commercial customers dwindling, steamboat owners increasingly turned to providing entertainment. Showboats, barges that brought theater to river towns, were uniquely American and had been around since the early 1800s. They regained popularity in the 1870s as they floated from town to town offering vaudeville, circuses, and Broadway-quality drama on elaborately decorated stages. Although showboats catered mostly to frontier towns, many did dock in New Orleans.

Another form of showboat was the lacy party barge known as a floating palace. These enormous gothic barges featured opulent staterooms, plush carpeting, twinkling chandeliers, shiny silver, and entertainment such as bands. In addition, floating palaces showcased Victorian-era culinary extravagance. In lavish dining halls filled with bone china and monogrammed linens, ordinary folks were able to eat from extraordinary menus that featured many New Orleans–inspired soups and entrées, such as gumbos, fricassees, and jambalaya. Similar delicacies had, of course, long been common in New Orleans restaurants. Rich in complex sauces, awash in imported wines, and lasting for hours, the city's European template for dining had been earning national gastronomic acclaim since the early 1800s. Mark Twain, who is credited with coining the term "floating palace," was so taken with French Creole cuisine that in 1884, after dining on a particularly toothsome pompano, he wrote, "New Orleans food is as delicious as the less criminal forms of sin."

Jazz and the dinner dance became trendy in the early 1900s when Captain John Streckfus started offering music-focused day, afternoon, and evening-long excursions from New Orleans to St. Paul, Minnesota. With no passenger sleeping cabins, the Streckfus line of steamers was able to construct huge art deco ballrooms, and over the years these boats featured such jazz greats as Louis Armstrong, Red Allen, Shorty Baker, Tab Smith, Clark Terry, and Jimmy Blanton. Kathryn and Linda Koutsky write in their book *Minnesota Vacation Days* (2006) that in addition to dancing to top-notch music, Streckfus patrons were able to dine in relative elegance on boats with "bubbling fountains, chic restaurants, gourmet buffets—and soda fountains decorated with pink elephants, purple snakes, and green monkeys."

In spite of all the gallant efforts to entertain, the steamboat could not compete with the Great Depression and modern technology such as movie houses. That, along with the more efficient train and automobile, brought to an end the common use of paddle wheelers in New Orleans in the early twentieth century.

DAWN OF THE CELEBRITY CHEF

Today the Port of New Orleans is the sixth largest in the country, and has been eclipsed worldwide by megaports. Over the years, however, the city has maintained its reputation

The palatial setting of later steamboats attracted pleasure-seekers and wealthy travelers . . . More comfortable than their "settin' rooms," more ornate than their prim and uncomfortable parlors . . . they saw the steamboat's cabin as a bewilderingly beautiful palace. The . . . glistening cut-glass chandeliers; the soft oil paintings on every stateroom door; the thick carpets that transformed walking into a royal march; the steaming foods piled high on the long linen cloth in the dining room, with attentive waiters standing at the traveler's elbow, waiting with more food, and gaily colored desserts in the offing—neither homes nor hotels . . . were ever like this.

—Herbert Quick, from *Mississippi Steamboatin': A History of Steamboating on the Mississippi and Its Tributaries* (1926)

as a food mecca. But when the Delta Queen Steamboat Company moved to New Orleans in 1985, it found many of the city's upscale restaurants just weaning themselves from dependence on convenience foods. In spite of the region's impressive culinary heritage and access to a world of fresh foodstuffs, many old-line restaurants had succumbed to the simplicity and economy of purchasing ingredients frozen or prepackaged. But that was changing. All over the United States, serious cooks and restaurants were reexamining their standards of quality, thanks in large part to celebrity chefs.

In the early 1980s public television began airing its *Great Chefs* series, with the first thirteen half-hour shows featuring restaurants in New Orleans. At the same time, California's Alice Waters and her state's farm-fresh produce became all the rage, and yuppies were lining up at hip restaurants for Mediterranean-influenced organic and seasonal foods. Waters's one-time business partner Jeremiah Tower and French-trained Wolfgang Puck became cult figures, as did New Orleans's favorite Cajun chef, Paul Prudhomme. Another local chef, John Folse, made headlines for opening Louisiana-style demonstration restaurants in Hong Kong, England, Canada, Japan, and Spain. With help from chefs Kim and Tim Kringlie of Baton Rouge, Mike Roussell of New Orleans, and Bruce Cain of Shreveport, Folse even opened a Cajun-Creole restaurant four blocks from the Kremlin for the Reagan-Gorbachev summit. These successful personalities, among others, prompted restaurants to reconnect with fresh produce, to learn how to use spices, to make more creative presentations, and to figure out just exactly what "fusion" meant.

The *Delta Queen*'s galley was definitely in on the food craze of the eighties. And during this time of culinary introspect, menus started becoming more sophisticated, especially with inventive lunch sandwiches, the option for smaller entrée portions, and updated seafood preparations, including dishes such as stuffed catfish and crawfish with pasta, as well as the ubiquitous Prudhomme creation of the time, blackened redfish. Interestingly, the boat's chefs tended to shy away from then-popular California fare and instead continued spotlighting Creole cuisine and that of the Deep South. Likely owing to its new corporate home and Prudhomme's Cajun movement, the galley even intensified the genre. True, age-old favorites such as beef Wellington, filet mignon with béarnaise sauce, and prime rib were still standard menu items. And fettucini alfredo and pasta genovese made frequent appearances. But theme dinners definitely leaned southern, with menus highlighting French Creole, Acadian, Mardi Gras, and Plantation cookery. Regular meals, too, were heavy with local dishes such as fried catfish, jambalaya, shrimp creole, rice pudding, and pecan pie.

This era's "southern" experience also focused on exemplary service, and the newly relocated Delta Queen Steamboat Company went all out to treat passengers like visiting luminaries. The 1984–86 edition of *Steamboatin'*, the company's promotional magazine, gives a flowery yet informative look into the regal atmosphere the *Mississippi Queen* and the *Delta Queen* tried to create:

Gracious Dining aboard the *Queens*

As the setting sun turns day to dusk, softly ringing chimes announce that dinner is served. The Master chefs daily create an endless selection of cuisine fit for royalty.

In true Riverboat fashion, four-course dinners offer Oysters Vieux Carré, Prime Rib of Beef and Southern Catfish—an old favorite of Mark Twain's. Attentive waiters meet your every request with a smile while our wine stewards are happy to help you select a fine bottle of domestic or imported wine to complement your meal. Soft piano music invites you to linger a little longer over your Pecan Pie, Baked Alaska or Praline Sundae.

In the morning, you'll be surprised how quickly you have regained your appetite once you're presented with the possibilities of a hearty Southern breakfast, made even more delightful as the sunlight breaks softly through the window offering a view of America just outside. Your palate will continually be tempted throughout the day as waiters emerge from the Galley with sumptuous lunches, afternoon tea hors d'oeuvres and delectable midnight buffets. It's all so grand, you might begin to think preparations for your stay aboard actually began over a century ago. Gracious dining on the river became a glorious tradition during the Great Steamboat era. It has reached true perfection aboard the *Delta Queen* and the *Mississippi Queen*.

Aside from changing its own way of looking at food, the Delta Queen Steamboat Company reacted to the nation's food obsession by hiring celebrated food writer Rick Rodgers to write a cookbook. In the early 1990s, Rodgers took a trip on the *Delta Queen*, and while on board, he laid the groundwork for his steamboat-themed cookbook, *Mississippi Memories* (1994). Rodgers's collection features tempting recipes such as Sweet-

and-Sour Spiced Swedish Beans; Wild Rice and Dried Cherries Salad; and Banana, Raspberry, and Peach Cookie Trifle. But even though these appealing choices appear in a book published by the Delta Queen Steamboat Company, none of the recipes came from *Delta Queen* steamboat chefs.

Taking a page from the 1800s, the *Delta Queen* also connected with the late twentieth-century eating craze by offering a "recipe sharing" program. During a scheduled time, all interested passengers met and submitted favorite recipes. Before the end of the trip, the cruise director typed them and distributed copies. Printed recipes also went home with passengers who took food-themed trips that sailed from New Orleans to shore stops on the lower Mississippi. Usually held during Christmastime, "Taste of the Mississippi" trips focused specifically on food and food demonstrations, while "Dixiefest" trips also offered jazz. The three- to seven-night Dixiefest trips began with a snazzy sendoff from the New Orleans dock and led to a single special performance on board the *Delta Queen* by celebrities such as Pete Fountain, Al Hirt, the Preservation Hall Jazz Band, and the Dukes of Dixieland.

For both themes, food demonstrations leaned heavily to Deep South dishes, and regular meals and jazz brunches filled passengers up with lots of local seafood, gumbos, and champagne. Participating guest chefs on the *Mississippi Queen* and the *Delta Queen* (and later the *American Queen*) included local greats such as Lazone Randolph of Brennan's; Curtis Moore from the Praline Connection; Gary Darling of Copeland's and Semolina's; Ann Dunbar of K-Paul's; Joe Cahn from the New Orleans School of Cooking; Mark Defelice of Pascal's Manale; Richard Hughes from the Pelican Club; Joel Shapiro of the Gumbo Shop; Carroll Thomas from Cajun Power Sauce Manufacturing, Inc.; and Kathy Starr, author of *The Soul of Southern Cooking* (1989), a book of authentic soul food recipes. After the show was over, passengers nibbled on preprepared samples. To finish off a day of cooking, anyone interested could join one of the *Delta Queen*'s chefs in decorating gingerbread houses and cookies, an activity that remained popular through 2008.

In 1986, a year after the Delta Queen Steamboat Company moved to New Orleans, the company fell under the umbrella of Sam Zell's Equity Group Investments, Inc. Two years later, the *Delta Queen* participated in the first Tall Stacks festival, a celebration of music, art, and riverboat heritage held every three or four years on the Ohio River at Cincinnati. Always attracting massive attention, through 2006 the *Delta Queen* made six consecutive appearances at the festivities.

During the eighties era of corporate maneuverings, promotions through the media and travel agencies resulted in a passenger capacity of 95 percent, with fares rising more than 28 percent and operating income shooting up accordingly. To end this prosperous decade in style, in 1989 the *Delta Queen* was named a National Historic Landmark.

Big red paddle wheel

TWO MORE *QUEEN*S ARE BORN

In 1992, the Delta Queen Steamboat Company again traded publicly, and it had no debt. More good news came in 1993 in the form of a SOLAS extension that was good until 1998. And with the nation's burgeoning consumerism and steamboating's renewed popularity, in 1993 the Delta Queen Steamboat Company contracted with McDermott Shipyard of Amelia, Louisiana, to construct a third New Orleans–based boat, the *American Queen*. This Victorian-inspired boat was designed with a paddle wheel but ran on modern diesel technology. She was built a gigantic 418 feet long and 89 feet wide, earning her the title of the world's largest cruising riverboat. She could accommodate 436 passengers in 222 staterooms, and had every imaginable modern luxury, including a formal dining room that aimed to copy the famous *J. M. White*'s opulence.

Decorative souvenir plate

Zell formed American Classic Voyages, and in 1993, he bought the bankrupt American Hawaii Cruises. He made American Classic Voyages the Delta Queen Steamboat Company's parent in 1994. A year later, the $60 million *American Queen* made her maiden voyage. In 1997, American Classic Voyages was able to spend $3.3 million to renovate the *Delta Queen*, stripping the boat's superstructure down to bare wood.

Things were looking so grand for the company that management ordered a fourth *Queen*, the 218-foot diesel-powered *Columbia Queen*. Built off the hull of a former casino boat in the style of classic historic river steamers, construction began on the 150-passenger boat at Leevac Shipyards, Inc. of Jennings, Louisiana, but was finished at Cascade General, Inc., in Portland, Oregon. The ultramodern *Columbia Queen* was designed with diesel engines and no paddle wheel. On May 27, 2000, she made her maiden voyage up the Columbia River through the Snake River Canyon to Lewiston, Idaho, and has always sailed in the Northwest.

ADJUSTING TO THE HURRIED 1990s

At the beginning of the 1990s, the super-health-conscious were already eating raw, and Martha Stewart was writing books on how to entertain properly. At the French Laundry restaurant in California, Thomas Keller was artfully serving tiny portions for astronomical prices, and tapas bars were on the scene. By the middle of the decade, the Food Network was up and running, and a gaggle of celebrity chefs were grilling anything edible and experimenting with artistic versions of Mexican, Greek, and Italian foods. But despite the food world's push to encourage both healthy eating and extravagance, this time period saw fast-food outlets more than double their sales. The decade's lightning-fast society did not want to stay home and cook. For those who still longed for Mom's home cooking, the pick-up and delivery of HMRs (home meal replacements) gained popularity, and precooked entrées, sides, and desserts were increasingly available in quick-service eating places and supermarkets.

It was not until this time that the *Delta Queen's* galley started offering light entrées and desserts approved by the American Heart Association along with a few vegetarian choices. In addition, passengers could choose an off-the-menu southern vegetable. Bowing to the lingering Cajun food phenomenon, everything was still a little spicy.

The mid-1990s galley also cleverly integrated prevailing trends by updating what was natural to the region (seafood in particular), and they avoided the overly stylized (i.e., objectionable) fads that would have turned off more traditional passengers. Of course, lots of things were still fried, and there was no shortage of rich desserts.

THE TIDE TURNS AGAIN

Right after the *Columbia Queen* started sailing, schedule-changing floods, lackluster sales in Hawaii, and a corporate attempt to sell to a mass market instead of an upscale niche all combined to cripple the Delta Queen brand. Making matters worse, after the World Trade Center attack on September 11, 2001, American Classic's cancellations increased by 30 percent and bookings declined by 50 percent. With the U.S. tourist industry in collapse, on October 19, 2001, American Classic Voyages filed for Chapter 11 bankruptcy. But even though the new century started on a sour note, *Delta Queen* fans could find solace in the past two decades, a prosperous, innovative period that produced not only memories, but a wealth of superior recipes, many of which remained favorites through 2008.

CHEDDAR-GARLIC GRITS SPOON BREAD

Yield: 6 servings

Recipe from the Delta Queen Steamboat Company pamphlet *Recipes from the Heartland*, August 2001

½ cup yellow cornmeal	2 large eggs, beaten
½ cup all-purpose flour	1½ cups milk, divided
½ cup old-fashioned grits (not instant)	1 cup shredded sharp Cheddar
1 tablespoon sugar	cheese (4 ounces)
1 teaspoon baking soda	1 cup corn kernels, thawed if frozen
1 teaspoon salt	1 garlic clove, minced
1 cup buttermilk, or 1 cup milk mixed	2 tablespoons unsalted butter, cut
with 1 teaspoon cider vinegar	into small pieces

Preheat oven to 400°F. In a large bowl, combine cornmeal, flour, grits, sugar, baking soda, and salt; whisk to mix. Stir in buttermilk and eggs. Add 1 cup of the milk along with cheese, corn, and garlic. Stir just to combine; do not overmix.

Place butter in a 10-inch round cake pan or cast-iron frying pan. Place pan in the oven and heat just until butter melts, about 3 minutes. Tip the pan to coat the bottom and sides with butter. Pour batter into buttered pan and sprinkle remaining ½ cup milk over the top.

Bake until golden brown, about 25 minutes. A toothpick inserted 2 inches from the edge of the pan will come out clean and the center will be barely set. Remove from oven and let stand 5 minutes. Serve warm.

LAGNIAPPE:

Turn this into a crab spoon-bread casserole by spreading 8 ounces of crabmeat on the bottom of the hot pan before pouring in the batter.

GAZPACHO

Yield: 8 servings

4 cups V8 vegetable juice

1 can diced tomatoes (15 ounces), drained

1¼ cups peeled, seeded, and
    diced cucumbers

½ cup diced carrot

½ cup diced celery

½ cup diced onion

½ cup diced green pepper

½ cup sliced scallions

2 tablespoons lemon juice

½ teaspoon granulated garlic

½ teaspoon Tabasco sauce

Salt and pepper

Sour cream (for garnish)

All vegetables should be cut into the same size small dice. Combine all ingredients except sour cream and mix well. Cover and refrigerate for at least 12 hours. Serve ice-cold in chilled soup cups. Garnish each serving with a dollop of sour cream.

ROAST DUCK and WILD RICE SOUP

Yield: 8 to 10 servings

Recipe from the Delta Queen Steamboat Company pamphlet *Recipes from the Heartland*, August 2001

2 tablespoons unsalted butter

6 scallions, chopped

4 ounces white mushrooms, thinly sliced

3 ribs celery, cut into ¼-inch slices

2 medium carrots, cut into ½-inch cubes

2 quarts duck stock (*recipe follows*)

¼ cup chopped fresh parsley

1½ teaspoons dried savory or thyme

1 teaspoon salt

¼ teaspoon freshly ground black pepper

¾ cup wild rice, well rinsed and drained

Reserved duck meat (*recipe follows*)

Sour cream (for garnish, optional)

Prepare Roast Duck and Stock at least 1 day in advance of making the soup.

Melt butter in a large pot over medium-low heat. Add scallions, mushrooms, celery, and carrots. Cover and cook until vegetables are soft, about 5 minutes. Add stock, parsley, savory, salt, and pepper. Bring to a simmer. Add wild rice and simmer over low heat, partially covered, until rice is tender, about 1 hour to 1 hour and 15 minutes. Add duck meat and heat through, about 5 minutes. Serve immediately, topping each serving with a dollop of sour cream if desired.

ROAST DUCK and STOCK

1 duck (4½ to 5 pounds), including neck
    and all giblets except liver
½ teaspoon salt
¼ teaspoon freshly ground black pepper
1 cup boiling water
1 large carrot, coarsely chopped
1 medium rib celery, coarsely chopped
1 large onion, coarsely chopped
1 cup plus 2 quarts cold water, divided
4 sprigs parsley
1 whole bay leaf
½ teaspoon dried thyme
¼ teaspoon whole black peppercorns

Preheat oven to 400°F. Rinse the duck, remove and discard excess fat from the tail cavity, and pat duck dry with paper towels. Sprinkle cavity with salt and pepper. With the upturned prongs of a searing fork, pierce the duck skin all over, being careful not to pierce the meat.

Place duck on a rack in a roasting pan and slowly pour boiling water over the duck. Roast, basting often with pan juices, for 45 minutes. Place carrot, celery, onion, duck neck, and giblets in the pan and continue to roast, basting often, until juices run clear when the thigh is pierced with a fork, about 1 hour. Remove from oven and set aside until duck is cool enough to handle. Remove as much meat as possible, discarding the skin and fat but reserving the carcass. Cut duck meat into ½-inch cubes, cover, and refrigerate.

Using a slotted spoon, transfer the vegetables, neck, and giblets to a large soup pot. Place the roasting pan over two burners on top of the stove and add 1 cup cold water. Bring to a simmer, scraping up any flavorful bits from the bottom of the pan, then pour pan juices into the soup pot.

Add duck carcass and wings to the soup pot along with 2 quarts cold water. Bring to a simmer over medium heat, skimming off any foam that rises to the top. Add parsley, bay leaf, thyme, and peppercorns. Reduce heat to low and simmer for 2 hours. Strain broth and cool to room temperature. Cover and refrigerate until well chilled, at least 4 hours or overnight. Discard fat that rises to the top of the stock.

CRAB and ASPARAGUS CHOWDER

Yield: 6 to 8 servings

Recipe from the Delta Queen Steamboat Company pamphlet *Recipes from the Heartland*, August 2001

½ cup (1 stick) butter

2 cups finely chopped asparagus stems

1 cup finely diced onion

½ cup flour

2 quarts chicken stock

½ pound potatoes, cooked and diced

Worcestershire sauce

Tabasco sauce

Salt

White pepper

1 cup heavy cream

2 cups crabmeat (for garnish)

1 cup cooked and diagonally sliced asparagus spears (for garnish)

Melt butter in a soup pot. Add asparagus stems and onion. Sauté for 4 minutes. Stir in flour to make a roux. Cook another 4 minutes. Add stock and simmer over low heat for 10 minutes. Strain through a fine strainer. Discard asparagus and onion.

Return liquid to soup pot, bring to a boil, then reduce heat and simmer for 2 minutes. Add potatoes and simmer for 5 minutes. Add Worcestershire sauce, Tabasco, salt, and pepper. Stir a few tablespoons of the hot soup into the cream, 1 tablespoon at a time, to temper; then blend tempered cream into soup. Heat through but do not boil. Ladle soup into bowls and garnish with crabmeat and asparagus slices.

THANKSGIVING TURKEY DRESSING

Yield: 12 to 15 servings (or enough to stuff a turkey) | Recipe courtesy of Sir Robin Hixson

This dressing can also be baked in a greased 2-quart baking dish at 375°F for about 45 minutes or until top is browned.

2 loaves French bread
¼ cup vegetable oil
3 ribs celery, finely chopped
2 large onions, finely chopped
1 large green bell pepper, finely chopped
2 pounds ground pork or beef, or
   1 pound of each

3 pints oysters, drained
Salt and pepper
1 medium bunch green onions, chopped
1 medium bunch fresh parsley, chopped
1½ teaspoons fresh thyme
2 eggs, beaten

Preheat oven to 350°F. Cut bread into 1-inch cubes. Spread bread cubes in a single layer on a baking sheet. Place in oven for 5 minutes to dry.

Heat oil in a Dutch oven. Add celery, onion, and bell pepper. Sauté until onion is translucent. Add pork or beef and sauté until cooked through. Drain off excess fat. Add oysters and cook until edges begin to curl. Add salt and pepper.

Soak bread in water, then squeeze bread dry. In a large bowl, combine bread, green onions, parsley, and thyme. Add bread mixture to meat and oyster mixture in Dutch oven and blend well. Simmer 15 minutes.

Add eggs and mix well. Remove from heat and cool. Do not stuff turkey until ready to bake. Bake turkey according to instructions on packaging.

EGGS CRAWKITTY

Yield: 8 servings

In the 1980s, Chef Gary Darling was with the New Orleans–based Copeland's restaurant chain, and he often gave demonstrations on both the Delta Queen and the Mississippi Queen. This dish derives its name from a crawfish hollandaise sauce used to top poached eggs and fried catfish. When the dish appears on menus in locales where it's hard to procure catfish and crawfish, it often retains the unusual name but makes substitutes for these regional ingredients.

Peanut oil for deep-frying

4 cups buttermilk

2 cups corn flour

1 teaspoon freshly ground white pepper

1 teaspoon salt

8 catfish filets (4 ounces each)

8 eggs, poached

Tasso Crawfish Hollandaise (*recipe follows*)

Snipped fresh chives (for garnish)

8 crawfish, boiled (for garnish, optional)

Heat oil to 350°F in a deep-fryer or large heavy saucepan. Pour buttermilk into a shallow pan or dish. Sift corn flour, pepper, and salt into another shallow pan. Dip catfish in buttermilk, then dredge in seasoned flour. Carefully place catfish in hot oil (a few pieces at a time) and fry until golden brown, about 3 minutes. Remove fish from oil with a slotted spatula and drain on paper towels. Place 1 piece of catfish on each dinner plate. Top with a poached egg and Tasso Crawfish Hollandaise. Garnish with chives and crawfish.

Louisiana produces 90 percent of the world's crawfish and 98 percent of crawfish consumed in the United States, with 70 percent of the annual crop eaten locally.

TASSO CRAWFISH HOLLANDAISE

Yield: about 3 cups

6 egg yolks

1 tablespoon water

2 cups (4 sticks) butter, melted

¼ to ½ teaspoon salt

Dash of hot pepper sauce

2 tablespoons fresh lemon juice

1 ounce tasso ham or double-smoked, thick-cut bacon, cut into strips

4 ounces cooked crawfish tails, sliced in half (about ½ cup)

1 tablespoon chopped green onions

Whisk egg yolks and water in the top of a double boiler over gently simmering water until mixture is thick and foamy, about 5 minutes. Remove top pan from double boiler. Gradually whisk in butter. Season with salt and hot pepper sauce. Stir in lemon juice. Set aside and keep warm.

Cook tasso in a small heavy skillet over medium heat until browned. Remove from heat. Stir in crawfish tails and green onions. Cool for 15 minutes. Gently fold tasso mixture into warm sauce. Serve immediately.

PRALINES

Yield: 1 to 50 candies, depending on size

Recipe and history courtesy of Joe Cahn, the self-proclaimed "Commissioner of Tailgating"

Chef Joe Cahn founded the New Orleans School of Cooking, and for years he was a celebrity judge in an annual Delta Queen Steamboat Company steamboat race from New Orleans to St. Louis. Usually held around July 4, the race was accompanied by activities such as banner contests, talent shows, and "floozy" contests, as well as lively praline-making demonstrations by Cahn on board both the Delta Queen and her rival.

Joe Cahn's history of pralines: The most popular New Orleans candy, pralines are made from two of Louisiana's top products—sugar and pecans. Pralines derive their name from Marshal du Plessis-Praslin (1598–1675), a Frenchman who offered almonds coated in cooked sugar to famous women along with his amorous intentions.

(Another legend says that the name praline *was coined by Praslin's personal chef, while yet another says it was bestowed by military rivals who had tasted the delicious treat. Some diners of the time also believed that the sugary confection prevented indigestion.)*

When Louisiana was settled by French colonists, native pecans were substituted for France's traditional almonds, and sugar made from Louisiana sugarcane was used. Recipes have been handed down from generation to generation.

NOTE:

To roast pecans, arrange nuts in a single layer on a sheet pan. Bake at 275°F for 20 to 25 minutes or until pecans are slightly browned. Watch carefully so they do not burn.

1½ cups shelled pecans (roasted, if desired; *see Note*)

1½ cups granulated sugar

¾ cup packed light brown sugar

½ cup milk

6 tablespoons (¾ stick) butter

1 teaspoon vanilla extract

Have sheets of buttered waxed paper, aluminum foil, or parchment paper ready for the hot pralines. If using waxed paper, be sure to place several sheets of newspaper or paper towels underneath to buffer the heat of the pralines as hot wax will transfer to the countertop or table.

Combine all ingredients in a large heavy saucepan. Bring to a boil and cook until soft-ball stage (238°F–240°F) is reached, stirring constantly. Remove from heat and continue stirring until mixture thickens. The candy will become creamy and cloudy, and the pecans will stay suspended in the mixture.

Working quickly, spoon hot candy onto prepared paper or foil. Cool pralines completely and store in a covered container.

SOUTHERN PRALINE PECAN PIE

Yield: 2 9-inch pies | Recipe courtesy of Kathy Starr

Food writer John Egerton believes that molasses pie was a precursor to pecan pie. And although no documentation exists, legend also has it that the French invented pecan pie in New Orleans right after they founded the city and discovered an abundance of pecan trees.

3 eggs

1 cup sugar

1½ cups light corn syrup

½ cup (1 stick) butter, melted

1½ teaspoons vanilla extract

1¼ cups shelled pecans

2 tablespoons plain white flour

2 unbaked 9-inch pie shells (*see page 141*)

Preheat oven to 375°F. Break eggs into a mixing bowl and beat slightly. Add sugar and beat until mixture is smooth. Add corn syrup, butter, and vanilla; mix well. In a small dish, combine pecans and flour, tossing to coat pecans evenly. Add pecans to egg mixture and blend gently. Pour filling into crusts and bake 35 to 40 minutes.

Sweet Potato Pie

SWEET POTATO PIE

Yield: 2 9-inch pies | Recipe courtesy of Kathy Starr

A guest chef for several Delta Queen holiday tours, Kathy Starr is the author of the acclaimed book "The Soul of Southern Cooking," a collection of recipes that were passed down from slaves.

5 medium sweet potatoes	2 teaspoons vanilla extract
3 eggs	1½ tablespoons baking powder
1½ cups sugar	⅓ cup evaporated milk
10 tablespoons (1¼ sticks) butter, melted	2 unbaked 9-inch pie shells (*recipe follows*)
2½ teaspoons ground nutmeg	

Wash and peel sweet potatoes. Place in a deep pot and cover with water. Simmer until tender, about 60 minutes.

Preheat oven to 350°F. Drain potatoes and beat until no lumps remain. Add eggs, sugar, butter, nutmeg, and vanilla; mix well. Blend baking powder with milk, then stir into potatoes. Pour filling into pie shells and bake for 50 minutes or until firm. Cool and serve.

PIE SHELLS

Yield: 2 9-inch pie shells | Recipe courtesy of Kathy Starr

2 cups plain white flour	¼ cup water
1 cup vegetable shortening	Dash of salt

Sift flour into a medium bowl. Add shortening, water, and salt. Stir with a fork until well blended. Do not add any more flour than needed to form dough. Too much flour will make the crust tough. Roll out dough for two 9-inch pie plates. Fit dough into pie plates and crinkle edges.

BANANA PUDDING

Yield: 7 to 8 servings | Recipe courtesy of Kathy Starr

4 eggs, separated

2¼ cups sugar

1 can evaporated milk (12 ounces)

1¼ cups water

¾ cup plain white flour

2 teaspoons vanilla extract

5 cups vanilla wafers

6 ripe bananas

Meringue (*recipe follows*)

In the top of a double boiler over gently simmering water, beat egg yolks until they are foamy. Add sugar, evaporated milk, and water, stirring constantly. Slowly stir in flour and beat until pudding thickens. Add vanilla.

Preheat oven to 350°F. In a deep 9" × 9" ovenproof baking dish, use one-third of each ingredient to make layers of vanilla wafers, bananas, and pudding. Repeat layers two more times. Top with meringue. Bake until meringue browns, about 15 minutes. Cool and serve.

MERINGUE

Yield: one topping for a 9" × 9" pan | Recipe courtesy of Kathy Starr

4 egg whites

¼ cup sugar

In a clean, dry mixing bowl, beat egg whites at high speed of electric mixer until they begin to turn fluffy. Gradually add sugar and beat until stiff peaks form.

Banana Pudding with Meringue

MISSISSIPPI MUD PIE

Yield: 6 to 8 servings

The Mississippi mud pie is named for the dark chocolate–colored banks of the Mississippi River. The recipe is believed to have originated in the state of Mississippi, and it became popular in the 1970s. Many Delta Queen chefs prepared similar versions of this perennial southern favorite. This recipe combines the best of them all.

1 recipe Chocolate Pecan Brownie (*recipe follows*)

1 recipe Coffee Ice Cream (*recipe follows*), or 1½ quarts purchased ice cream, softened

1 recipe Whipped Cream (*recipe follows*)

½ cup chocolate syrup (homemade or purchased), warmed

½ cup pecan pieces (for garnish)

Bake brownie and cool in pan. Spread ice cream evenly over the entire brownie. Cover and place in freezer until ice cream is firm. Top with whipped cream and freeze again. When ready to serve, cut into equal portions and top with chocolate syrup. Garnish with pecans.

CHOCOLATE PECAN BROWNIE

4 ounces unsweetened chocolate

1 cup (2 sticks) unsalted butter, softened

4 whole eggs

1¾ cups sugar

1 teaspoon vanilla extract

½ teaspoon salt

1 cup all-purpose flour

1 cup pecan pieces

Preheat oven to 375°F. Grease an 8" × 11" × 2" baking pan. Melt chocolate, then cool. Beat butter in a medium bowl until light. Add eggs, sugar, vanilla, and salt; mix until light and fluffy. Stir in chocolate and flour. Fold in pecans. Pour into prepared pan and bake for approximately 30 minutes. Remove from oven and cool in pan.

COFFEE ICE CREAM

Yield: about 1½ quarts

COFFEE REDUCTION:

4 cups coffee simmered until liquid is reduced to ¼ cup. Two teaspoons instant coffee granules mixed with 2 tablespoons water may be substituted.

2 cups whole milk	4 eggs
1½ cups heavy cream	¼ cup coffee reduction
1 can evaporated milk (12 ounces)	½ teaspoon vanilla extract
1 cup sugar	¼ teaspoon salt

In a medium saucepan, combine milk, cream, and evaporated milk; heat to scald, watching carefully so the mixture does not burn. Remove from heat and add sugar. Stir until sugar dissolves.

In a medium bowl, beat eggs, coffee reduction, vanilla, and salt. Slowly add milk mixture, whipping continuously.

Pour mixture back into the saucepan and cook over low heat, stirring constantly, until mixture thickens slightly, about 5 minutes. Strain to remove any hard particles. Cool to room temperature, then freeze in an ice cream freezer according to manufacturer's directions.

WHIPPED CREAM

Yield: about 5 cups

2 cups heavy whipping cream	2 teaspoons chocolate liqueur
½ cup confectioners' sugar	

Combine all ingredients in a chilled mixing bowl and whip until stiff peaks form.

9   Saved Again, a Couple of Times

AT THE BEGINNING of 2003, with the *Delta Queen, Mississippi Queen,* and *American Queen* languishing in New Orleans, a cadre of *Delta Queen* faithful were headlong into a campaign to find a new owner for the boats. Their wooing eventually paid off with the Buffalo-based Delaware North Company winning all three for $80 million at an auction that May. (The *Columbia Queen* was not part of the package, and was later purchased by a company called Great American River Journeys.)

Delaware North is one of the world's biggest food service and hospitality providers, with customers including major league baseball parks, the Kennedy Space Center, and Yosemite National Park. The company is even credited with inventing sports concessions, so assuredly it knew how to cater to tourists. But did the *Delta Queen*'s new owner know anything beyond nachos and pizza?

The *Queen*'s galley soon happily learned that the megacorporation, like many leading restaurants of the time, was committed to organics and self-sustainability, as was Certified Master Chef Roland G. Henin, the leader of the corporation's Annual Chefs' Summit at the Culinary Institute of America at Greystone, located in Napa Valley, California. In addition to exposure to trendy recipes, chefs from the *Delta Queen, Mississippi Queen,* and *American Queen* who attended these conferences were also encouraged to seek out local and organic ingredients. Regional sustainability was not new to the New Orleans–based chefs, who for years had been serving such Louisiana specialties as crawfish, catfish, grouper, oysters, and redfish, along with local mustards, hot sauces, rice, and produce. Duly impressed, the new owner decided to advertise the boats' regional cuisine. Organics, on the other hand, never found their way onto the *Queens*' menus, strictly because of cost. But the boats' chefs did pay attention to the Monterey Bay Aquarium's Seafood Watch and stopped using the overfished sea bass.

Things were going well with Delaware North at the boats' corporate helm, and in 2004, the *Delta Queen* was inducted into the 2003 National Maritime Hall of Fame. But luck once again turned against the boat when, in August 2005, Hurricane Katrina, the most catastrophic hurricane in U.S. history, devastated the central Gulf Coast and the city of New Orleans. With the *American Queen* docked safely in Memphis, the hurricane sent the *Mississippi Queen* and the *Delta Queen* scurrying up the Ohio River and upper Mississippi and out of harm's way. All three boats came out unscathed, but tragically many Delta Queen Steamboat Company employees were left homeless. The storm also forced cancellation of several months of scheduled trips. The economic loss was too much, and Delaware North was forced to put the three boats up for sale.

Enter Ambassadors International, a cruise, marine, and travel company that bought the Delta Queen Steamboat Company in April 2006. In June of that year, the corporation launched the Seattle-based Majestic America Line to focus exclusively on a newly amassed fleet of inland river boats that included all three *Queens* and eventually even the *Columbia Queen.*

Once again, life on the *Delta Queen* changed significantly. With New Orleans still in shambles, the new owner decided that the city would no longer exclusively be the *Delta Queen*'s home port. Instead, the boat temporarily had several port cities, including Galveston, Memphis, Cincinnati, Pittsburgh, Louisville, Nashville, and St. Louis—as well as New Orleans. Majestic America also made numerous improvements, along with freshening up the *Queen* with new paint, mattresses, and high-thread-count linens. In an attempt to attract a broader range of clientele, the boat was now called a "boutique ship." No longer the Delta Queen Steamboat Company, the new company also discarded everything with the old corporate logo, including the waiters' vests. A few waiters gifted their old vests to a table of lucky repeat passengers who soon started "Vest Night," a designated evening during trips when the vests' new owners who were present wore their cherished souvenirs.

The Orleans Room menu was also updated, and it now included dishes from the Pacific Northwest. Chef Howie Velie, a nationally acclaimed food writer and currently a lecturing instructor at the Culinary Institute of America, spent the year 2006 overseeing the executive chefs, sous chefs, and cooks for Majestic America Line. His vision of steamboat cuisine coincided with the national trend toward honest yet visually appealing food, and he jazzed up the old menus in a way that brought accolades from connoisseurs yet left most traditionalists satisfied that they'd been served their favorites.

Above: Chef Howie Velie

Right: Gallery view of Fort Henry Bridge over the Ohio River at Wheeling, West Virginia

The years following saw even more updated recipes and modern presentations, and eventually a few regulars began complaining that the new eats tasted like "restaurant" food. After the home office eliminated two institutions—a once-a-trip chicken-and-ribs picnic lunch and a hot dog broiler in the Texas Lounge—there was grumbling. When the bread pudding recipe changed, chefs actually received hate mail. Then chowder replaced gumbo, and there was near mutiny.

In no time, the chefs brought back the old regulars such as gumbo, and they started using the traditional bread pudding recipe. The picnic came back, and so did the hot dogs. But even though these familiar favorites were resurrected, many of Majestic's new recipes did take root. Menu choices such as spinach risotto and Bucatini all'Amatriciana had been unexpected, but once passengers got used to the change, these dishes rapidly became new favorites.

FANCY FRIED CHICKEN

Yield: 4 servings | Recipe courtesy of Chef Howie Velie

4 boneless, skinless chicken breasts,
    pounded evenly flat
2 cups Marinade for Fancy Fried Chicken
    (*recipe follows*)

Oil for deep-frying
½ cup white cornmeal
½ cup all-purpose flour

Place chicken breasts in a bowl with marinade. Cover and refrigerate at least 24 hours.

Heat oil to 350°F in a skillet or deep-fryer. Combine cornmeal and flour in a shallow bowl. Drain chicken and discard marinade. Dredge chicken in cornmeal mixture, then carefully place in hot oil. Cook until internal temperature of chicken is 165°F, approximately 10 minutes. Remove from oil and drain well. The fried chicken can be held in a 250°F oven for up to 1 hour; after that, the chicken will dry out.

MARINADE for FANCY FRIED CHICKEN

Yield: about 2 cups | Recipe courtesy of Chef Howie Velie

1½ cups buttermilk
3 tablespoons olive oil
1½ tablespoons lemon juice
1½ tablespoons chopped fresh parsley
1 teaspoon garlic powder

1 teaspoon onion powder
1 teaspoon rubbed sage
½ teaspoon white pepper
½ teaspoon salt

Combine all ingredients in large bowl and whisk to blend. Cover and refrigerate if not using right away.

FRIED CHICKEN SALAD

Yield: 4 servings | Recipe courtesy of Chef Howie Velie

6 cups salad greens, rinsed and drained
Assortment of toppings
  (bacon, hard-boiled egg, cucumber,
  tomato, crumbled bleu cheese, etc.)

4 Fancy Fried Chicken breasts (*see page 149*),
  cut into ½-inch slices
Buttermilk Ranch Dressing (*recipe follows*)

Arrange greens on 4 chilled plates. Add desired toppings and 1 chicken breast to each serving. Drizzle with buttermilk ranch dressing.

BUTTERMILK RANCH DRESSING

Yield: 1 cup | Recipe courtesy of Chef Howie Velie

½ cup Marinade for Fancy Fried Chicken (*see page 149*)
½ cup bottled ranch dressing

Combine marinade and ranch dressing in a small bowl. Cover and refrigerate until ready to serve.

SMASHED POTATOES

Yield: 2 servings | Recipe courtesy of Chef Howie Velie

1 pound red-skinned potatoes
10 tablespoons (1¼ sticks) butter
½ cup cream

3 tablespoons chopped fresh parsley
Salt and pepper

Place potatoes in a medium saucepan and cover with water. Boil for 20 minutes or until very soft, then drain. "Smash" potatoes and mix in butter, cream, parsley, salt, and pepper.

Never reuse marinade after it has been used to marinate chicken.

PIMIENTO CHEESE

Yield: 1 cup | Recipe courtesy of Chef Howie Velie

Chef Velie likes to melt this popular southern sandwich filling between slices of fried green tomatoes.

⅓ cup shredded Cheddar cheese

⅓ cup mayonnaise

⅓ cup minced canned pimiento or roasted red pepper

Combine all ingredients and mix well. Cover and refrigerate until ready to serve.

LOBSTER BATON ROUGE

Yield: 4 servings | *Adapted from a recipe by Chef Howie Velie*

½ cup (1 stick) butter

1 cup sliced okra (fresh or frozen)

1 cup chopped onion

½ cup diced carrot

½ cup diced celery

½ cup diced green bell pepper

2 tablespoons chopped fresh parsley

1 tablespoon Cajun seasoning (*see page 27*)

½ cup all-purpose flour

3 green onions, diced

3 cups good Chardonnay wine

2 cans diced tomatoes (12 ounces each)

1 cup lobster, fish, or chicken stock (or water)

½ teaspoon snipped fresh chives

½ teaspoon fresh sage

½ teaspoon fresh thyme

2 cups canned lobster (meat intact) or shelled crawfish, or the meat of 4 1-pound lobsters

4 puff pastry squares (each large enough to cover top of serving dish), baked

Melt butter in a large heavy-bottomed sauté pan. Add okra, onion, carrot, celery, green pepper, parsley, and Cajun seasoning. Cook over medium-high heat until vegetables are well browned but not charred. Add flour and cook until well browned, 5 to 6 minutes. Add green onions, wine, tomatoes, stock, chives, sage, and thyme; mix well. Add lobster and cook for only 10 minutes (any longer and the meat will get tough and chewy).

Serve in a low-rimmed bowl or pasta plate and top with a square of puff pastry.

CHEF'S NOTE:

"This is similar to a rich, fancy gumbo with a stew quality. The puff pastry makes it seem lighter and adds a crunch factor. We used to cut the puff pastry in the shape of the Louisiana State Capitol building because we typically served this dish the night we arrived in Baton Rouge."

LOW COUNTRY SHRIMP BOIL

Yield: 6 servings | Recipe courtesy of Chef Howie Velie

Because of heavy African and Caribbean influences, the food of the low country (coastal Georgia and South Carolina) is in many ways similar to south Louisiana's cuisine, especially seafood preparations. The low country shrimp boil resembles Louisiana's crawfish boil in that each region's dish features boiled spiced shellfish. Both crowd-pleasers are also often cooked with corn, potatoes, and sausage, and are typically served outdoors on picnic tables covered with newspaper.

8 cups water

1 lemon, cut into wedges

1 cup Savannah Spice Blend (*recipe follows*)

2 pounds raw shrimp, peeled and deveined

In a large kettle, combine water, lemon, and Savannah spice blend; bring to a boil. Add shrimp, and as soon as the water returns to a boil, remove kettle from heat. Drain off water but do not rinse shrimp. Set aside to cool. Place shrimp in a serving dish and dust with more Savannah spice blend.

SAVANNAH SPICE BLEND

Yield: 2 cups | Recipe courtesy of Chef Howie Velie

1 cup Old Bay seasoning

1 cup Cajun seasoning (*see page 27*)

Combine seasonings and mix well. Store in covered container.

The low country shrimp boil is also known as Frogmore stew and Beaufort stew.

Low Country Shrimp Boil

FRIED CATFISH with CREOLE TOMATO SAUCE

Yield: 4 servings | Recipe courtesy of Chef Howie Velie

Vegetable oil for frying

1 recipe Marinade for Fancy Fried Chicken
   (*see page 149*)

½ cup white cornmeal

½ cup all-purpose flour

4 catfish filets (5 to 7 ounces each)

Dirty rice, rice pilaf, or red beans and rice
   (use your favorite recipe)

1½ cups Creole Tomato Sauce (*recipe follows*)

Chopped fresh parsley (for garnish)

Chopped scallions (for garnish)

Heat oil to 350°F in a deep-fryer or heavy, deep skillet. Pour marinade into a shallow dish. Combine cornmeal and flour in another shallow dish. Dip catfish in marinade, then dredge in cornmeal mixture. Gently shake off extra cornmeal, then carefully place fish in hot oil. Do not crowd deep-fryer or skillet. Fry until fish is thoroughly cooked, 5 to 7 minutes depending on the thickness of the filets. To serve, place a filet on a bed of your choice of rice. Spoon Creole tomato sauce over the top and garnish with parsley and scallions.

CREOLE TOMATO SAUCE

Yield: about 4 cups | Adapted from a recipe by Chef Howie Velie

2 tablespoons olive oil

3 scallions, finely diced

1 rib celery, finely chopped

1 white onion, finely diced

1 green bell pepper, finely diced

1 red bell pepper, finely diced

½ cup plus 2 tablespoons chopped
   fresh parsley, divided

2 tablespoons all-purpose flour

1 cup chicken stock

1 cup white wine

2 cans diced tomatoes (12 ounces each),
   undrained

1 teaspoon fresh thyme

½ teaspoon dried sage

Pinch of Cajun seasoning (*see page 27*)

Heat oil in a large skillet. Add scallions, celery, onion, bell peppers, and ½ cup parsley. Sauté until vegetables begin to wilt (do not brown). Add flour and cook for 5 minutes, stirring often and keeping heat low so mixture will not brown.

Add stock and wine and simmer for 1 to 2 minutes. Add remaining parsley, tomatoes (with juice), thyme, sage, and Cajun seasoning. Simmer for at least 1 hour, stirring occasionally.

CHEF'S NOTE:

"Contrary to popular notion, Creole food is not always hot and spicy. On the other hand, Cajun food is [typically] highly seasoned. Creole cuisine is more refined and has lots of tomatoes in the recipes. Cajun food has less tomato and a lot more spice and browned roux."

It is best to prepare the Creole Tomato Sauce a day in advance of serving so the flavors will meld fully.

SOUR CREAM RAISIN PIE

Yield: 1 9-inch pie

Although much creamier, this traditional Midwest holiday dessert is a close cousin to the Amish "funeral pie," a raisin pie given to console grieving families.

Recipes for sour cream raisin pie can be traced back to the 1800s, with the arrival of Russian and German immigrants to America's heartland.

1⅓ cups sour cream	3 egg yolks, beaten
¾ cup plus 2 tablespoons sugar	1½ cups water
2 tablespoons all-purpose flour	1 cup raisins
½ teaspoon ground cinnamon	1 9-inch pie crust, baked and cooled
¼ teaspoon ground nutmeg	1 cup heavy cream, chilled
⅛ teaspoon ground cloves	

In a medium saucepan, mix together sour cream, 1 cup sugar, flour, spices, and egg yolks.

Whisking constantly, bring to a boil over medium heat. Lower heat to a bare simmer and cook, stirring constantly, 1 minute. Remove from heat and allow to cool while preparing raisins.

Bring water to a boil in a small saucepan. Add raisins and simmer 3 minutes. Remove from heat and let raisins soak 5 minutes. Drain raisins well and stir into filling mixture.

Pour filling into pie shell. Refrigerate until set, at least 3 hours.

In a mixing bowl, beat cream until peaks start to form. Add remaining 2 tablespoons sugar and beat until stiff. Spread whipped cream over pie. Slice and serve.

Seafood Gumbo

SEAFOOD GUMBO

Yield: 1 gallon, 12 to 14 servings

2 cups diced onion

1½ cups diced green bell pepper

1¼ cups diced celery

¼ cup plus 2 tablespoons vegetable oil, divided

2 whole bay leaves

1 tablespoon minced garlic

2 teaspoons salt

½ teaspoon cayenne

½ teaspoon black pepper

½ teaspoon white pepper

½ teaspoon dried thyme

¼ teaspoon dried oregano

2 dashes Tabasco sauce

1 tablespoon tomato paste

2 quarts seafood stock

1 cup dark roux (*see page 24*)

1 pound smoked pork sausage, sliced into ½-inch rounds

1 pound crawfish tail meat with fat

1 pound medium shrimp, peeled and deveined

½ pound crabmeat, picked over to remove bits of shell

1 cup sliced okra (⅓-inch slices)

Cooked white rice

2 bunches green onions, chopped

In a large soup pot, briefly sauté onion, bell pepper, and celery in ¼ cup oil. Add bay leaves, garlic, salt, cayenne, peppers, thyme, oregano, and Tabasco. Sauté until onion is translucent. Add tomato paste and cook 1 minute. Add stock and bring to a boil. Reduce heat and simmer for 15 minutes, skimming foam from top if necessary.

Add roux and mix well. Cook for 5 minutes. Add sausage and return to a simmer. Cook for 15 minutes. Add crawfish, shrimp, and crabmeat. Cook gently for 10 minutes, then remove bay leaf and remove from heat.

Heat remaining 2 tablespoons oil in a skillet over medium-high heat. Add okra and fry to seal, about 5 minutes. Stir into gumbo.

Serve gumbo over rice in soup bowls. Garnish with green onions.

10 Themes and Traditions

IN ADDITION TO the food-themed cruises in the 1980s and '90s, the *Delta Queen* often offered specialty trips that tied in with events at stops on shore. Sometimes these themes were advertised, but often passengers boarded and then learned to their surprise that their trip was focusing on such topics as the Civil War, fall foliage, Natchez's antebellum homes, or wilderness passages that traced the westward routes of pioneers along the Ohio, Tennessee, and Cumberland rivers. Every once in a while, the boat even embarked on highly specialized jaunts, including a Victorian-themed trip through the Gulf Intracoastal Waterway from New Orleans to Galveston, Texas, or a "trampin' trip" devoted entirely to impromptu shore stops.

Even when following a theme, almost all trips featured a much-anticipated picnic and a captain's dinner. And while chefs usually altered menus to reflect a trip's theme and location, they rarely tinkered with the core entrées for these latter two events, with picnics offering traditional outdoor favorites such as fried chicken or ribs, and captain's dinners always featuring beef.

MARDI GRAS

The mystery and nostalgia of New Orleans have always been a magnet, and were especially so to the high-spirited Tom Greene in the 1940s. Captain Fred Way writes that whenever Greene was sailing on a Greene Line boat headed for New Orleans, as they approached Baton Rouge, Greene would wire ahead to New Orleans and reserve banquet rooms at such fabled restaurants as Antoine's, Arnaud's, Galatoire's, and Broussard's. There he would pay for lavish meals for fifteen or so selected passengers, and

Gala Champagne Party
AND
Captain's Dinner
MISSISSIPPI STEAMBOAT STYLE

HORS D'OEUVRE DELICACIES A LA *DELTA QUEEN*
CHILLED CHAMPAGNE MARDI GRAS   CAPTAIN'S PUNCH

STEAMBOAT SHRIMP COCKTAIL

FRENCH MARKET CHILLED RELISH TRAY

TENDER SLICES OF BEEF   DOVER SOLE EN WHITE WINE
from the eye of the prime rib

PADDLEWHEEL POTATOES   BROCCOLI w/HOLLANDAISE SAUCE

TOSSED GREENE SALAD, Choice of Dressing

OL' MAN RIVER ROLLS

DUTCH APPLE PIE with sprinkles of cheddar   CREME DE MENTHE PARFAIT

BOURBON ST. COFFEE   NATCHEZ TEA   MEMPHIS MILK

Undated captain's dinner menu

then end the evening at a music hall listening to live Dixieland jazz. At least once on these New Orleans trips, Greene would throw a champagne party "on the house" for everyone on the boat and host a few banquets. So by the time the *Delta Queen* left the Cincinnati harbor on February 19, 1949, for her first Mardi Gras trip, the shipping line had already made fifteen trips to the annual event. This capricious background story makes it easy to understand why, during the days of the Greene family, the twenty-plus-day *Delta Queen* Mardi Gras trips to the Crescent City filled up quickly.

Given that the boat's home port was Cincinnati, the timing of Mardi Gras (early spring) was also a stroke of luck for the Greenes. As Fred Way put it, the *Delta Queen's* "blue-ribbon, high-class, top-fare" voyage not only boosted spirits but, after a long winter layup, also bolstered the company's bottom line. In 1951, the fare for a twenty-one-day Mardi Gras trip was $275. This was a comparative bargain, especially since the *Queen* served as a floating hotel in New Orleans and offered a convenience that eliminated the hassle any visitor to Mardi Gras experiences, that of trying to find a bathroom.

Early *Delta Queen* Mardi Gras trips docked in New Orleans for up to four days, with passengers offered the luxury of reserved seats to the Rex, Comus, and Proteus parades, and even to the Krewe of Bacchus Carnival Ball. The cookhouse crew must have joined in the fun too. Old-timers report that during many early Mardi Gras shore stops, the *Delta Queen* did not provide dinner for passengers, and instead encouraged them to try a few New Orleans restaurants.

In the *Queen's* later years, Mardi Gras trips were still occasionally offered, but most of these docked in New Orleans for only one or two nights. But regardless of the time of year, Mardi Gras masks and beads could be found scattered about the boat's lounges, and for many years these purple, green, and gold trinkets were "fashionably" worn by wait staff at captain's dinners.

Creole food, of course, figured big on Mardi Gras trips. New Orleans's Creole cuisine started from a complex mingling of French, African, Spanish, and Native American ingredients. Since the city's founding in 1718, local cooks have taken foods from all these cultures and created unique dishes such as gumbo, jambalaya, shrimp creole, po-boy sandwiches, and infinite preparations with fish and oysters—all popular *Delta Queen* menu items. Trained chefs invented some of these specialties, but the vast majority were cobbled together by African Americans, immigrants, and common housewives who lacked familiar ingredients or who had sparse pantries. Bread pudding, one example of a product of necessity, has been jazzed up so much by locals that this dish, although consumed nationally, is usually associated with New Orleans. It was also a perennial favorite on the *Delta Queen*.

SHRIMP CREOLE

Yield: 6 servings

2 tablespoons butter

1 teaspoon vegetable oil

2 ribs celery, diced

2 cloves garlic, minced

1 medium onion, diced

½ cup diced green bell pepper

2 tablespoons all-purpose flour

2 cups tomato sauce

1½ cups seafood stock

Juice of ½ lemon

2 whole bay leaves

¼ teaspoon sugar

Salt

Cayenne

2 pounds medium shrimp, peeled
and deveined

Cooked white rice

¼ cup chopped green onions (for garnish)

Melt butter in a heavy pot. Add oil, celery, garlic, onion, and bell pepper. Sauté until onion is transparent.

Add flour and blend well. Add tomato sauce, stock, lemon juice, bay leaves, sugar, salt, and cayenne. Cover and simmer over medium heat for approximately 30 minutes, stirring occasionally. Add shrimp and simmer 15 minutes, uncovered. Remove bay leaves.

Serve over rice. Garnish with green onions.

Muffuletta N'Awlins

MUFFULETTA N'AWLINS

Yield: 4 servings | Recipe courtesy of Chef Terry Newkirk

The aroma of the olive salad alone is enough to perk up any appetite, and the sandwich was always popular when it appeared on the Delta Queen lunch menu.

- 1 loaf muffuletta bread or any other round Italian loaf (10 inches)
- 4 ounces Genoa salami, thinly sliced
- 4 ounces Italian ham (*capocollo*), thinly sliced
- 4 ounces provolone cheese, thinly sliced
- 1 cup Olive Salad (*recipe follows*)

Slice bread in half like a hamburger bun. Layer meats and cheese on bottom half of bread. Top with olive salad and then with top half of bread. To serve, cut in quarters.

OLIVE SALAD

Yield: about 3 cups

- 2 cups coarsely chopped pimiento-stuffed green olives, drained (reserve liquid)
- 2 tablespoons red wine vinegar
- 1 tablespoon minced garlic
- 1 teaspoon dried oregano leaves
- ½ teaspoon black pepper
- ⅓ cup olive oil
- ¼ cup diced celery
- ¼ cup cocktail onions, drained
- 1 tablespoon small capers, drained

In a medium glass bowl, combine olive liquid, vinegar, garlic, oregano, and pepper. Slowly whip in olive oil. Add olives, celery, onions, and capers; mix well. Cover and refrigerate 8 to 10 hours or overnight. Bring to room temperature before assembling sandwich.

Sicilian immigrant Signor Salvatore Lupo generally gets credit for inventing the muffuletta sandwich at his French Quarter market, Central Grocery, in New Orleans.

NEW ORLEANS–STYLE BARBECUE SHRIMP

Yield: 4 servings | Recipe courtesy of Chef Herbert C. Cade Jr.

Although Chef Cade grills his shrimp, this New Orleans classic is not typically prepared anywhere near a barbecue pit. According to food critic Tom Fitzmorris, barbecue shrimp was invented in 1955 at New Orleans's Pascal's Manale restaurant, when a customer asked the Italian owner to replicate "a dish he had in Chicago but couldn't describe well." No one is sure how the word barbecue was added to the dish's name, but we do know that barbecue shrimp is considered one of Louisiana's top Creole dishes.

16 fresh shrimp (16/20 count), peeled (leave tail intact) and deveined	¼ cup clam juice
6 tablespoons unsalted butter, melted, divided	3 tablespoons Worcestershire sauce
2 tablespoons Cajun seasoning (*see page 27*)	1 teaspoon hot pepper sauce
¼ cup finely diced onion	⅓ cup heavy cream
2 tablespoons vegetable oil	2 tablespoons chopped fresh parsley
1 clove garlic, minced	½ teaspoon black pepper
¼ cup white wine	¼ teaspoon minced fresh rosemary
	1 lemon, thinly sliced
	1 loaf French bread, cut in 1-inch slices

Rinse shrimp and drain on paper towels. In a large bowl, combine shrimp with 3 tablespoons butter and Cajun seasoning. Toss gently until shrimp are well coated. Set aside.

Combine onion and oil in a skillet. Cook until onion is lightly browned. Add garlic and cook, stirring constantly, for 1 minute. Add wine and simmer to reduce by half. Add clam juice, Worcestershire sauce, and hot pepper sauce. Simmer until liquid is reduced by one-third.

Add cream, parsley, pepper, and rosemary. Cook until mixture is reduced by half. Add remaining 3 tablespoons butter and blend well. Add lemon slices. Set aside.

Heat grill for cooking shrimp. Grill shrimp until they are curled and pink. Arrange shrimp in shallow soup plates (4 per plate) and top with sauce. Serve with French bread for dipping.

New Orleans–Style Barbecue Shrimp

Delta Queen Bread Pudding with Bourbon Sauce

Although corporate headquarters encouraged consistency between the Mississippi Queen *and the* Delta Queen, *individual chefs created their own recipes and added their own touches. Here's a comparison of bread pudding recipes from the two boats:*

DELTA QUEEN BREAD PUDDING

Yield: 8 servings

3 eggs	1½ teaspoons vanilla extract
1½ cups sugar	½ cup coarsely chopped pecans, roasted
¼ cup (½ stick) unsalted butter, melted	½ cup raisins
1 tablespoon ground cinnamon	5 cups French bread cubes, dried for
1 teaspoon ground nutmeg	5 minutes in a 325°F oven
2 cups heavy cream	2 cups Bourbon Sauce (*recipe follows*)

Break eggs into a mixing bowl and beat until frothy. Beat in sugar, butter, cinnamon, and nutmeg. Beat in cream and vanilla. Add pecans and raisins, and mix gently.

Place bread cubes in a lightly oiled 11" × 7" baking pan. Pour egg mixture over bread and mix well. Let sit 30 minutes, occasionally stirring so all of the bread is fully soaked.

Preheat oven to 325°F. Bake 45 minutes or until pudding is puffy and brown. To serve, cut into squares and top with bourbon sauce.

BOURBON SAUCE

Yield: 3 cups

1 cup (2 sticks) butter	1 cup heavy cream
1 pound (2½ packed cups) dark brown sugar	¼ cup bourbon

Melt butter in a medium saucepan over medium heat. Add brown sugar and blend well. Stir in cream and bring to a boil. Reduce heat and stir in bourbon.

Turn the page for Mississippi Queen *Bread Pudding with Whiskey Sauce.*

MISSISSIPPI QUEEN BREAD PUDDING

Yield: 12 servings | Recipe courtesy of Chef Karea Anderson

Chef Karea cooked for a few years on the Mississippi Queen, *and she laughingly admits that galley duty on a steamboat "wasn't for the weak or faint of heart." She now supervises a hospital cafeteria and has placed in several national cooking contests. Anderson credits the Delta Queen Steamboat Company with making her the success she is today.*

1 pound white bread or French bread	1½ tablespoons ground cinnamon
1 cup raisins	4 cups whole milk
3 large eggs	2 tablespoons vanilla extract
1½ cups sugar	Whiskey Sauce (*recipe follows*)

Preheat oven to 325°F. Spray a 13" × 9" pan with cooking oil. Cut bread into small chunks and put in pan. Sprinkle raisins over bread.

In a medium bowl, combine eggs, sugar, and cinnamon. Add milk and vanilla; mix well. Pour egg mixture over bread, making sure all the bread is saturated.

Bake for 1 hour and 15 minutes or until pudding is very firm. Cool 10 minutes. Cut into squares and serve warm with whiskey sauce.

WHISKEY SAUCE

Yield: about 1 cup | Recipe courtesy Chef Karea Anderson

1 cup brown sugar	½ cup heavy cream
½ cup (1 stick) butter	3 tablespoons whiskey

Combine brown sugar, butter, and cream in a heavy saucepan. Cook over medium heat until sugar dissolves. Bring to a boil, then reduce heat and simmer 5 minutes. Remove from heat and cool for a couple of minutes. Stir in whiskey.

KENTUCKY DERBY DAYS

Horse racing is without question the highlight of Kentucky Derby week, but during that same frenetic time period, a steamboat race also draws massive attention to Louisville. There, in 1963, the *Delta Queen* first raced against the hometown *Belle of Louisville*. Almost every year after, through 2008, the two boats did battle the Wednesday before the big horse race. Through the years, riverboats including the *Julia Belle Swain*, the *Natchez*, the *Spirit of Jefferson*, and the *Belle of Cincinnati* occasionally raced, but the traditional rivalry always was between the *Belle of Louisville* and the *Delta Queen*.

As with many steamboat races, this one too was dubbed "The Great Steamboat Race." But to veteran onlookers, this particular contest really was "the one." The event started with a musical battle between the boats' calliopes. Then a cannon blasted, and up to one hundred thousand spirited onlookers, many with barbecue pits and picnic baskets, started cheering along the Indiana and Kentucky riverbanks. The course for the competition would be altered when water was high on the Ohio River, but typically it was a round-trip, fourteen-mile route from Louisville's Clark Memorial Bridge to Six Mile Island, and took about one and a half hours.

During the years she participated, the *Queen* usually carried some 280 race-day passengers. Free-flowing alcohol and a Dixieland band set the mood, and riders on both boats exchanged lots of banter and boasting. Good-spirited trickery was expected and sometimes outright cheating occurred. But the competing steamers also did everything they could to win legitimately. Before the 1964 race, the *Belle of Louisville* even went to the trouble of offloading a five hundred–pound galley stove and a heavy refrigerator. The effort apparently paid off because that year the *Belle* won.

The winner of the steamboat race took home the Golden Antlers for a year. Historically, antlers depict supremacy and speed on the river. Going back to the nineteenth

Captain Paul Underwood pointing to the mint box near the paddle wheel, 1960 (Photo © *The Courier-Journal,* reproduced by permission)

century, an upside-down broom signified a "clean sweep," meaning that a boat had won all of her races.

The *Queen's* final Kentucky Derby race against the *Belle of Louisville* was April 30, 2008. With the threat of the *Queen's* demise hanging heavy, special activities were held, including a "Tea with the *Queen*" party and a Mardi Gras party. On that melancholy day, the *Queen* beat out her old nemesis. As a final tribute, fireworks lit up the sky as the *Delta Queen* left the wharf. After all their years of competition, the final score between the two boats was *Belle of Louisville,* 22; *Delta Queen,* 20.

Kentucky cuisine means salty hams, savory stews, mile-high biscuits, and anything made with bourbon. Derby time on the *Delta Queen* also meant overflowing buffets of caviar, smoked oysters, and boiled shrimp. And of course, nothing says Kentucky more than mint juleps, and the *Delta Queen's* bartenders took their juleps seriously. The story goes that the drink was so popular in the 1960s that the crew grew tired of making emergency landings to track down mint. To solve the problem, the captain attached two wooden boxes to the stern for growing the crucial ingredient for mint juleps—spearmint.

The suitcase-sized wooden mint boxes resided in front of the *Queen's* paddle, where river spray provided just enough moisture for optimum spearmint growth. Unfortunately, over time, the boxes rotted. And the health department reportedly had concerns about bacteria that lurks in rivers, so the boxes were never replaced. But for many years, the mint boxes provided fresh mint, as well as a good topic of conversation.

STEAMBOAT MINT JULEP

This recipe was given to *Delta Queen* passengers in 1965. It is shared here in its original wording courtesy of the Cincinnati Museum Center, Cincinnati Historical Society Library.

In a 10-ounce Collins glass, combine ½ ounce (1 tablespoon) simple syrup [*see Note*], ½ ounce Southern Comfort (or to taste), and 13 fresh mint leaves. Muddle to release juice from mint leaves. Pack glass firmly with crushed ice. Pour bourbon whiskey (Kentucky variety, of course) in slowly to top. Slide bar spoon down inside of glass and jiggle a few strokes (this mixes the drink and frosts the glass). Put a nice sprig of mint on top, sprinkle with powdered sugar, and add a straw and Confederate flag. Sit in a deck chair and sip quickly.

SIMPLE SYRUP:

Combine equal parts of white sugar and water in a saucepan. Bring to a slow boil, stirring often, and cook until sugar dissolves. Remove from heat and cool before using.

KENTUCKY CHICKEN–RICE CHOWDER

Yield: 6 servings

3 tablespoons butter	1 clove garlic, minced
1 rib celery, medium dice	5 cups chicken stock
1 medium onion, diced	¼ cup blond roux (*see page 24*)
1 cup sliced fresh mushrooms	2 cups diced cooked boneless, skinless
¾ cup diced carrot (medium dice)	chicken breast (½-inch dice)
½ cup diced green bell pepper	¾ cup heavy cream
(medium dice)	2 tablespoons sherry
½ teaspoon white pepper	2 cups cooked white rice
¼ teaspoon black pepper	Salt and pepper
½ teaspoon granulated garlic	Chopped fresh parsley (for garnish)

Melt butter in a large pot. Add celery, onion, mushrooms, carrot, bell pepper, white and black peppers, and granulated and fresh garlic. Sauté until onion is wilted. Add stock and bring to a boil, then reduce heat to a simmer. Cover and cook 20 minutes.

Add roux and whip to blend. Simmer approximately 10 minutes, uncovered.

Add chicken, cream, and sherry. Simmer 10 minutes, uncovered. Reduce heat and add rice. Heat through. Adjust seasoning and consistency. Ladle into bowls and garnish with parsley.

STEAMBOAT SALAD with *DELTA QUEEN'S FAMOUS* PEPPER-DILL SALAD DRESSING

Yield: 4 servings | Recipe courtesy of Sir Robin Hixson

4 cups tossed salad greens (mixture of
    iceberg, romaine, and leaf lettuces)
½ cup shredded red cabbage
20 strips carrot (julienned)
4 cherry tomatoes, halved

8 black olives
8 red onion rings (⅜-inch thick)
Delta Queen's Famous Pepper-Dill
    Salad Dressing (*recipe follows*)

In a large bowl, combine lettuces and cabbage, tossing to mix well. Arrange lettuce mixture on salad plates and top each serving with carrot strips, cherry tomato halves, black olives, and onion rings. Drizzle with dressing.

DELTA QUEEN'S FAMOUS PEPPER-DILL SALAD DRESSING

Yield: 3 cups | Adapted from a recipe by Sir Robin Hixson

2 cups mayonnaise
½ medium white onion, minced
¼ cup buttermilk
1 tablespoon dried dill weed
1 tablespoon lemon juice
1 tablespoon grated Parmesan cheese

1 tablespoon tarragon vinegar
2 teaspoons black pepper
1½ teaspoons Tabasco sauce
1 teaspoon dry mustard
1 teaspoon sugar

Combine all ingredients and blend well. Cover and refrigerate for 24 hours before serving. If dressing is too thick, thin with water or buttermilk.

Steamboat Salad with *Delta Queen*'s Famous Pepper-Dill Salad Dressing

BAKING-POWDER BISCUITS

Yield: 8 to 12 biscuits (depending on size of cutter) | Recipe courtesy of Chef Herbert C. Cade Jr.

2 cups all-purpose flour

2½ teaspoons baking powder

½ teaspoon salt

⅓ cup vegetable shortening

¾ cup whole milk

Preheat oven to 450°F. In a medium bowl, whisk together flour, baking powder, and salt. Add shortening and work in with a fork, pastry blender, or your fingers until mixture is crumbly. Stir in milk to form a soft dough that can be easily handled. Do not overmix. On a lightly floured board, knead dough gently 15 to 20 times.

Roll dough to ¾-inch thickness. Cut biscuits closely together with a 2- or 3-inch floured cutter, pushing straight down and pulling up without twisting. Reroll scraps and cut again.

Place biscuits on ungreased baking sheets—just touching for soft biscuits or ½ inch apart for crusty sides. Bake 10 to 12 minutes or until golden brown.

RELIVING THE CIVIL WAR

The *Delta Queen*'s Civil War trips featured lectures by university professors and authors, and were usually filled with hard-core history buffs who knew as much about the Civil War as the boat's expert guest historians. Regardless of the level of expertise, however, everyone was entranced when the *Queen* took them back to the 1860s.

On board, a historian dressed as Abraham Lincoln might appear and give his recollections. Sometimes reenactors in full uniform performed authentic drills. Guest singers sang period battle songs, and musicians, including the widely acclaimed Bobby Horton, played antique instruments. Shore excursions included stops at such sites as Day's Gap, Alabama, where an April 1864 confrontation touched off a series of skirmishes known as Streight's Raid. Passengers roamed the streets of Paducah, Kentucky, where General Nathan Bedford Forrest had raided the town for supplies. Another favorite, Shiloh National Military Park, gave passengers a chance to see the site of the first major battle in the western theater, a bloodbath of twenty-four thousand casualties and the clash that opened both sides' eyes to the frightening realization that, yes, this war was real.

Northerners ate relatively well during the Civil War years, especially when compared to the blockade-induced empty pantries that forced southerners to cook whatever they could grow. Consequently, during these lean years, pork and corn were central to the southern diet, with corn the base for dishes such as hoecakes, pone, and hominy. All parts of the pig were used, with much of it landing in the smokehouse. Consumption of not-so-prime cuts such as chitlins (intestines) and "middlins" (salt pork) was a necessity. And although these two items were usually absent from the *Delta Queen*'s menus, on every trip, cooks offered plenty of ham and bacon and other southern Civil War–era favorites including fried catfish, fried green tomatoes, grits, and cobblers.

SKILLET CORNBREAD

Yield: 6 servings

3½ tablespoons bacon drippings, divided	¾ teaspoon salt
¾ cup sifted all-purpose flour	1¼ cups yellow cornmeal
1 tablespoon sugar	1 large egg, beaten
2½ teaspoons double-acting baking powder	1 cup whole milk

Preheat oven to 425°F. Grease a 10-inch cast-iron skillet with 1 tablespoon of the bacon drippings. Heat skillet in oven until it is sizzling hot.

Meanwhile, sift together flour, sugar, baking powder, and salt. Add cornmeal and mix well. Add egg, remaining bacon drippings, and milk. Stir and blend all ingredients with a few strokes. Do not overmix.

Pour batter into hot skillet. Bake for approximately 30 minutes or until done.

FRIED GREEN TOMATOES with CAJUN BEURRE BLANC SAUCE

Yield: 6 servings | Recipe courtesy of Chef Paul Wayland-Smith

Charleston food writer and culinary historian Robert F. Moss recently shocked the culinary world when his research revealed that the fried green tomato does not have southern roots at all. Moss dug up several published recipes dating as far back as 1873, but they were all from cookbooks in the Northeast and Midwest, and likely had a link to Jewish immigrants. To many southerners' disbelief, it is highly probable that recipes for fried green tomatoes did not reach the American South until the early to mid-twentieth century.

Vegetable oil for frying

3 green tomatoes (unripened red tomatoes), cut into ¼- to ⅜-inch-thick slices

1 cup all-purpose flour seasoned with ½ teaspoon salt and ¼ teaspoon cayenne pepper

Buttermilk or egg wash (1 whole egg combined with 3 tablespoons water or milk and beaten slightly)

1 cup Zatarain's Fish-Fri (seasoned cornmeal)

½ to 1 pound cooked crawfish tails, peeled

Cajun Beurre Blanc Sauce (*see page 178*)

Heat ½ inch vegetable oil in a deep skillet. Dredge tomato slices in seasoned flour. Dip in buttermilk or egg wash. Dredge in seasoned cornmeal. Carefully place tomato slices in hot oil (do not crowd skillet) and fry for about 2 minutes per side or until golden brown. Remove from skillet and drain on paper towels.

To serve, place 3 tomato slices on each serving plate. Top with crawfish and Cajun Beurre Blanc Sauce.

CAJUN BEURRE BLANC SAUCE

Yield: about 2¾ cups | Recipe courtesy Chef Paul Wayland-Smith

1½ cups white wine

2 shallots, minced

1 whole bay leaf

1 clove garlic, crushed

1 fresh lemon, halved

1 teaspoon cracked black peppercorns

1 cup heavy cream

2 cups (4 sticks) butter, cut into 1-inch pieces

1 tablespoon Blackened Seasoning
  (*recipe follows*)

In a heavy saucepan, combine wine, shallots, bay leaf, garlic, lemon, and peppercorns. Simmer over low heat until liquid is reduced by half.

Add cream and simmer to reduce by half. Slowly add butter, one piece at a time, whipping continuously and alternately placing the pan on and off the heat. Strain, then add seasoning and mix well.

BLACKENED SEASONING

Yield: 1¾ cups

10 tablespoons (1¼ sticks) unsalted butter,
  softened

½ cup vegetable oil

⅓ cup paprika

¼ cup salt

1 tablespoon garlic powder

1 tablespoon onion powder

1 teaspoon black pepper

1 teaspoon cayenne

1 teaspoon white pepper

½ teaspoon dried basil

½ teaspoon dried oregano

½ teaspoon dried thyme

Combine all ingredients and blend thoroughly. Cover and store in refrigerator.

CHICKEN NEW MADRID

Yield: 4 servings

One of the oldest American cities west of the Mississippi River, New Madrid was the center of the devastating 1811 earthquake, among the most powerful to hit the United States.

🖙

This dish was named for a popular Delta Queen shore stop, New Madrid, Missouri.

🖘

4 boneless, skinless chicken breasts (8 ounces each), pounded thin
1 recipe Kiev Butter (*recipe follows*)
½ cup all-purpose flour
½ teaspoon salt, divided
½ teaspoon white pepper, divided
1 egg
2 tablespoons water

⅓ cup bread crumbs
⅓ cup cracker crumbs
¼ teaspoon dried basil
¼ teaspoon dried oregano
¼ teaspoon dried parsley
¼ teaspoon dried thyme
Vegetable oil for deep-frying

Rinse chicken and blot dry with paper towels. Wrap each chicken breast around one portion of Kiev butter, sealing very tightly with toothpicks. Freeze overnight or until firm.

In a shallow bowl, stir together flour, ¼ teaspoon salt, and ¼ teaspoon white pepper. In another shallow bowl, beat together egg and water. In a third shallow bowl, combine remaining salt and white pepper, bread crumbs, cracker crumbs, basil, oregano, parsley, and thyme; stir to mix.

Preheat oven to 350°F. Heat oil to 325°F in a deep-fryer or heavy pot. Dredge chicken in flour, dip in egg wash, and roll in seasoned crumbs. Carefully place chicken in hot oil and deep-fry to a golden brown, about 6 minutes. Remove chicken from oil and place on a baking sheet. Finish in oven until internal temperature of chicken reaches 160°F.

KIEV BUTTER

Yield: about ½ cup

½ cup (1 stick) butter, softened
Juice of ½ lemon
1 clove garlic, minced
1 tablespoon white wine

1 tablespoon finely chopped fresh parsley
Pinch of black pepper
Pinch of salt

Combine all ingredients in a mixing bowl and cream together well. Shape mixture into a 4-inch block. Wrap in plastic and freeze. When ready to use, slice into four equal portions.

ROAST PORK LOIN with 3-CHILE JUS

Yield: 8 servings | Recipe courtesy of Robert J. Harrington

1 boneless pork loin roast (3 to 4 pounds)

1 tablespoon minced fresh chives

1 tablespoon minced fresh garlic

1 tablespoon fresh thyme leaves

Salt and black pepper

Juice of 1 lime

1 tablespoon olive oil

1 serrano chile pepper, minced and seeds and membrane removed

1 poblano chile pepper, minced and seeds and membrane removed

1 tablespoon minced chipotle chile pepper

¼ cup sherry

1¼ cups chicken stock

1 tablespoon cornstarch

Preheat oven to 325°F. Rub pork loin with chives, garlic, thyme, salt, and pepper. Roast pork loin until the internal temperature reaches 165°F.

Remove pork loin from roasting pan and allow to rest while making sauce. Pour off any excess fat that has accumulated in the bottom of the pan, leaving 1 tablespoon.

Place roasting pan over burners on stove top and add lime juice, olive oil, and the serrano, poblano, and chipotle chiles. Add sherry and cook over low heat to deglaze, stirring to loosen the particles from the bottom of the pan.

Add stock and bring to a simmer. Mix cornstarch with a little water to make a slurry. Add to mixture in roasting pan. Cook, stirring often, until sauce thickens.

Slice pork loin and top each serving with 2 to 3 tablespoons of 3-Chile Jus.

A CAJUN COUNTRY CHRISTMAS

Between 1755 and 1763, the English deported more than ten thousand French Acadians from Nova Scotia for refusing to pledge allegiance to the King of England. Known as the *Grand Dérangement* (great expulsion), the tragic forced migration lasted more than eight years and sent broken families to such far-flung places as England, Martinique, New England, Virginia, and Georgia. Eventually, some thirty-five hundred ended up in Acadiana, the twenty-two French-speaking parishes south and west of New Orleans. There, on the bayous, swamps, and prairies, the Cajuns (English corruption of the word *Acadian*) have peacefully farmed and fished for hundreds of years. Today their descendants number more than two hundred thousand.

Beginning in the 1980s, at Christmastime the *Delta Queen* would deck out in Victorian finery for Cajun-themed trips through Acadiana's muddy and critter-infested bayous and to little-known Louisiana towns such as Morgan City, Houma, Krotz Springs, French Settlement, and St. Francisville. There, those interested were able to speak with, or at least listen to, users of the Cajun language. They also went on guided tours of Avery Island, home of Tabasco sauce, and Eunice's Liberty Theater, where they danced the *fais-do-do* to local and ancient Cajun music. All along the way, they saw the quiet beauty of rice and sugarcane fields, crawfish ponds, and cypress-filled swamps, scenes foreign to most of the nation but commonplace in rural Louisiana.

At the end of the trip, passengers were treated to the Cajun Christmas tradition of *feux de joie* (fire of joy), a blazing bonfire on the river's levee. According to Cajun legend, the flickering firelight shows Papa Noël the route for delivering his toys. The fiery ritual was started over two hundred years ago, and is still re-created at hundreds of locations on small-town levees just above New Orleans every Christmas Eve.

Aside from music and bonfires, robust food also identifies the Cajuns, a notoriously easygoing yet traditional lot that still stews okra and simmers *sauce picante* in black iron pots that have been handed down for generations. On shore stops, it was not unusual for local hosts to offer passengers tastes of such delicacies as alligator. Boiled crawfish were plentiful in season, and boudin, a spicy rice and pork dressing stuffed in casings, was always well received. On board, menus burst with treats such as gumbo, Acadian seafood bisque, trout la fête, and crawfish cooked into étouffées, pies, or fritters. If there was room for dessert, there were always sweets such as pecan pie or rice pudding. Any free time could be spent sipping eggnog and decorating gingerbread houses and cookies.

ACADIAN BISQUE

Yield: 10 to 12 servings | Recipe courtesy of Chef Terry Newkirk

3 tablespoons butter

2 ribs celery, finely diced

2 cloves garlic, minced

1 large onion, finely diced

½ cup finely diced green bell pepper

1 teaspoon dried thyme

½ teaspoon dried oregano

¼ teaspoon dried basil

¼ teaspoon granulated garlic

¼ teaspoon cayenne

¼ teaspoon black pepper

Pinch of white pepper

1 tablespoon paprika

2 teaspoons tomato paste

2 quarts seafood stock

1 pound small shrimp (150/200 count), peeled and deveined

½ cup blond roux (*see page 24*)

1 cup heavy cream

¼ cup brandy

¼ cup sherry

¼ cup white wine

3 cups whole milk, heated

½ pound crabmeat, picked over to remove bits of shell

½ pound crawfish tail meat, cooked

½ cup chopped green onions (for garnish)

Whipped cream (for garnish)

Melt butter in a large soup pot over medium-high heat. Add celery, garlic, onion, bell pepper, thyme, oregano, basil, granulated garlic, cayenne, and peppers. Sauté until onion is translucent. Add paprika and tomato paste. Sauté 2 minutes. Add stock and bring to a boil, then reduce heat to a simmer and cook 30 minutes.

Add shrimp and bring to a boil, then reduce to a simmer. Add roux, blending and whipping until mixture is smooth and thick. Add cream, brandy, sherry, and wine. Bring to a boil, then reduce heat to a simmer and cook 30 minutes.

Remove from heat and add hot milk. Blend well. Add crabmeat and crawfish. Return to heat just until heated through. Adjust seasoning and consistency. Garnish with green onions and whipped cream.

CRAWFISH FRITTERS

Yield: 10 fritters

½ rib celery, minced

½ cup minced yellow onion

¼ cup minced green bell pepper

2 tablespoons minced red bell pepper

1 tablespoon chopped fresh garlic

1 tablespoon chopped fresh parsley

1 tablespoon minced jalapeño chile pepper

½ pound crawfish tail meat

½ cup grated Parmesan cheese

1 egg

2 teaspoons baking powder

2 teaspoons Cajun seasoning (*see page 27*)

Pinch of sage

2 tablespoons all-purpose flour

Vegetable oil for deep-frying

Remoulade Sauce (*recipe follows*)

In food processor, combine celery, onion, bell peppers, garlic, parsley, and jalapeño chile pepper. Process until vegetables are finely minced. Transfer to a mixing bowl and add crawfish, Parmesan cheese, egg, baking powder, Cajun seasoning, and sage. Add flour and mix well. Set aside for 30 minutes.

Heat oil to 350°F in a deep-fryer. Using a soup spoon, carefully drop batter into hot oil (a few at a time) and cook until golden brown. Turn fritters during cooking so they brown evenly. Use a slotted spoon to remove from hot oil. Drain on paper towels. Serve with remoulade sauce.

REMOULADE SAUCE

Yield: 2 cups

This recipe is representative of the many versions prepared by Delta Queen chefs.

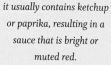

Remoulade originated in France as a mayonnaise-based sauce similar to tartar sauce. In Louisiana, it is spicier and it usually contains ketchup or paprika, resulting in a sauce that is bright or muted red.

1 cup mayonnaise

½ cup finely minced celery

½ cup finely minced green onion

¼ cup prepared horseradish

¼ cup chopped fresh parsley

2 tablespoons Creole mustard

1½ tablespoons Worcestershire sauce

1 tablespoon chili sauce

1 tablespoon minced fresh garlic

1 tablespoon prepared mustard

1 tablespoon white vinegar

2¼ teaspoons paprika

1 teaspoon salt

1 teaspoon Tabasco sauce

½ teaspoon lemon juice

Combine all ingredients and blend well. Cover and refrigerate until chilled.

SHRIMP ÉTOUFFÉE

Yield: 8 servings

2 tablespoons vegetable oil

1 rib celery, diced

1 clove garlic, minced

1 small green bell pepper, diced

½ large onion, diced

⅔ teaspoon dried thyme

⅓ teaspoon granulated garlic

3½ cups shrimp stock

1 tablespoon tomato paste

¼ cup dark roux (*see page 24*)

2 pounds shrimp (40/50 count), cooked, peeled, and deveined

1 tablespoon lemon juice

1 teaspoon Worcestershire sauce

½ teaspoon salt

¼ teaspoon black pepper

Few drops of hot sauce

Hot cooked rice

Lemon wedges, chopped green onions, and parsley (for garnish)

Heat oil in a medium-sized, heavy-bottomed saucepan. Add celery, garlic, bell pepper, onion, thyme, and granulated garlic. Sauté until onion is transparent.

Stir in stock and tomato paste. Simmer 10 minutes.

Add roux, stirring and whipping well. Simmer on low heat 15 minutes.

Add shrimp, lemon juice, Worcestershire sauce, salt, pepper, and hot sauce. Adjust seasoning and consistency.

Serve étouffée over rice. Garnish with lemons, green onions, and parsley.

Shrimp Étouffée

GINGERBREAD HOUSE and COOKIE ORNAMENTS

For many years, during the holidays, a chef guided passengers through the sticky but fun steps of making cookie ornaments and gingerbread houses. The following recipe makes enough for a small (approximately 5" × 7") house, or up to three dozen cookie ornaments, depending on the size of the cookie cutters. (This recipe is from the Delta Queen Steamboat Company's 1995 souvenir booklet "Old-Fashioned Holidays: Great Guest Chefs." The booklet does not include a pattern, but the walls, roof, and chimney can all be easily fashioned from stiff cardboard.)

Supplies:

Cookie sheets

Silicone paper

2 rectangular (12" × 16") cake boards, covered with Fanci-Foil wrap

1 piece of Styrofoam approximately 1 to 1½ inches high, cut to fit inside walls of house, covered in Fanci-Foil

Food coloring, if desired for colored icing

Ingredients for Gingerbread (*recipe below*)

Ingredients for Royal Icing (*recipe below*)

Assorted trims (candy canes, fruit striped gum, gumdrops, hard candy, puffed cereal, edible glitter, ready-made royal icing pieces, sugar cones for trees)

Paring knife

Rolling pin

GINGERBREAD RECIPE

Yield: enough for a 5" × 7" house or up to 3 dozen cookie ornaments

5½ cups all-purpose flour

2 teaspoons ground cinnamon

2 teaspoons ground ginger

1 teaspoon ground cloves

1 teaspoon ground nutmeg

1 teaspoon salt

1 teaspoon baking soda

1 cup shortening

1 cup sugar

1¼ cups unsulfured molasses

2 eggs, beaten

In a large mixing bowl, combine flour, cinnamon, ginger, cloves, nutmeg, salt, and baking soda. Mix well. Heat shortening in a large saucepan over low heat until just melted, not hot. Add, in order, sugar, molasses, and eggs. Mix well. Cool slightly, then add 4 cups of the flour mixture. Mix well. Turn out onto a lightly floured surface and knead in remaining dry ingredients by hand. Add a little more flour, if necessary, to make a firm dough.

NOTE:

Dough can be wrapped in plastic wrap and stored in the refrigerator for up to 1 week. Remove dough from refrigerator 3 hours prior to rolling so it is soft and workable. You will need one recipe of dough to make the gingerbread house.

Preheat oven to 375°F. Place one-third of the dough on a lightly floured cookie sheet. Press dough to flatten. Dust a rolling pin with flour and, rolling from the center, roll out dough on the cookie sheet to approximately ¼-inch thickness. (You may need to place a dampened towel under the cookie sheet to prevent the pan from slipping as you roll out the dough.)

Place gingerbread house patterns on dough and cut around them with a sharp knife. Carefully remove patterns and excess dough.

Bake in preheated oven 10 to 12 minutes for large pieces and 6 to 8 minutes for smaller pieces. (Do not combine large pieces and small pieces on the same baking sheet because of the difference in baking times.) Check frequently to avoid overbrowning. Loosen pieces with a spatula after baking to prevent sticking. Cool on pan.

Repeat this process with remaining dough and pattern pieces.

ROYAL ICING

Yield: about 3 cups

> 4 cups sifted confectioners' sugar (about 1 pound)
> 6 tablespoons water (use 5 tablespoons for stiffer icing)
> 3 level tablespoons meringue powder

Combine all ingredients in a large mixing bowl. Beat at medium speed of electric mixer for 7 to 10 minutes or until stiff peaks form. If icing becomes too thick, thin with 1 to 2 teaspoons corn syrup.

For decorating, you will need:

> Decorating bags (for icing)   Spatula
> Decorating tips No. 2 and No. 8   Cooling rack with drip pan

NOTE:

Icing can be stored in an airtight container. Rewhip before using.

HINT:

To make a sturdy, quick-setting "glue," slowly melt 2 cups sugar in a saucepan. Dip edges of wall, chimney, etc., in melted sugar and press pieces together.

PICNICS

For many passengers, the single best meal served on the *Delta Queen* was the "picnic," a family-style lunch served toward the end of the trip. On that day, a clanging triangle summoned passengers to long benches covered in red gingham. Although the accoutrements fluctuated through time, waiters usually dressed like cowboys or baseball players, and a band set the mood by playing country-western ballads. The meal itself included picnic standards such as fried chicken, catfish, barbecue, corn on the cob, baked beans, butter beans, potato salad, and watermelon. And no matter the temperature or the time of year, that day always felt like the Fourth of July.

Around 1991, a passenger sneaked a few oversized plastic ants onto the picnic tables. They were such a hit that, for years after, waiters supplied the plastic critters and let them charmingly "crawl" all over the tables and even onto passengers' folksy bibs. The ants became such an expected part of the festivities that repeat passengers could tell them apart and actually gave them names (Antoine was a popular "pet").

CAJUN POTATO SALAD

Yield: 4 servings | Recipe courtesy of Chef Terry Newkirk

1 pound Red Bliss "B" (small red) potatoes

1 cup diced onion

1 rib celery, diced

½ cup mayonnaise

⅓ cup Creole mustard

Salt and pepper

Cut unpeeled potatoes into quarters or halves. Boil potatoes until they are tender but not mushy or overdone. Drain. While still warm, toss potatoes with all remaining ingredients. Cover and refrigerate at least 20 minutes. Adjust seasonings as desired.

BLACK BEANS

Yield: 6 servings

2 cups dried black beans, picked over	½ of a whole bay leaf
½ medium onion, diced	½ teaspoon cumin
½ rib celery, diced	½ teaspoon thyme
¼ green bell pepper, diced	½ teaspoon salt
1 teaspoon granulated garlic	¼ teaspoon black pepper

Place beans in a large bowl and cover with 2 inches of water. Soak 8 to 10 hours or overnight. Drain.

Place beans in a heavy soup pot and cover with ½ inch of water. Add all remaining ingredients.

Bring to a boil, then reduce heat and simmer, partially covered, until beans are tender and begin to get creamy, about 2 to 3 hours, adding more water during cooking if needed. Cooking time will vary depending on age and moisture content of beans. Remove bay leaf before serving.

SUMMERTIME SNOWBALLS

Yield: 6 servings | Recipe courtesy of Chef Terry Newkirk

6 large scoops vanilla ice cream, formed into balls	1 pint strawberries, hulled and quartered
1 can sweetened flaked coconut (3½ ounces)	4 tablespoons sugar, divided
	1 cup whipping cream
	Cookie wafers or chopped nuts (for garnish)

Roll scoops of ice cream in coconut so they are well coated. Place "snowballs" on a pan or plate lined with wax paper and keep in freezer until ready to serve.

Sprinkle strawberries with 3 tablespoons sugar. Let stand 15 minutes.

Whip cream with remaining 1 tablespoon sugar. When ready to serve, divide strawberries among 6 champagne glasses or sherbet dishes. Top each with a "snowball" and crown with a rosette of whipped cream. Garnish with a cookie or nuts.

BABY BACK RIBS

Yield: 3 servings

1 rack pork baby back ribs (12 bones)	Pinch of cayenne
¾ cup barbecue sauce	Pinch of garlic powder
2 tablespoons orange marmalade	Pinch of dried oregano
1 tablespoon honey	Pinch of black pepper
1 tablespoon soy sauce	Pinch of white pepper
Pinch of dried basil	Pinch of dried thyme

Poach or steam rib rack until tender, about 1 hour.

In a medium bowl, combine all remaining ingredients to make a sauce.

Preheat oven to 275°F. Brush rib rack liberally with sauce and place on a foil-lined baking pan. Bake 30 minutes, turning and basting with sauce three times.

To serve, cut into 3 portions of 4 ribs each.

THE CAPTAIN'S DINNER

Here's to you all,
And we want you to know
Our sentiments honest and real.
May your days be as bright
And your hearts be as light
As the spray from our old paddle wheel.

—Boatmaster's toast to passengers during *Delta Queen's* captain's dinners

Anyone who has cruised on an ocean liner, or even watched the television series *Love Boat*, is surely familiar with the captain's dinner, an end-of-the-cruise dining extravaganza hosted by the ship's captain. The affair is usually formal or semiformal, with extra-special food selections appearing on this night. Customarily, a handful of lucky passengers receive invitations to sit at the captain's personal table, and those few who are chosen are the envy of the ship.

The captain's table was born of necessity. During the height of European immigration to America, ship passengers often did not have much to eat. And since the delivery of half-starved cargo would have hurt business, ship captains often invited the more needy to dine with them on the last day of the trip. According to a 1977 *Delta Queen* captain's dinner menu, Greene Line Steamers actually brought the tradition of a captain's dinner to America's inland waters. Although the last-night-out dinner was a fixture on ocean liners, Mississippi steamboats had paddled along for some 140 years without hosting the traditional affair.

Delta Queen captains did not have a set procedure for selecting invited guests; they chose frequent passengers or those celebrating special events, such as honeymooners, while some passengers outright asked for invitations. Written invitations arrived in staterooms a day or two before the dinner, and invitees RSVPed to the purser's office. In later years, these chosen guests also enjoyed predinner cocktails in the Betty Blake Lounge, the area that had been the dining room in California. In 2008, this was a comfortable living room of plump Victorian furniture, Greene family portraits, John Stobart prints, and display cabinets of silver antiques. In the Orleans Room at the long captain's table, name cards guided invited guests to their places; as with all meals on the *Delta Queen*, everyone in the Orleans Room received the same menu. And for this one night only, there was just one seating, and somehow all passengers were served at the same time.

Letha Greene's *Long Live the Delta Queen* colorfully details a mid-1900s captain's dinner. In Greene's day, officers wore white uniforms, just as they did in 2008 (although there is evidence that some wore blue in the interim). While dinner jackets and tuxedos were expected of male passengers at Greene's dinners, in later years, suits were the norm. But regardless of the guests' attire, captain's dinner night always was a festive occasion, and, as evidenced by this passage from Greene's book, was particularly so during the time when that night's menu offered much more than the paddleboat's usual countrified fare:

> [The captain's dinner is] a highlight of the last day of a cruise, and always followed a generous, lively champagne party. The steward ordered a handsome floral centerpiece for the long table, which extended the length of the dining room. The chef and pantrymen did an extra special job of preparing a variety of tasty hors d'oeuvres. There was a huge bowl of fresh shrimp with a tangy delectable sauce dip, caviar, smoked oysters, sautéed chicken livers, the like of which I have never tasted elsewhere, fancy cheeses with special cocktail spreads and crackers, and dozens of other delicious dishes which appealed to smell, taste and sight.

Although it was a special evening, only one or two entrée choices were ever offered for a captain's dinner. Back in the 1950s and '60s, fanciful captain's dinner sides included such selections as Ol' Man River Rolls, Gangplank Celery, Riverboat Olives, and Greene Salad. Captain's dinner menus from the 1970s did not change much from trip to trip, with the usual relish tray of green and ripe olives, celery, carrots, tiny sweet and dill pickles, and radishes; and wedge salad with choice of jarred dressing. Salads, sides, and soups changed with the times, but through 2008, the entrée stuck close to tradition with offerings of prime rib and fish.

While a "recent" vintage of sparkling California wine was served as part of the meal, connoisseurs usually opted to purchase a better bottle from the Mark Twain Service Bar, the bar adjoining the Orleans Room. Often, with folks warmed up by whatever wine they had chosen, most of the room ended the meal by kicking up their heels behind the maître d', who led a second-line dance, the New Orleans equivalent of a conga line, complete with umbrellas, colored beads, and "do-rags" made from napkins.

This final-evening gala always was unforgettable, not only for those lucky enough to sit with the captain but for everyone celebrating the end of a memorable cruise.

CRAWFISH *EN CROÛTE*

Yield: 12 2-inch pieces

1 puff pastry sheet, 10" × 15", thawed if frozen	¾ teaspoon paprika
1 egg	1¼ cups seafood stock
1 tablespoon water	2 tablespoons blond roux (*see page 24*)
2 tablespoons butter	¼ cup sherry
¼ cup chopped green onions (plus extra for garnish)	1 cup heavy cream
1 teaspoon Cajun seasoning (*see page 27*)	1 pound crawfish tail meat with fat
¼ cup tomato sauce	1 tablespoon fresh lemon juice
	Lemon slices or wedges (for garnish)

Preheat oven to 375°F. Place pastry on a lightly floured surface (such as a cutting board) and cut in half. You should have two sheets measuring 7½" × 10" each. Combine egg and water in a small bowl and beat together to make egg wash. Brush egg wash on top of one pastry sheet. Place second pastry sheet on top and press lightly.

With a 2-inch biscuit cutter, cut out 12 pastry circles (do not separate pastry sheets). Place pastry circles on a cookie sheet. Bake until deep golden brown, about 9 minutes. Remove from oven. With a sharp paring knife, cut out pastry centers to form cavities. (If you are not serving this dish right away, you can keep shells in an airtight container at room temperature until ready to serve. Reheat shells in a 400°F oven before serving.)

Melt butter in a heavy, deep saucepan. Add green onions and Cajun seasoning. Sauté 1 minute. Add tomato sauce and paprika. Sauté until hot and bubbly.

Add stock and bring to a boil, then reduce heat to a simmer. Add roux and whip until mixture is smooth and thick.

Add sherry and simmer 1 minute. Add cream and simmer to reduce by one-third.

Add crawfish. Bring to a boil, then reduce heat and simmer 10 minutes.

If too thick, adjust consistency with stock or cream. Stir in lemon juice.

Arrange pastry shells on dinner plates and spoon crawfish mixture into the shells. Garnish with green onions and lemon slices or wedges.

Crawfish *En Croûte*

CREAM of FIVE ONION SOUP

Yield: 8 servings | Recipe courtesy of Chef Paul Wayland-Smith

1 cup (2 sticks) butter

2 cups flour

1 cup sliced leeks, white parts only

1 cup julienned red onion

1 cup julienned yellow onion

½ cup chopped shallots

¼ cup chopped fresh garlic

1 cup Madeira wine

6 cups vegetable stock

2 cups heavy cream

Salt and pepper

Dash of Worcestershire sauce

Dash of Tabasco sauce

⅓ cup chopped green onions or canned french-fried onions (for garnish)

Melt butter in a heavy soup pot. Add flour and cook, stirring constantly, to make a light roux.

Add leeks, red and yellow onions, shallots, and garlic. Cook 3 to 5 minutes.

Add wine; stir and cook until liquid is reduced by half. Stir in stock. Bring to a boil, then reduce heat to a simmer and cook 30 minutes.

Add cream and blend. Add salt, pepper, Worcestershire sauce, and Tabasco. Adjust seasoning. Garnish with onions.

CREAMED SPINACH

Yield: 4 servings | Recipe courtesy of Sir Robin Hixson

1 pound fresh spinach

½ teaspoon salt

4 slices bacon, finely chopped

1 clove garlic, minced

1 small onion, finely chopped

2 tablespoons flour

⅛ teaspoon black pepper

1 cup milk

Pick over and rinse spinach thoroughly. Place spinach and salt in a medium saucepan, cover tightly, and cook until tender, about 5 minutes. (Do not add water.) Drain spinach thoroughly and chop fine.

Cook bacon, garlic, and onion in a heavy saucepan until onion is soft. Blend in flour and pepper. Add milk gradually, stirring constantly until mixture boils. Cook 1 to 2 minutes. Add spinach to sauce and mix well.

STEAMED LOBSTER

Yield: 2 servings

2 lobster tails (8 ounces each)

2 wooden skewers

½ cup (1 stick) butter

1 lemon, cut into wedges (for garnish)

Using a knife or kitchen shears, split bottom side of lobster tails lengthwise. Remove meat from shell in one piece and remove vein. Insert a wooden skewer down the length of each tail to prevent curling.

Fill a pot with a steaming rack with water and bring to a boil. Place lobster tails on rack, cover pot, and steam for 8 minutes or until done.

While lobster is steaming, melt butter in a small saucepan over medium-high heat. Boil for 30 seconds, then remove saucepan from heat and let sit 2 minutes. Skim off solids, then pour drawn butter into 2 small ramekins, leaving the watery liquid in the pan.

Serve lobster with drawn butter and lemon wedges.

MARINATED BEEF TENDERLOIN

Yield: 10 servings

1 beef tenderloin (5 pounds), trimmed

1 recipe Marinade for Beef (*recipe follows*)

2½ cups demi-glace

Pat beef dry with a paper towel. Combine tenderloin and marinade in a medium bowl, turning tenderloin to coat all sides with marinade. Cover with plastic wrap and refrigerate 8 to 10 hours or overnight.

Preheat oven to 425°F. Prepare hot grill and sear meat until it is brown on all sides. Finish in oven until temperature reaches 118°F (rare). Cover with aluminum foil and let sit 15 minutes.

Place demi-glace in a small saucepan and bring to a simmer. To serve, place ¼ cup demi-glace sauce on each dinner plate. Top with slices of tenderloin.

MARINADE FOR BEEF

Yield: 1¼ cups

½ cup vegetable oil

¼ cup soy sauce

¼ cup red wine

2 tablespoons red wine vinegar

1 clove garlic, chopped

1 teaspoon dried basil

1 teaspoon dried oregano

1 teaspoon dried thyme

Combine all ingredients in a mixing bowl. Whisk to blend.

CRÈME DE MENTHE PARFAIT

Yield: 1 serving | Recipe courtesy of Captain Bob Reynolds

This simple dessert was a favorite at captain's dinners from the 1950s all the way through the 1970s.

1 large scoop vanilla ice cream

Reddi-wip canned whipped cream

1 ounce crème de menthe

1 maraschino cherry

Pack ice cream into a parfait glass. Pour on crème de menthe. Squirt on Reddi-wip and top with a cherry.

11 Passing Time aboard the *Queen*

FROM THE TIME OF the Greenes through 2008, a daily newsletter would let *Delta Queen* passengers know about the next day's stops at towns that dotted the boat's route, and it also listed available guided tours. But what did passengers do when they did not want to disembark for shore trips? The *Delta Queen* did not have a swimming pool, casino, theater, beauty salon, or spa. The Wi-Fi computer connection was not reliable. Cell phone service was even more hit-or-miss, and the only television was somewhere down in the crew's quarters. All told, this absence of modern-day gadgets was enough to make "connected" newcomers question their decision to book a trip.

At least at first.

Thinking that they had to do something, some novices read books in the Forward Cabin Lounge, an alluring space with cherry tables and original stained-glass windows, and where snacks such as fruit, coffee, tea, and homemade cookies were always available. Some nestled into the wood-trimmed sofas in the Betty Blake Lounge and wrote poetry. Others played cards, pieced together jigsaw puzzles, browsed the gift shop, tried a hand at the calliope, or flew kites from the fantail.

Delta Queen historians (employees at various times known as "riverlorians" or "discovery guides") gave lectures and boat tours throughout the day. Occasionally a storyteller was on hand to mesmerize with old-fashioned tales. A few passengers even made their way to the Texas Lounge to hit the hooch early. But in the end, almost everyone found themselves doing the most fun thing of all—absolutely nothing.

Books, newspapers, diaries, and Internet blogs are filled with accounts from passengers and travel writers rhapsodizing about their favorite *Delta Queen* pastime: the pleasure of relaxing in rockers and chairs on the boat's galleries. There the beguiled

succumbed to the gentle pursuit of shore gazing. And whether written by cruise critic or retiree, all these recollections say essentially the same thing, that this quiescence took them back to a simpler time—back one hundred glorious, blood-pressure-lowering years.

On a fast-moving current, the *Delta Queen* could travel up to 14 mph downstream, and upstream the average was a rousing 6 mph. But it was easy to relax on a boat that was so slow, and especially on one that was so quiet. About the only noise that broke the elegant serenity was water rhythmically splashing off the paddleboards and gentle swells washing ashore. The sights, too, were tranquil, yet intriguing. Catfish rolled in muddy waters. Goliath plantation homes peeked up from behind levees. Coal-laden barges and tugboats glided by, and the occasional osprey and eagle would be spotted fishing. At times the watching turned into waving—at children on the shore, at cars on bridges honking their horns, at small boats shimmying up to the boat's side. To the *Queen's* mostly well-heeled and well-traveled passengers, none of it was extraordinary— yet somehow it all was.

AFTER THE SUN GOES DOWN

The *Queen's* nighttime entertainment also helped take minds away from everyday cares. After dinner, the Orleans Room was transformed into an old-fashioned music hall. Dining tables were pushed back, tablecloths were replaced, and a stage was set up. When the band started warming up, inhibitions soon flew out the window.

In the innocent days of Letha Greene, a phonograph record played over the PA system signaling the beginning of the evening's entertainment. In *Long Live the Delta Queen*, Greene notes that the events usually began with a bingo game or a hat or costume contest. There were sing-alongs, the "Lemon Race," and participatory team games with such names as "Army and Navy," "Battle of the Banks" (for the two river banks), or "Baseball." The main attractions were organists and accordion players whose tunes stimulated passengers to cut a rug with dances such as the Virginia reel and the Pawpaw Patch. In later years, passengers were treated to some form of live jazz, ragtime, Dixieland, or blues—good, honest, homegrown music that would have been a hit on any stage.

Drawing on steamboating's rich jazz history, in December 1972, the *Delta Queen's* "interlocutor" (entertainment director), Vic Tooker, orchestrated a widely publicized "Good Time Jazz Cruise," a rollicking romp that began in New Orleans and took passengers upriver to jazz balls in Vicksburg and Memphis. Written accounts reveal that on this trip, jam sessions broke out, cocktails flowed freely, and many guests gave in to spontaneous dancing. In the midst of all this frivolity, passengers did find time to eat. Myron Tassin's book *Delta Queen: Last of the Paddlewheel Palaces* (2004) gives a detailed look at a menu from that cruise that, although more refined than in earlier years, still was not ahead of its time. Tassin, however, was impressed as he judged a lunch of tuna salad, corned beef and cabbage, and blackberry pie as "ample and delicious." His "hearty" dinner one night was a choice of veal cordon bleu or the time-honored liver with onions, and strawberry shortcake. Tassin particularly enjoyed the captain's dinner, an "impressive affair" with champagne and the officers all decked out in blue, a night when the chef "outdoes himself" with what we now know as the ubiquitous last-night dinner of prime rib of beef, this meal also offering Dover sole.

The versatile Tooker, band leader of the long-running Riverboat Ramblers, had started out by playing on board with his parents. A small sampling of other entertainers who lit up the Orleans Room's stage includes pianists Eric Rosser, Tony Schwartz, and Bill Wiemuth; clarinetists Glenn Wilson and Walter Kross; bassist Johnny Powers; banjo players Fred Dodd, Robin Hopkins, Danny Barker, and Lowell Schreyer; guitarist Paul Penta; ragtime players Dick Hardwick, Hayle Osborne, Steve Spracklen, and Jazzou Jones; and singers Laura Sable, Amy Baker, and Annie LeBeau. Another favorite was Phyllis Dale, the "Red Hot Mama" who, for ten years, donned an outrageous red hat and dress and belted out jazz and blues. Also, comedians such as Justin Wilson did stand-up comedy.

The *Delta Queen*'s cast of performers was so entertaining that in her last decade of service, readers of several Condé Nast magazines ranked the boat's entertainment among the best, even when compared to ocean liners.

ANY TIME IS SNACK TIME

When passengers weren't dancing, singing, reading, or idling away their time, between-meal snacks were on lots of folks' minds. Beginning early in the morning, it was easy to sniff out pastries, juices, and coffee in the Forward Cabin Lounge. By late morning, the aroma of popcorn was wafting out of the Texas Lounge, and hot dogs were warming up on the bar. Throughout the day, fruit bowls, cookie trays, tea canisters, and coffee pots were kept well stocked.

Although tea had always been offered on the *Delta Queen*, when the beverage gained superstar status in the United States in the 1980s, the galley started offering afternoon teas with rotating menus featuring cookies, petits fours, beignets, chocolate-dipped strawberries, fruit tarts, and finger and pinwheel sandwiches. Another afternoon institution, happy hour, started around 3:00 P.M. in the Texas Lounge. Sometimes sing-alongs erupted, even among the teetotalers, and everyone enjoyed enticements such as cheese, fruit, guacamole, fried chicken strips, catfish nuggets, Swedish meatballs, and (a passenger favorite) fried mini-Reubens.

Of course, regular meals always showed up on time, and if a day full of nonstop eating wasn't enough, there was always the late-night buffet. On most trips, after the night band shut down and while a self-named group called the Night Owls was starting to sing in the Texas Lounge, the Orleans Room was transformed once again, this time into a giant food bar. To much fanfare, waiters would roll in tables piled high with foods reflecting a theme. Cajun Night would feature boiled shrimp or crawfish, shrimp creole, or headcheese, a southern pork specialty. Oriental Night might include egg rolls, fried rice, or that favorite soup of 1950s cooks, beef yaka mein. Those who stayed up to partake, however, usually did so for the decadent desserts. Any given night might offer blueberry cobbler, tiramisu, assorted fruit tarts, cookies, or brownies. A fruit or cream pie was usually available, as were irresistible cakes. At the end of the day, no one went to bed hungry. But if a passenger's stomach did start growling in the night, someone on watch in the galley was always willing to make a sandwich.

Remarkably, all of this eating took place on a boat with a single dining room that doubled as a theater and a Sunday chapel. But this rustic multitasking was part of the *Delta Queen*'s charm. The steam engine, the bright red paddle, the rich woods, the calliope—they all more than made up for the lack of frills. The *Delta Queen* was a moving, living time machine. And for most passengers, this authenticity trumped convenience any day, providing the perfect setting to enjoy doing nothing.

BEER-BATTERED BRIE

Yield: 12 servings

Vegetable oil for deep-frying

3 rounds well-chilled brie cheese
(5 inches each)

3 cups Beer Batter for Brie (*recipe follows*)

1 cup Raspberry Sauce (*recipe follows*)

1 can mandarin orange sections
(11 ounces)

Fresh mint sprigs (for garnish)

Heat oil to 350°F in a deep-fryer. Cut each cheese round into 4 equal wedges. With a long fork, dip each wedge in batter, coating fully. Carefully place cheese wedges in hot oil (a few at a time) and deep-fry until golden brown, about 3 minutes.

Spread 3 tablespoons raspberry sauce over the serving area of each dinner plate. Place a wedge of fried brie on each plate. Garnish with orange sections and mint.

BEER BATTER for BRIE

Yield: 3 cups

1⅔ cups all-purpose flour

2 teaspoons salt

½ teaspoon ground white pepper

4 egg yolks, beaten

2 tablespoons butter, melted

1½ cups flat beer

In a medium bowl, combine flour, salt, and pepper. In another bowl, blend egg yolks and butter. Slowly add beer to egg yolk mixture, stirring constantly. Add egg yolk mixture to dry ingredients and blend well. Cover and refrigerate for 4 hours.

RASPBERRY SAUCE

Yield: about 1¾ cups

1 pint fresh raspberries

1 cup water

¼ cup sugar

1 cup purchased melba sauce

1 teaspoon cornstarch

1 tablespoon raspberry liqueur
(optional) or water

In a saucepan, combine raspberries, water, and sugar. Cook until mixture is reduced by one-half. Add melba sauce and blend. Mix cornstarch with raspberry liqueur until smooth. Stir cornstarch into raspberry mixture and cook, stirring constantly, until sauce thickens. Strain before serving.

POPCORN SOUP

Yield: 4 servings | Recipe courtesy of Sir Robin Hixson

Popcorn soup in America can be traced back to the seventeenth century, when the Great Lakes Iroquois Indians made the dish from popcorn popped in earthenware placed in hot sand. Colonial housewives also served popcorn doused with milk and sugar as a breakfast cereal.

2½ cups fresh corn kernels, chopped

3½ cups milk, divided

3 tablespoons butter

½ medium onion, chopped

3 tablespoons flour

1 teaspoon salt

Dash of pepper

½ cup half-and-half

1 cup popped popcorn

Cook corn in 1 cup of the milk until tender.

Melt butter in a medium saucepan. Add onion and sauté until soft. Stir in flour, salt, and pepper. Add remaining 2½ cups milk, half-and-half, and corn and milk mixture. Simmer until soup thickens.

To serve, ladle into bowls and garnish with popcorn.

Popcorn Soup

COCONUT BEER-BATTERED SHRIMP

Yield: 10 servings

Vegetable oil for deep-frying

2½ pounds large shrimp, peeled (leave
tail intact) and deveined

4 cups Beer Batter for Shrimp (*recipe follows*)

5 cups flaked coconut (1 pound)

3 cups Honey Mustard Sauce (*recipe follows*)

Heat oil to 325°F in a deep-fryer. Dip shrimp in beer batter, then dredge in coconut to coat. Carefully place shrimp in hot oil (a few at a time) and deep-fry until golden brown, about 1 minute. Serve hot with honey mustard sauce.

BEER BATTER for SHRIMP

Yield: 4 cups

2⅔ cups all-purpose flour

2 teaspoons salt

½ teaspoon black pepper

4 egg yolks, beaten

2 tablespoons butter, melted

1¾ cups flat beer

In a medium bowl, combine flour, salt, and pepper. In another bowl, blend egg yolks and butter. Slowly add beer, stirring constantly. Add egg mixture to flour mixture and blend well. Cover and refrigerate for 4 hours. Thin with a little more beer if batter is too thick.

HONEY MUSTARD SAUCE

Yield: 3 cups

1½ cups honey

1½ cups creole mustard

Combine honey and mustard, and mix well. Cover and refrigerate. Bring to room temperature before serving.

RATATOUILLE

Yield: 6 to 8 servings | Adapted from a recipe by Sir Robin Hixson

This dish of stewed and layered summer vegetables was originally cooked by peasants who lived around Nice, the Mediterranean resort town in southern Provence.

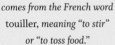

The word ratatouille *comes from the French word* touiller, *meaning "to stir" or "to toss food."*

2 pounds eggplant, peeled and diced

3 medium zucchini (1½ pounds total), peeled and diced

Salt

¾ cup olive oil, divided

2 onions (1 pound total), thinly sliced

3 bell peppers (1½ pounds total), any color, seeded and cut into thin strips

Freshly ground black pepper

3 large tomatoes (1½ pounds total), peeled, seeded, and diced

4 cloves garlic (3 minced and 1 whole, peeled)

2 bay leaves

1 small bouquet garni (fresh parsley, thyme, and oregano tied together in a cheesecloth bag)

Place eggplant and zucchini in separate nonreactive bowls (glass or stainless steel). Sprinkle lightly with salt and set aside for 20 minutes.

Heat half of the olive oil in a skillet. Add onions and cook until onions are soft but not brown. Remove onions from skillet.

Add bell peppers to skillet and sauté, then remove from skillet.

Drain eggplant. Add to skillet and sauté, then remove from skillet. Drain zucchini. Add to skillet and sauté, then remove from skillet.

Pour remaining olive oil into a heavy-bottomed pot. Add layers of vegetables in the following order: onion, eggplant, tomatoes, zucchini, and peppers. Season with salt and pepper. Add minced and whole garlic, bay leaves, and bouquet garni. Cover and cook for 1 hour over gentle heat, being careful not to let vegetables stick to bottom of pot. Serve hot or cold.

Tiramisu

TIRAMISU

Yield: 8 large or 24 mini servings | Adapted from a recipe by Chef Herbert C. Cade Jr.

Some food historians believe that tiramisu, Italy's famous sweet, coffee-infused "pick-me-up," was invented in the 1600s to honor Grand Duke Cosmo III, who was visiting Siena, in the northwestern province of Tuscany. Another story says that the dessert was created much later, in the 1960s or '70s, in the town of Treviso, in Italy's northeastern province of Veneto, at either the Ristorante El Toulà or Le Beecherie. Regardless of its origin, tiramisu is arguably Italy's most famous cake, and since the 1990s it has been a staple on American restaurant menus.

8 eggs, separated, plus 2 whole eggs
1⅓ cups confectioners' sugar
1⅓ cups cake flour
⅔ cup strong coffee

⅔ cup coffee liqueur
1 recipe Tiramisu Filling (*see page 212*)
Powdered cocoa (for garnish)

Best made a day ahead. Preheat oven to 375°F. Generously oil a 13" × 18" × 1" sheet pan.

In a large bowl, beat 8 egg whites until they hold soft peaks. Fold in confectioners' sugar and beat until stiff.

In a medium bowl, beat 8 egg yolks and 2 whole eggs on medium-high speed until light-colored and thick, about 5 minutes. Fold yolks into egg whites. Fold in flour.

Spread mixture smoothly and evenly in prepared pan. Bake until light brown, about 12 minutes. Remove from oven and cool 1 minute in pan, then turn out onto lightly floured parchment paper on a hard surface and cool completely.

Cut cake into three 13" × 6" rectangles. Combine coffee and coffee liqueur. Generously brush both sides of one cake layer with coffee mixture and place on a serving platter. Spread one-third of the tiramisu filling over cake layer. Repeat this procedure two more times with remaining cake layers and filling, stacking the layers on the serving platter and ending with filling.

Cover and refrigerate at least 12 hours. Sift cocoa powder over top. To trim and cut smooth pieces, dip a sharp knife in hot water before cutting into 8 pieces. (To serve up to 24, cut cake into two equal rectangles instead of three. Fill with half the coffee mixture and filling, and top with the remainder. Slice into small squares.)

TIRAMISU FILLING

Yield: 1 quart | Recipe courtesy Chef Herbert C. Cade, Jr.

¾ cup sweet Marsala wine, divided

3 egg yolks

3 tablespoons sugar

1⅓ cups heavy cream

8 ounces mascarpone cheese or cream cheese, at room temperature

¾ teaspoon unflavored gelatin

In a medium metal bowl, whip ½ cup Marsala, egg yolks, and sugar. Place bowl in a pan of barely simmering water and whisk until mixture is the consistency of soft pudding, about 4–5 minutes. Remove bowl from pan and beat on medium speed of electric mixer until cool.

Whip cream in a large bowl until stiff peaks form. Gradually add egg yolk mixture and mascarpone, alternately folding in small amounts of each. (Be sure cheese is soft or filling will be lumpy.)

In a small saucepan, combine remaining ¼ cup Marsala and gelatin. Heat just until wine boils and gelatin dissolves, stirring to blend. Stir a few tablespoons of cheese mixture into gelatin and mix well, then fold all of the gelatin mixture into cheese mixture and blend well.

BLACK-BOTTOM CHEESECAKE

Yield: 8 servings | Adapted from a recipe by Sir Robin Hixson

2 cups chocolate wafer crumbs

¼ cup (½ stick) butter, melted

¾ teaspoon ground cinnamon

2¼ pounds cream cheese, at
room temperature

1½ cups sugar

4 eggs

¼ cup green crème de menthe

¼ teaspoon peppermint extract

¼ teaspoon salt

½ cup semisweet chocolate chips

¼ cup sour cream

Preheat oven to 325°F. Grease and flour a 10-inch springform pan.

In a large bowl, combine chocolate wafer crumbs, butter, and cinnamon. Blend until mixture holds together. Press into bottom of springform pan. Set pan aside.

In a large bowl, combine cream cheese, sugar, and eggs. Beat at medium speed of electric mixer until light and smooth. Stir in crème de menthe, peppermint extract, and salt. Add chocolate chips and sour cream, and stir just to mix. Pour evenly over crust in prepared pan.

Bake 45 to 50 minutes, or until an instant-read thermometer inserted in the center reads 150°F. Turn off heat and leave cake in oven with door closed for 60 additional minutes.

Refrigerate cheesecake in pan for at least 4 hours. To serve, run a knife around the inside of the pan and remove springform rim.

12 The Cookhouse

THE DELTA QUEEN's meals were almost always "happy interludes," but in the boat's later years, the modern trend toward around-the-clock cruise eating was a challenge for the cookhouse of an authentic steamboat. The biggest problem was the galley's small size. Compared to the cooking areas of the *Mississippi Queen* and *American Queen,* the *Delta Queen*'s galley was tiny, only about 15' × 15', with barely enough room for its usual complement of 14 crew members to maneuver. With so little space, wait staff were required to remain in the dining room, and were only allowed in the galley for a pickup or to bring items into the scullery area. "Hanging out" in the galley was definitely not allowed, and the maître d' was charged with strictly enforcing that policy.

Galley safety was, of course, paramount. Always aware of the danger of fire, the crew worked mostly with electric appliances, including a flat-top electric stove with totally closed burners and electric chafing dishes in the buffets. Heavy-gauge stainless steel sheathed the ceilings and walls, and the whole area was protected by an elaborate sprinkler and chemical fire-suppression system.

Probably the closest call the *Delta Queen* had with fire was in the mid-1960s when the boat's old oil-burning stove caused timbers in the deck above to smolder. Luckily the potential catastrophe was quickly averted. The crew reacted so swiftly that the boat did not even have to go ashore. After a safe new electric marine stove was installed, the old stove was retired. It probably would have made a good museum piece, but rumor has it that the cast-iron relic "somehow" fell overboard in an undisclosed location in the Mississippi River.

Even though the galley was air-conditioned, it was sometimes hot. And between shouted orders, rushing busboys, and a constant barrage of jokes, the area was often loud.

Genuine southern cooking is a tradition on steamboats, and mealtimes will be happy interludes. Modern refrigeration cabinets are stocked with the choicest cuts of meat, fish and fowl, likewise a tempting array of fresh vegetables. Meals are served in traditional steamboat style.

—*from a 1951 Greene Line Steamers brochure*

But the cramped space was well ventilated. And most chefs feel it was laid out efficiently, with its small service table between the cold and hot areas, a dishwashing area off to the side, and a large walk-in refrigerator and a freezer at the back of the room. Some of the electric appliances included deep-fryers, a double convection oven, and a broiler. The stove had four burners, a high temperature hot plate, and two dry ovens under the burners. Next to the stove sat a piece of equipment used often—the electric tilting skillet, a rectangular braising pan with six-inch sides and a tilting mechanism that made it easy to pour liquids. The tilting skillet was used to make pancakes and for grilling, and was the natural choice for cooking stewlike dishes such as étouffée and beef stroganoff.

The few items that did not run on electricity were powered by steam from the boat's boilers. In the days of the Greene family, the coffee percolator was located in the pantry aft of the dining room and it was heated by steam. Although the percolator was eventually replaced, through 2008 steam was piped up to two kettles, a steam-powered warming table, and a double-bayed vegetable and rice steamer that had been used since the boat was first built.

In later years, a typical galley staff consisted of a chef, a sous chef, two or three first cooks, three in pantry prep, five scullery workers to scrub pots and run the electric dishwasher, and one crew steward in charge of crew meals. The crew worked twelve-hour shifts, seven days a week, and from four- to six-week periods. The galley was generally open from four a.m. until midnight, and all crew were required to clean up their stations to FDA standards by the end of their shifts.

Most food prep was done just a few hours before service because there was not enough storage area, and also so that items would remain fresh. Courses were prepared in service protocols—salads, soups, appetizers, entrées, and dessert. Cold service foods were typically prepared ahead and placed in the galley's cooler for the wait staff to draw upon as needed. Appetizers and desserts were pre-plated, while hot food was plated toward the end of the appetizer and salad course. The staff pretty much knew when they would be hit with each course rush, and it was up to the executive chef to ensure they were prepared for it.

Different menus greeted diners at every meal. The price of all food was included in the trip fare, but passengers were encouraged to tip the wait staff, bus persons, and the maître d'. In 2008, a cold breakfast buffet appeared at 6:30 A.M. for early risers. Later, full hot breakfasts were made to order, and twice during a trip the galley set up elaborate omelet and waffle stations. These displays, along with the galley's fluffy biscuits, prompted many diners to give the *Delta Queen*'s breakfasts their highest marks. Lunch offered soups, salads, sandwiches, and a hot entrée or two, and was open seating.

Keeping with sailing custom, dinner was the largest meal. Back in the seventeenth century, ships served travelers meager breakfasts and lunches, but dinners were more substantial. To accommodate all the evening's food, passengers of this era received their multiple dishes on easily stowed square trays, and from these bountiful trays came the term "square meal." On the *Delta Queen,* dinner was the only meal with reserved seating. Typically both prix fixe (referring to a complete meal) and à la carte (individual item) menus were offered, with the latter featuring two choices of appetizers, along with salads, soups, fish, poultry, meat, and vegetables and, in later years, at least one health-conscious choice.

The galley must have found ways to work around its significant physical limitations because passengers remember that meals were almost always hot and on time. And when the time came for lunch and dinner, mealtime was heralded in style. Harking back to the *Queen*'s California roots, the two meals were announced by the melody from a four-note, 1920s-era Deagan dinner chimes. First played around the decks and then sounded over the intercom, this quaint call to the dining room was so endearing that one passenger had an identical instrument made as a gift for her husband.

Surprisingly, the boat's motion rarely affected the ability to cook or serve food. Since the *Delta Queen* operated inland, rough water was hardly ever a problem. Locking through a dam or bumping a lock wall occasionally shook things up a bit, but not

Above left: Dinner chimes calling passengers to the Orleans Room

Above right: Dining table in the Orleans Room, 2008

enough to delay service. However, one major mishap did ruin a captain's dinner. On May 15, 1982, while 187 passengers were enjoying prime rib and champagne, a fast current forced the *Delta Queen* to tangle with a dam in St. Louis. The abandon-ship bells were sounded. Fortunately all passengers disembarked unhurt, but a cook named Greg Dudley did suffer a broken collarbone.

Until 1991, a significant galley impediment was the availability of potable water. Typical of many older riverboats, the *Delta Queen,* for most of her time on the Mississippi, carried three different water systems. One tank held filtered river water for bathroom sinks and showers. At times, this water had a "distinctive" smell and usually looked light yellow. During Lower Mississippi trips in the spring, this water was sometimes so dark that land-based fire hydrants were tapped to help lighten the color. Since water from this tank was suitable only for washing, sinks bore signs that said "DO NOT drink." A second system contained river water strictly to flush toilets, while another much smaller tank held water for drinking and cooking. This drinkable supply was filled up from local sources using designated pipes, but its limited amount forced cooks to be judicious.

During her Sacramento years, the *Delta Queen* carried approximately 8,000 gallons of potable water for her 125-mile Sacramento to San Francisco run. While undergoing her 1947 remodeling at Pittsburgh's Dravo Shipyard, the addition of another tank

Above left: View of the Ohio River from the Orleans Room

Above right: Applauding maître d' Darryl Reed

increased potable water capacity to 15,000 gallons, a substantial improvement, yet not nearly enough for cooking and heavy-duty dishwashing machines. The old filtered river water system was replaced in 1991 when the boat was fitted with a new hull and the crew areas below decks were rebuilt to allow for a new, larger clean-water tank. Filled from municipal water systems, the new tank held up to 70,000 gallons and was cleaned, tested, and inspected regularly. This upgrade not only gave the galley relief, but it also took a burden off the crew who, before then, had to explain the complicated three-tank water system to passengers. The treatment plant for wastewater was comprised of three MSD (marine sanitation device) units, and solid trash was removed in port.

SERVICE WITH FLAIR

Service in the Orleans Room was performed by a uniformed staff that averaged six servers and four assistant servers. In the early years, the galley steward was in charge of the galley, its crew, and the menus, and he had his hands and eyes on every food item turned out, testing for taste, temperature, and appearance. In later years, those duties were divided, with the kitchen staff reporting to the executive chef and the wait staff reporting to the maître d'.

Each table in the Orleans Room had assigned waiters who cheerfully made substitutions, quickly picked up names, and, after the first day, usually remembered drink preferences. At times, especially during management changes, there were glitches; but on the whole, dining room service was reportedly exceptional. An unnamed travel writer

You're fed three times a day, plus a 10:30 moonlight buffet, all of it above average, none of it resembling the lavish spreads on the Love Boat. We thought the food improved after touring the galley and wondering how the cooks turned out 1,500 plates of food each day from a room that didn't seem much bigger than our cabin.

—*Waterloo (IA) Courier*, July 1992

for the *Pasadena (CA) Star-News* summed up this coddling best by noting that each table's personal waiter "proceeds to pamper him in a way he'd probably like to get accustomed to for the rest of his life."

This love of job and people did not seem a corporate gimmick. A good illustration was the maître d' in charge of the dining room from 1995 through 2008, Darryl Reed, who could chat with passengers about their grandchildren while simultaneously training a new hire on a complicated table setting. Most servers, like Reed, worked on the boat for many years. A large number originated from New Orleans, a city known for its proficient waiters—a mature, genuinely friendly group that does not blink at a requirement to wear a tuxedo—and where it is not uncommon for some to spend entire careers at one restaurant.

Through the years bonds developed, and repeat passengers requested service from favorites such as Mo, Byron, Jim, Benard (who was always requested by the actress Helen Hayes), Antwon, Red Dog, Choo Choo, Travis, and Ortis. Apart from tending tables and making diners comfortable, these servers were also a source of entertainment. A running joke was the supposed recycled bread pudding. At dessert time on the third night of a trip, a solemn waiter would inform the table, "We have three-day-old bread pudding with warm whiskey sauce, this with blueberries." Day four would be "four-day-old bread pudding," maybe with raisins. This comedic drama went on through the entire trip, and passengers disembarked for home never really knowing if they'd been part of a joke. (The bread pudding was always a passenger favorite and it never did *taste* stale.)

THE CREW NEEDS TO EAT TOO

In early steamboat history, cookhouse crews, compared to deckhands, had it relatively cushy with plenty of food, the carpet of the main deck floor to sleep on, and a work location farther away from boiler explosions. Naturally, all eighty members of the *Delta*

Queen's crew slept in beds, and no one gave explosions a second thought. And food, although less varied than what was served to passengers, was more than ample.

In later years, the blue benches and small warming table in the cafeteria-style crew mess were not considered elaborate. But the room was comfortable, especially compared with what crews had to endure in the paddleboat's early days. Letha Greene writes that on the *Delta Queen*'s first trips, passengers ate in the yet-unnamed dining room on the relatively cool Main Deck while, surrounded by heat generated by the old stove, the crew gnawed through their food in the searing hot cookhouse in the hold. At the time, the service crew took their meals in two dining rooms in the hull, one for maids and a separate one for men, both, of course, un-air-conditioned. Crew members recall that the stove, the cast-iron "monster" inherited from the *Queen*'s California days, did more than make the galley unbearably hot; the appliance's No. 1 fuel oil, stored in drums in the head of the boat, added to the misery by sometimes "flavoring" baked goods with the smell of kerosene. Due to the heat, the crew dining room was eventually moved up to the corners of the stern end of the main dining room, separate from passengers but still in full view. In the early 1950s, the port side of the area was sectioned off for the crew's dining room and the starboard side was transformed into a cocktail lounge.

Oftentimes the crew had its own designated cook. Rated as a beginning position, this job typically attracted cooks who were adept at conventional home-style cooking. Occasionally, however, their menus deviated from the expected. The trendiest experiment with crew food occurred during the early 1970s, when then-owner Overseas National Airways decided to serve the crew soul food. True, foods largely associated with early twentieth-century African Americans had been on-board favorites in earlier years. But by this time, every *Delta Queen* crew member, regardless of race or background, was used to a contemporary diet. Items such as sow's ears and boiled collards were therefore not met with much enthusiasm. Mainstream menus reappeared after only a few weeks.

Also, a move in the 1970s to unionized crew labor created, at least initially, an unintended galley problem. Union rules required that employees receive three hot meals a day, a mandate not necessarily embraced by the crew, and certainly not by the cooks. Now, instead of sandwiches for lunch, the galley had to cook something hot for a crew that likely could not get around to eating it until it was cold. That quandary created strain all around.

Crew menus from the 1980s show that vegetable choices tended to be conventional, such as corn, potatoes, broccoli, and beans. And while entrées leaned more toward chicken than prime rib, the crew was well fed and they generally gave the galley praise. Some even complained that the *Delta Queen*'s galley was responsible for their "steamboat figures," a river term for carrying a few extra pounds.

Here is a typical weekday crew dinner menu from this period:

Tossed salad with dressings	New potatoes
Cold meat and cheese	Entrée du jour
Swiss steak	Yellow squash
Grilled fish, Creole	Dessert du jour

MURDER IN THE COOKHOUSE

Unfortunately, all was not calm during the boat's seemingly congenial period in Cincinnati. Tempers sometimes ignited, as evidenced by the galley's most tragic chapter. As reported in the *Charleston (WV) Gazette,* on a payday in June 1960, a contentious card game turned into a knife-and-razor battle between a chef named Floyd Matthews, who had been cooking on the river since 1914, and a butcher named Eddie Nolan. Reminiscent of steamboat brawls that were common a hundred years earlier, the two men scuffled on the floor with their weapons treacherously flying. Unable to break them up, crew members turned a fire hose on the two. Unfortunately for Matthews, they were too late.

Captain Doc Hawley was master on this ill-fated trip and in the pilothouse at the time of the incident. The house phone rang with the chief engineer, Cal Benefiel, a man of few words, at the other end announcing, "Floyd's been cut." Thinking that an encounter with a rotary meat slicer was the culprit, Hawley grabbed an elementary first aid kit and ran to the pantry, where everyone was in a state of shock. After viewing the gory scene in the galley below, he soon realized that mercurochrome and adhesive bandages were not enough.

Hawley ran up to the dining room to summon Dr. Robert Hudson, who was dining with Letha Greene. Hudson's first comment was, "You told me nothing serious ever happens." Hawley had talked Dr. Hudson into coming on board in place of the boat's regular physician, Dr. Eckert, and had offered him a room, meals, free access to the bar, and the promise that "nothing serious ever happens. Just bring your best bedside manner and some sugar pills." After Dr. Hudson pronounced Matthews "quite dead," he turned to Hawley saying, "You realize you have a murderer on board, don't you?"

Nolan was put off at the next lock and into the hands of the State Police. His wounds landed him in the hospital, but he recovered. As soon as he was discharged, he was tried and convicted, with fifty percent of witnesses claiming it was self-defense and fifty percent claiming premeditation. Nolan served one year and one day for his crime. After he was released, Nolan went back to the *Delta Queen* and asked for a job, but the captain wasn't hiring.

CHEFS THROUGHOUT THE YEARS

As in most long-running restaurants, the quality, temperament, initiative, and creativity of the *Delta Queen's* cooks fluctuated. Several learned their craft in the kitchens of both high-end and low-end restaurants and hotels. Many had little training at all, while, especially in later years, some were formally trained. Their longevity also varied widely. A typical twelve-hour workday in shifts of four to six weeks on and two weeks off prompted many chefs to show up for just one trip. But even more found the arrangement to their liking, and with support from understanding families, some stayed around for many years.

The much-advertised African American "southern chefs" from the paddleboat's early days were mostly old-line Greene Steamer employees who were schooled in whipping up folksy fare such as cornbread, fried catfish, hush puppies, Kentucky hams, mashed turnips, mustard greens, and candied yams. Often, domestic crew positions were filled with a good employee's family members, and whether they be porter, waiter, or cook, it was not unusual to have several relatives working for the company at the same time.

It would be impossible to list the names of all the galley's employees, but a few who contributed their talents in the boat's early Mississippi River years included George Peters and Charley Clay. Walter Hicks, a veteran of the Corps of Engineers boats, manned the stove in the 1960s and, according to Hawley, baked the best chess pie ever made. The head chef for the 1970 season was Willie Taylor, and although males still dominated the galley, that year Jean Thrash and Evelyn Michael occupied the position of *Delta Queen* "salad girls." Robert Jackson was a long-time chef in the transitional days during most of the 1970s, and his biggest distinction was that he cooked for President Carter's trip. Among the many other cooks of this period were Alan Weisling and Jerry Held.

When the 1980s ushered in its obsession with food (and with those who prepared it), the *Delta Queen* started hiring more public-savvy chefs. Sir Robin Hixson was chief

The first African American department head on the *Delta Queen* was Franklin Miles from Memphis, who was named chief steward in the late 1960s.

1968 *Delta Queen* Galley Crew

Chief steward
  (Homer Green)
Second steward
Chef
2 morning cooks
2 after-watch cooks
1 pantryman
1 storekeeper
7 dining room waiters
3 dishwashers
1 pot washer

steward in the early 1980s. A former executive chef with the Baton Rouge Hilton, Hixson made substantial personnel and menu changes. Adrian Johnson was his maître d', and Thomas March was a prominent chef.

Terry Newkirk served as executive chef on the *Mississippi Queen* and the *Delta Queen* from 1989 to 1993. He specialized in Cajun and Creole cuisine, and holds several gold medals from American Culinary Association competitions. Aside from creating exciting new dishes, Chef Newkirk made a tremendous contribution by testing and standardizing all of the Delta Queen Steamboat Company's recipes. He performed the colossal task on a winter layover, and many of the recipes from a resulting in-house cookbook were popular on the *Delta Queen* through 2008. Also during this era, Dr. Robert J. Harrington, dean of the Chef John Folse Culinary Institute at Nicholls State University in Thibodaux, Louisiana, spent a summer cooking on the *Delta Queen*.

Although it was rarely achieved, consistency between the galleys of the *Mississippi Queen*, the *American Queen*, and the *Delta Queen* was always a goal. As with Newkirk, another notable chef who worked hard to reach this elusive uniformity was Paul Wayland-Smith. Chef Paul began his career in New York restaurants. He worked his way up to a position with the Delta Queen Steamboat Company in 1989, and for many years was the company's corporate chef. Along the way, he married a former *Mississippi Queen* employee, and the couple's young children, when not in school, were often found cruising on the *Delta Queen* with their daddy.

In the *Delta Queen*'s later years, Lincoln Nixon was a familiar face in the galley. Around the same time, two female cooks—Jeannette Gerarve, known as Aunt Lucy, and Audrey Harbor, affectionately known as Mom—both brought smiles to the crew's faces with their no-nonsense cooking and much-respected discipline and advice. Around the beginning of the twenty-first century, another important figure appeared in the galley— Chef Herbert C. Cade Jr., who served as the *Delta Queen* executive chef through 2008. Hailing from upscale hotel restaurants in New Orleans, Chef Cade was often quoted as saying that he, like Mary Greene and Tom Greene long before him, would do whatever possible to make a passenger happy. He proved that point by filling special orders and scribbling down favorite recipes for passengers. Once he even whipped up a wedding cake at a moment's notice. Cade was also celebrated for his omelet-flipping expertise. Cade's job was made easier with help from hardworking pros including Mark Goller and Joyce Ballard.

Like all the chefs before him, Chef Cade consistently mastered the near-impossible feat of plating fifteen hundred meals each day. In addition to churning out meals at a phenomenal pace, the galley went out of its way to suit every lifestyle, medical need, and allergy, including one with a challenging sensitivity to water. This attentiveness won

The biggest crowds in the galley were during meals when all the cooks, salad folks, dishwashing crew, plus waiters and busboys were in and out. Waiters shouting orders to the cooks, cooks hollering for a certain dish, plate, or bowl from the dishwashers, cooks shouting at the salad people, etc., etc.

—Captain Bob Reynolds (recalling his high school days as a *Delta Queen* dishwasher)

prodigious accolades. Long-time passenger Jane Carey admits that this policy of food accommodation was a prime reason she kept returning. Jane, like many passengers, appreciated that chefs offered heart-healthy, vegetarian, and alcohol-free dishes, and that at least one person staffed the galley twenty-four hours a day for food "emergencies."

The Orleans Room habitually received higher marks than the dining rooms on the *Delta Queen*'s sister boats on the Mississippi. Since the *Delta Queen* was much smaller than the *Mississippi Queen* and the *American Queen,* presumably the galley was able to pay more attention to each plate and to special requests. On the rare occasion when the chef did let a diner down, complaints were loud and clear. The *Delta Queen*'s regulars considered the boat more a home than a public retreat. And when you're sitting at Grandma's dinner table and you want your fish fried instead of broiled, you do not hold your tongue. The running joke among executive chefs was that they had the first pass at setting menus, but it was the *Queen*'s guests who had ultimate control.

HAM, CHEESE, and RED BELL PEPPER OMELET

Yield: 1 serving

2 tablespoons butter, divided
¼ cup diced red bell pepper
3 large eggs
¼ teaspoon salt

¼ teaspoon ground black pepper
¼ cup ham, ¼-inch dice
½ cup shredded cheddar cheese, divided

Preheat broiler. Melt 1 tablespoon butter in a heavy small skillet over medium heat. Add bell pepper to skillet; stir until crisp-tender, about 2 minutes. Transfer sautéed peppers to a bowl.

Beat eggs, salt, and black pepper in a small mixing bowl until well blended. Heat remaining tablespoon butter in the same skillet over medium heat. Pour in egg mixture and cook until edges are slightly firm, about 1 minute. Using a fork, lift omelet edges and let uncooked eggs flow underneath cooked eggs until all egg is set, about 2 minutes. Sprinkle red bell pepper, ham, and half of cheese over omelet. Fold omelet in half and transfer to a plate. Sprinkle with remaining cheese and broil until cheese melts, about 1 to 2 minutes. Serve immediately.

BLACK-EYED PEA SALAD

Yield: 8 servings | Recipe courtesy of Chef Howie Velie

Black-eyed peas, also known as cowpeas, are actually legumes, and documents show that they were brought to the West Indies by West African slaves in 1674. The vegetable appeared in Georgia and South Carolina a short time later, and it is credited with saving the lives of many starving southerners during the Civil War. Rice, pork, and black-eyed peas form the basis for hoppin' john, a low country one-pot meal created in pre–Civil War America.

3 cups canned black-eyed peas, rinsed
    and drained well
2 cups finely diced seedless cucumber
1 red onion, finely diced
½ cup finely chopped fresh parsley

½ cup extra virgin olive oil
2 tablespoons cider vinegar
1 teaspoon black pepper
1 teaspoon salt

Combine all ingredients in a large bowl and mix well. Cover and refrigerate until chilled.

Black-eyed peas are still extremely popular in the American South, and many southerners eat them on New Year's Day for luck.

FRIED GREEN TOMATOES with REMOULADE SAUCE

Yield: 6 servings | Adapted from a recipe by Dr. Robert J. Harrington

During Dr. Harrington's stint on the Delta Queen, *this version of fried green tomatoes was served as a regular starter course choice.*

3 firm green tomatoes (medium size)	3 dashes Louisiana hot sauce
Salt and pepper	⅔ cup cornmeal
½ cup all-purpose flour	¼ cup canola oil
2 eggs, beaten	1 cup Remoulade Sauce (*see page 183*)
¼ cup milk	Microgreens (for garnish)

Cut tomatoes into ½-inch slices and sprinkle with salt and pepper. Let stand for 15 minutes. Use a three-step breading procedure: 1) dredge each tomato slice in flour; 2) dip floured slices in mixture of eggs, milk, and hot sauce; 3) shake off excess liquid and coat with cornmeal.

Heat oil in a skillet over medium heat. Carefully place breaded tomato slices in hot oil (a few at a time) and fry for 4 to 6 minutes on each side or until golden brown.

Season with salt and pepper. Arrange on individual plates and drizzle each serving with 1½ tablespoons remoulade sauce. Garnish with microgreens.

CORN and CRAB BISQUE

Yield: 2 quarts, 6 to 8 servings | Adapted from a recipe by Chef Terry Newkirk

2 tablespoons butter

1 small carrot, diced

1 clove garlic, minced

1 small onion, diced

½ rib celery, diced

¾ teaspoon dried thyme

½ teaspoon granulated garlic

¼ teaspoon white pepper

Pinch of black pepper

Pinch of cayenne

1 quart seafood stock

1¼ cups fresh corn kernels

3 tablespoons blond roux (*see page 24*)

1 cup heavy cream

2 tablespoons sherry

1 pound jumbo lump crabmeat, picked over to remove bits of shell

Melt butter in a large, heavy-bottomed pot. Add carrot, garlic, onion, celery, thyme, granulated garlic, and peppers. Sauté until onion is transparent. Do not brown.

Add stock and bring to boil, then reduce heat to a simmer. Add corn and simmer 15 to 20 minutes.

Add roux, mixing and whipping well. Simmer until soup thickens. Stir in cream and sherry. Simmer and adjust consistency, adding more cream or stock if too thick. Add crab. Simmer 2 minutes without stirring. Serve hot.

BUTTERNUT SQUASH BISQUE

Yield: 2 quarts, 6 to 8 servings | Recipe courtesy of Chef Terry Newkirk

1 large butternut squash, halved
   and seeded
4 cups water
½ cup (1 stick) butter
½ rib celery, finely diced
½ medium onion, finely diced
½ green bell pepper, finely diced
½ cup all-purpose flour

4 cups heavy cream
2 chicken bouillon cubes
½ teaspoon ground nutmeg
Salt and pepper
Unsweetened whipped cream
   (for garnish)
Toasted sliced almonds (for garnish)

In a large kettle with a cover, steam squash in water until soft, about 15 minutes. Remove squash and reserve cooking liquid. When squash is cool enough to handle, peel off skin and discard. Purée squash and set aside.

Melt butter in a heavy soup pot. Add celery, onion, and bell pepper. Sauté until onion is translucent. Add flour and cook over medium heat 3 to 4 minutes, whisking constantly to prevent lumps.

Add reserved cooking liquid, stirring and whisking to make a smooth, thick base. Add squash and simmer over low heat for 5 minutes.

Add cream, bouillon cubes, nutmeg, salt, and pepper. Simmer 10 minutes. Adjust taste and consistency. Garnish with whipped cream and almonds.

Butternut Squash Bisque

CAJUN CRAWFISH and PASTA

Yield: 10 servings | Adapted from a recipe by Chef Terry Newkirk

½ cup (1 stick) butter

2 bunches green onions, chopped, divided

1 tablespoon Cajun seasoning (*see page 27*)

4 cups heavy cream

1 pound crawfish tail meat with fat

½ pound smoked pork sausage, sliced and blanched

2 dashes Tabasco sauce

1 pound rotelli pasta, cooked according to package directions

Heat butter in a heavy-bottomed soup pot over high heat. As butter melts and bubbles, add half of the green onions and Cajun seasoning. Cook briefly. Add cream and simmer until liquid is reduced by one-half.

Add crawfish and mix well. Add smoked sausage and Tabasco. Adjust seasoning. Stir in remaining green onions and serve over pasta.

STEAK WINONA

Yield: 2 servings | Adapted from a recipe by Chef Terry Newkirk

The Delta Queen *often made stops at the picturesque town of Winona, Minnesota, a lumber town that was a former refueling stop for steamboats.*

> 4 tournedos of beef tenderloin (3½ ounces each)
> ½ cup Green Peppercorn Sauce (*recipe follows*)

Broil steaks to taste. Top each steak with 2 tablespoons sauce and serve immediately.

GREEN PEPPERCORN SAUCE

Yield: ½ cup

1 tablespoon butter	2 tablespoons brandy
2 tablespoons finely chopped shallots	½ cup demi-glace
2 tablespoons green peppercorns with brine	2 tablespoons heavy cream

Melt butter in a small heavy-bottomed saucepan over medium-high heat. Add shallots and sauté briskly. Do not brown.

Add peppercorns and brine. Cook briskly until almost all of the liquid evaporates.

Add brandy but do not stir. Very carefully ignite the liquor. When the flame goes out, add demi-glace and cream, mixing well. Simmer until mixture is reduced to ½ cup.

LEMON CREPES

Yield: 4 servings

2 tablespoons cornstarch	2 tablespoons butter
1 cup sugar	3 large egg yolks, slightly beaten
¼ teaspoon salt	8 6-inch Crepe Shells (*see page 260*)
½ cup orange juice	1 cup Lemon Sauce (*recipe follows*)
3 tablespoons lemon juice	Confectioners' sugar for dusting
1 teaspoon grated lemon peel	

To make filling, in a medium saucepan combine cornstarch, sugar, salt, orange juice, lemon juice, lemon peel, and butter.

Cook 5 minutes over low heat, stirring constantly. Remove from heat and whisk half of mixture into egg yolks.

Add egg yolk mixture to mixture in pan and cook over low heat 3 minutes, whisking constantly. Remove from heat and cool completely, stirring occasionally.

Cover with plastic film and refrigerate until ready to use. Can be made 1 day ahead.

To serve, spread 2 tablespoons filling in center of each crepe. Fold and roll. (Filled crepes can be refrigerated up to 2 hours.)

Place 3–4 tablespoons warm Lemon Sauce on each of 4 dessert plates. Place 2 filled crepes on each plate. Dust with confectioners' sugar and serve.

LEMON SAUCE

Yield: 1½ cups

1 lemon, halved	2 tablespoons cornstarch
1 cup water	½ teaspoon vanilla extract
¾ cup sugar	

Squeeze juice from lemon halves into a medium saucepan. Chop lemon halves coarsely and add to pan. Add water and sugar and bring to a boil. Dissolve cornstarch in ⅓ cup water and add to boiling mixture. Stir in vanilla and simmer 3 minutes. Remove from heat. Strain and keep warm until ready to serve.

13   Mimosas, Beer, and Ghosts

BARBARA HAMEISTER OF Ohio made forty-four trips on the *Delta Queen*, and she recounts a story from her third trip, in 1984, when she was traveling to the world's fair in New Orleans. An early riser, Barbara was leaning against an outside gallery rail on the second morning of the trip, enjoying the quiet. All of a sudden, she distinctly felt that someone was standing next to her. She turned around to say hello, but no one was there. The next morning, while at the same place, she felt the same presence, but again she saw that she was alone. The third morning, after again sensing she had company, she whirled around fast enough to glimpse the misty figure of a tall, large man dressed in a white uniform. As she watched, the apparition slowly faded away. Thinking back, Barbara says she probably should have been frightened, but she wasn't. Somehow she felt comfortable with her newfound friend. She had the distinct impression that the misty figure was enjoying watching her and was delighted to share in the peaceful calm.

Several old-timers believe that Barbara's vision could have been Captain Tom Greene. But Barbara, along with many others who intimately know the *Queen*'s history, believes that he was Captain Ernie Wagner, "The Big E," master of the *Delta Queen* in the 1960s and '70s. (A riverboat can have several captains but only one master, who is in charge of the boat's entire operation.) Wagner, a legend in *Delta Queen* history, was instrumental in outfitting the boat to meet mandated SOLAS safety requirements. He died in 1979.

The most celebrated ghost on the *Delta Queen* made her presence widely known. Bartenders, stewards, captains, and passengers have all filtered back reports that the *Delta Queen* was home to the spirit of an elderly woman. Occasionally she wore a green bathrobe. Several times the woman had been spotted climbing the stairs to the pilot-

Cave-In-Rock, Illinois . . . In 1797 one Samuel Mason came out here to the cave and set up a trap for travelers. Advertising the place as "Wilson's Liquor Vault and House of Entertainment," blazoned in large letters across the rock, he enticed weary and thirsty boatmen to stop. Few of them ever went away alive.

—Virginia S. Eifert in *Log of the Steamboat Delta Queen*, a travel guide for trips from Cincinnati to New Orleans

Inside the pilothouse

house or sitting in staterooms, and once she was held responsible for knocking drinks off a bar table.

Alan Brown's book *Haunted Places in the American South* (2002) chronicles that one passenger reported that the woman stared at her through a window. Another passenger, who was ill, swears that one night the woman tucked her in bed and wiped her sweaty forehead. According to Brown, yet another passenger glimpsed the woman walking around in the Betty Blake Lounge, while a crew member insists that an invisible person whispered in his ear, the soft voice starting a chain of events that led him to find a leaky pipe that could have potentially sunk the boat.

Many of those who saw the kindly woman remember that she looked just like the figure in a painting hanging on the wall in the Betty Blake Lounge. That painting featured Captain Mary B. Greene, the former Greene Line Steamers owner who, like her husband Captain Gordon, was a rigid opponent of selling alcohol aboard the *Delta Queen*. Right after Captain Mary passed away on board in 1949, the *Delta Queen* started serving alcohol from its new bar. Soon passengers started complaining about strange knocking sounds coming from the general direction of room 109, Captain Mary's old room. After the boat's engineers searched every inch and found nothing, a medium was called in and identified the location of the noise—room 109. In 1992, when the container holding the ashes of Mary's old friend Captain Fred Way made its final trip on the boat, problems with the electricity had the crew scrambling, and they soon learned that the source of the problem began in room 109.

Captain Doc Hawley remembers a few brushes with the posthumous Captain Mary (he says the crew always called her Captain Mary, not the widely publicized name "Ma Greene"). On a cold Cincinnati night in the off-season, Hawley's normally docile Doberman, Duke, was in the lobby and, unprovoked, started growling. With the hair on his neck standing, the dog suddenly tensed up and seemed ready to spring into action, the whole while fiercely barking at stateroom 109. Hawley had found a stowaway in a nearby stateroom a week before, and he fully expected to find another. Grabbing a billy club, he tiptoed into the room and found nothing, not even a rat or a bug. The well-respected and level-headed Hawley is convinced that on that particular night, his normally laid-back dog had sniffed out Captain Mary.

Captain Hawley was also on board for the most unsettling Captain Mary visitation. One night in 1962, a towboat that needed to put an injured crewman ashore attempted to land on the *Delta Queen's* starboard side amidships. Due to flood conditions, the landing became a "crash," throwing the boat into the outboard side of the *Delta Queen's* newly constructed cocktail lounge and causing considerable damage. Jumping out of bed in the stateroom just above, Hawley ran out on deck and discovered that the motor vessel's name was the *Mary B*. And since Captain Mary's maiden name was Becker and she was famously against the consumption of alcohol, both the location of the mishap and the runaway boat's name raised knowing suspicions. Before she died, Captain Mary had made a pragmatic decision to allow a small bar on the Greene Line's *Gordon C. Greene*. But since she was adamant that no such vice be allowed on the *Delta Queen*, those who knew her immediately surmised that the *Mary B* "accident" was hardly ac-

'Tis the human touch in this world that counts,
The touch of your hand and mine,
That means much more to the fainting heart
Than shelter, bread or wine.
For shelter is gone when the night is o'er,
And bread lasts merely a day,
But the touch of the hand,
And the sound of the voice
Will live in our soul always.

—Captain Mary B. Greene's last-night toast

Above: Punch bowl

Opposite: Texas Lounge

cidental. Hawley's call to Letha Greene the next morning brought, at first, silence. Then Captain Mary's daughter-in-law responded, "The old lady strikes again."

Friends who knew Captain Mary do not fear her; they respect her. Only five feet tall, Captain Mary was not only an expert at handling boats; she could also spin a wild tale, and she loved to dance. The first woman to earn both a master's and a pilot's license, she was so well respected in the boating community that after her death the city of Covington, Kentucky, honored her with a life-size bronze statue overlooking the Cincinnati riverfront. And aside from forbidding alcohol, her story is one of a woman who dedicated everything to the steamboats that she loved in life . . . and possibly still loves in death.

In the boat's later years, alcohol was served from the Mark Twain Service Bar (just off the dining room and the only bar for many years) and in the Texas Lounge, and typical trips carried four bartenders. Most of the time, the Texas Lounge was serving mimosas, screwdrivers, and Bloody Marys by 10:00 A.M. Daily mixed drink specials were announced at 3:00 P.M., and included artful presentations such as margaritas, martinis, and lemonade and iced tea juleps. In spite of an expansive repertoire, however, one of the most popular alcoholic drinks was beer, with microbrews the favorites.

By the 1990s, sightings of the legendary river woman had begun to dwindle. No one could explain her snub, but everyone hopes that Captain Mary did finally approve of the two on-board bars.

> He [Tom Greene] upset the family tradition and opened a bar aboard the *Delta Queen,* and for the last night out of port he instigated a barbarous "Grab Bag Party" which many guests recall with groans and a fleeting hot flash of head throbs and aspirin tablets. All of the leftover liquor, regardless, was poured into a punch bowl. Those who tipped glasses filled with this aqua regia deserved what they got—at least it cost them nothing.
>
> —Captain Frederick Way Jr. in *Ships and the Sea* magazine (1953)

All drink recipes are courtesy of bartender Brandon Gipson.

MIMOSA

Yield: 1 drink

The mimosa is closely related to the Buck's Fizz, a champagne drink created in 1921 at London's Buck's Club, and which contains triple sec or orange liqueur, along with more orange juice.

2 ounces champagne
2 ounces orange juice

Orange slice (for garnish)

Pour champagne into a tall flute glass. Top with orange juice. Garnish with orange slice.

BLOODY MARY

Yield: 1 drink

The Bloody Mary was originally concocted from only tomato juice and vodka, either by bartender Fernand Petiot at Harry's New York Bar in Paris in 1920, or by actor George Jessel in 1939. The origin of the drink's name is just as unclear as the drink's beginnings. But according to Tabasco hot sauce historians, the drink was not named for England's "bloody" Queen Mary I, but instead came from "a bartender at Harry's New York Bar in Paris" who claimed that "one of the boys suggested we call the drink 'Bloody Mary' because it reminded him of the Bucket of Blood Club in Chicago, and a girl there named Mary." It is certain that Fernand Petiot came to the King Cole Bar in New York's St. Regis Hotel in 1934, and it was there that he added seasoning, including Tabasco sauce, to the drink that either he or Jessel invented.

Coarse salt
Ice
1 ounce vodka
3 drops Tabasco sauce

Spicy V8 vegetable juice
Olive, pickled okra, and pickled green
   beans (for garnish)

Salt the rim of a tall glass and fill with ice. Stir in vodka, Tabasco, and enough V8 juice to fill the glass. Garnish with an olive, pickled okra, and 2 green beans.

Mimosas

Iced Tea Julep

SALTY DOG

Yield: 1 drink

Coarse salt

Ice

1½ ounces gin

Grapefruit juice

Salt the rim of a rocks glass and fill with ice. Add gin. Fill glass with grapefruit juice and stir.

CAPE COD

Yield: 1 drink

⅓ cup cranberry juice

1½ ounces vodka

Ice

Lime slice (for garnish)

Pour cranberry juice and vodka over ice in a rocks glass and stir. Garnish with lime.

ICED TEA JULEP

Yield: 1 drink

5 fresh mint leaves, plus a full sprig of
  mint for garnish

1 ounce simple syrup (*see page 171*)

Shaved ice

3 ounces Jim Beam bourbon

1 ounce brewed tea

In a tall glass, muddle mint and simple syrup with a muddler or the back of a spoon. Fill glass with ice. Add bourbon and tea, and stir briskly. Garnish with a mint sprig.

STOLI RASPBERRY COSMO

Yield: 1 drink

Ice

2 ounces Stolichnaya raspberry vodka

⅔ ounce (4 teaspoons) Triple Sec

Splash of cranberry juice

Splash of Rose's lime juice

Lemon twist (for garnish)

Fill a shaker with ice and add vodka, Triple Sec, cranberry juice, and lime juice. Shake and strain into a chilled cocktail glass. Garnish with lemon.

14 The End?

BEGINNING IN 1966, when Congress first passed the Safety at Sea Act, the *Delta Queen* was exempted from adhering to the regulation a total of nine times. Since the law's inception, *Delta Queen* owners had gone to tremendous lengths to ensure safety, including informing passengers about the boat's potential fire hazard, conducting emergency drills, installing sophisticated fire suppression systems, using only fireproof paints, and undergoing at least six Coast Guard inspections each year. And after the 1970 battle with Congress and Representative Garmatz, approval seemed to be routine. But all that changed in August 2007 when the *Delta Queen*'s tenth SOLAS renewal attempt hit a snag more deadly than any hidden river stump. That year, none of the precautions seemed to matter. And if lawmakers were to have their way, the steamboat's exemption was going to be allowed to expire November 1, 2008, when she would only be allowed to sail with a maximum of fifty passengers. The boat could not generate enough income without a permit to sail overnight with her full complement of 174, and she would then be forced to dock as a restaurant or hotel, or sail only for daily excursions, this potential fate the same and as unsavory as it had been in 1970.

As chronicled in an October 25, 2007, *New York Times* article, the reason for not exempting the *Queen* was highly controversial. The *Delta Queen*'s biggest critic in Congress, Representative James Oberstar of Minnesota, cited safety concerns, while Ambassadors International, the then-owner of Majestic America and the *Delta Queen*, blamed politics and a workers' union the company had abandoned. Oberstar and the union expressed outrage at the accusation, and that debate raged on and on. But regardless of the reason for the congressional threat, terrified *Delta Queen* loyalists did not waste time pointing fingers. Instead, in this Internet age, Web sites immediately sprang up urging

Build all-steel diesel riverboats for those who want comfort and more safety. But keep the Delta Queen *for those who want to cling to a bit of history. There's a place in America for both.*

—William Muster, March 15, 1970

"Save the *Delta Queen*" banner

proponents to contact representatives and senators. Determined employees produced a video plea through YouTube. Flyers, banners, stickers, and T-shirts were available for sale online, and bloggers kept the faithful informed about rallies, legislation, and numerous media reports.

During 2008, management continued efforts to extend the *Queen*'s congressional exemption, but just in case, Majestic America did not schedule any trips for the boat after October 31. That year, the *Queen*'s itinerary also included a farewell tour schedule, and with her staterooms almost always full, she made good-bye stops in places such as St. Francisville, Louisiana; Maysville, Kentucky; Cape Girardeau, Missouri; Alton, Illinois; Clarksville, Tennessee; Point Pleasant, West Virginia; and Helena, Arkansas—all small towns that had, for years, welcomed the *Queen* as a natural part of their landscape, and also depended on her for revenue. And on these riverbanks, as had happened almost forty years earlier, heavy-hearted mayors, high school bands, and townsfolk gathered to wish the grand old lady well. Among them, there was scarcely ever a dry eye.

In the middle of all the conflict, in early 2008, Ambassadors International decided to focus on other ventures, and it put its Majestic America Line up for sale, including the *Delta Queen,* along with six other boats. With this news, worried fans, along with crew members fearful of losing their jobs, knew that only a miracle would save the vessel, especially since a high-spirited presidential campaign was outshining the SOLAS debate. Local news organizations and a few national cable channels were covering the *Delta Queen*'s story, but national television and radio networks were overwhelmingly focused on the contest between Senators Barack Obama and John McCain.

Then the unthinkable happened. Unlike the past, this time no savior came. No matter how much the boat's champions pleaded, no buyer or congressional exemption could be conjured up. And with the SOLAS deadline just a day away, on October 30, 2008, in

Delta Queen gangplank

Memphis, the *Delta Queen* unloaded what was to be her last load of overnight passengers.

At midnight on October 31, 2008, the *Delta Queen*'s SOLAS exemption expired. With a skeleton crew, the boat steamed down to New Orleans, where she was tied up to wait for an unknown fate. By the end of the year, no new owner had yet appeared, and the *Queen*'s then-owner, Majestic America, ceased to exist.

FANS GALORE

The *Queen* faced and overcame adversity for most of her life. More than a story of a cat with nine lives, however, the *Delta Queen*'s tale is one of living and incomparable history. This tangible connection with America's past has attracted a large number of devotees. Many are former passengers, some of whom are serious students of steamboat history. And they will quickly tell you that the cookhouse should be called a cookhouse, not a galley. A trip is a trip, not a cruise, and mercy on the unfortunate who calls the boat a ship. (Anything big enough to carry smaller vessels is a ship, while vessels built for inland navigation are boats.)

Another fervent group is made up of the many employees who worked on board, some for decades, and who can spout off every blueprint detail of this 1920s-era steamboat. Former crew members are also quick to give credit for the boat's longevity to the men and women who captained her over the years—greats including Louden, Wilkinson, Underwood, Richie, Williams, Zang, Dugger, Palmore, Chengery, Theony, Hawley, and Wagner, to name a few.

Then there's the cadre of fans who freely admit to having a mild interest in steamboats, but who are absolutely "nutsy" about the *Queen*. These faithful knew all the captains, the wait staff, bartenders, and their families. When not sailing on the boat, it was not unusual for those who lived near a shore stop to bring the crew cookies, home-grown tomatoes, or fudge. Many delivered roses out of backyard gardens. Some even ran to local grocery stores for the galley crew.

Yet another group is the admirers who have never actually taken a *Delta Queen* trip, but all their lives have watched her tie up to their town docks. For as long as most folks remember, the *Delta Queen* was as much a part of the Natchez scenery as its bluffs and Spanish moss. She was as common as catfish on the Tennessee River and poplars along the Cumberland. She was as cherished as Maysville, Kentucky's Rosemary Clooney and, like a sultry blast of the blues, brought a smile to the residents of Memphis. The last authentic representation of the early steamboat, she characterizes the vessel that tremendously aided the growth of great cities such as Pittsburgh, Cincinnati, Louisville, and St. Louis, and that spawned hundreds of smaller communities like Madison, Indiana—the picturesque town that Charles Kuralt called "the princess of the rivers." *Delta Queen* fans can be found in each of these locales.

All this adulation and respect is well earned. In her lifetime, the *Queen* traveled more than two million miles and carried more than five hundred thousand passengers. Over the years, rooms were added and rearranged, but fundamentally, the boat does not look or operate much differently than the elegant packet she was in the 1920s. Her leaded glass still sparkles in the sun, and her serene white galleries provide inviting shade. Through 2008, the capstan still ran on steam, and at isolated areas along the rivers, deckhands still hopped ashore to "choke a stump" (tie on to a tree). When it was time to move, the magnificent red paddle wheel still effortlessly turned and pushed the *Queen* to her widespread destinations. And through it all, her engines and boilers, all older than 85 percent of the U.S. population, performed flawlessly, this mechanical feat alone leaving scores in awe.

AMERICA'S STEAMBOAT

The *Delta Queen*, the only floating Historic Hotel of America, has always been owned by Americans, and since the late 1940s, she has always advertised that she strictly hired an "All-American" crew. Following the tenets of democracy, accommodations were unpretentious. Public areas were open to everyone, and at mealtime everyone received the same menu.

The paddleboat's food overwhelmingly tilted to the American South, and to her many passengers, these homey meals were generally considered excellent. However delicious, though, what the galley dished up could never have competed with the popularity of this legendary boat. But just as food was a big part of nineteenth-century steamboating, satisfying dining was important to the total *Delta Queen* experience.

In the Orleans Room, enjoyable dining naturally included openness to food trends, yet fried food was never out of fashion and cream was usually a crucial ingredient in soups and desserts. Without a doubt, many of the galley's dishes could have appeared on the menus of high-end restaurants; but just as many could have been found on family dinner tables in the 1920s. This point is punctuated by a look at the boat's most frequently requested recipes, a list that includes age-old favorites such as oyster stew, red beans and rice, seafood gumbo, shrimp creole, fried catfish, Mississippi mud pie, and apple brown betty. Time had a way of getting blurred on the *Delta Queen*. She was the last of a bygone era, always proudly stubborn about what she was. And to her many devoted passengers, this disconnect with the twenty-first century was just fine.

FRENCH TOAST

Yield: 4 servings | Adapted from a recipe by Chef Herbert C. Cade Jr.

Versions of French toast go all the way back to fourth-century Rome, and milk-soaked and fried stale bread was extremely common throughout Europe during the Middle Ages. This breakfast and dessert treat is called "French" toast because it was popularized in the United States by French immigrants.

Like the French, Louisiana's Cajuns call this dish pain perdu (lost bread).

8 slices French bread (½ inch thick)
1 cup whole milk
3 large eggs
2 tablespoons sugar
¼ teaspoon salt

Pinch of ground cinnamon
Pinch of ground nutmeg
3 tablespoons unsalted butter, melted
Confectioners' sugar (for garnish)
Fresh strawberries (for garnish)

Place bread in a single layer on a sheet pan. Bake at 200°F for 1 hour to dry.

In a medium bowl, combine milk, eggs, sugar, salt, cinnamon, and nutmeg. Whisk until smooth.

Heat a skillet over medium heat and brush with butter. Dip bread slices in milk mixture and let soak until thoroughly saturated. Place slices in skillet, a few at a time, and cook, turning once, until both sides are golden brown. To serve, place 2 slices of French toast on each plate. Dust with confectioners' sugar and garnish with strawberries.

MARINATED MUSHROOMS

Yield: 4 servings

1½ cups Italian Dressing (*recipe follows*)
1 can tomato sauce (8 ounces)
½ pound button mushrooms, rinsed
   and quartered

2 tablespoons diced pimientos
Leaf lettuce
Chopped fresh parsley (for garnish)

Combine Italian dressing and tomato sauce in a mixing bowl. Add mushrooms and pimientos; mix well. Cover and refrigerate for at least 4 hours.

To serve, line salad plates with leaf lettuce and top with marinated mushrooms. Garnish with parsley.

ITALIAN DRESSING

Yield: 1½ cups

¾ cup olive oil
½ cup red wine vinegar
1 clove garlic, minced
1 tablespoon finely chopped shallot
1 teaspoon sugar

½ teaspoon dried basil
½ teaspoon dried oregano
½ teaspoon dried thyme
Salt and pepper
1 egg white, beaten until frothy (*see Note*)

Combine all ingredients except egg white in a mixing bowl. Whip to blend. Fold in egg white. Skim foam off top.

❧

NOTE:

*This recipe contains
a raw egg white. There
is a small chance of
salmonella poisoning
when consuming
raw eggs.*

❧

ANTIPASTO (ITALIAN SALAD)

Yield: 6 servings | Adapted from a recipe by Sir Robin Hixson

1 head Belgian endive, leaves separated,
    or 4 cups mixed looseleaf lettuce

6 radishes, sliced

1 rib celery, thinly sliced

2 tomatoes, each cut into 6 wedges

6 artichoke hearts

2 hard-boiled eggs, each cut into 6 wedges

12 anchovy filets

6 slices provolone cheese, each slice
    cut into 4 pieces

6 slices Italian hard salami, each slice
    cut into 4 pieces

18 black olives

6 sprigs fresh parsley

Italian Dressing (*see previous recipe*)

Arrange ingredients on individual salad plates as follows: endive or lettuce, radish, celery, tomato, artichoke, egg, anchovy, cheese, salami, and olives. Top with a sprig of parsley and drizzle with Italian dressing.

CORN and POTATO CHOWDER

Yield: 1 gallon, 12 to 16 servings | Recipe courtesy of Chef Paul Wayland-Smith

3 cups canned sweet corn, drained

1 cup heavy cream

2 teaspoons sugar

Pinch of saffron

2 tablespoons butter

2 ribs celery, diced

1 medium carrot, diced

1 medium onion, diced

¼ cup flour

1 cup finely diced ham or Canadian bacon

Pinch of Italian herbs

Dash of Tabasco sauce

Dash of Worcestershire sauce

Salt and pepper

2 quarts chicken stock

2 cups diced new potatoes (unpeeled)

Fresh parsley (for garnish)

In a large bowl, combine corn, cream, sugar, and saffron. Cover and refrigerate for 4 to 6 hours to infuse flavors.

Melt butter in a soup pot. Add celery, carrot, and onion. Sauté until vegetables are soft.

Add flour and mix well to make a roux. Cook roux for 5 minutes. Add ham, Italian herbs, Tabasco, Worcestershire sauce, salt, and pepper; blend well.

Slowly add stock, stirring until mixture is smooth. Cook 20 minutes. Add potatoes and cook until tender.

Add reserved corn mixture and heat through. Adjust seasoning. Ladle hot soup into bowls and garnish with parsley.

BAYOU STUFFED CATFISH with CAJUN BEURRE BLANC SAUCE

Yield: 6 servings | Adapted from a recipe by Chef Paul Wayland-Smith

6 boneless catfish filets (6 ounces each), skinned

2 cups Stuffing (*recipe follows*)

Vegetable oil for frying

1 cup seasoned flour

1 cup buttermilk

2 cups Zatarain's Fish-Fri (seasoned cornmeal)

1 recipe Cajun Beurre Blanc Sauce (*see page 178*)

Lemon wedges (for garnish)

Lay fish skinned side up and top each filet with ¼ to ⅓ cup stuffing. Roll tightly, cover, and refrigerate until firm.

Preheat oven to 350°F. Heat oil to 350°F in a deep-fryer. Dredge chilled fish rolls in seasoned flour, dip in buttermilk, and coat with seasoned cornmeal. Carefully place fish rolls in hot oil and deep-fry until light brown, about 2 minutes.

Remove fish from deep-fryer and place on a sheet pan. Finish in oven until internal temperature of fish is 150°F. To serve, top with Cajun beurre blanc sauce and garnish with lemon.

STUFFING

Yield: about 6 cups | Recipe courtesy Chef Paul Wayland-Smith

½ pound jumbo lump crabmeat, picked over to remove bits of shell

Baked cornbread (3" × 6" × 1" loaf), crumbled

1 cup chopped cooked spinach

¼ cup pine nuts, toasted

1 tablespoon Creole mustard

Salt and pepper

Combine all ingredients in a mixing bowl and mix well.

SEASONED FLOUR:

flour mixed with seasoned salt, garlic and/or onion powder, and other spices of your choice.

Leftover stuffing can be made into a casserole by stirring in some chicken stock until consistency is thin but not runny. Place in an oiled baking dish, and bake at 350°F for 40 to 45 minutes.

SESAME CHICKEN

Yield: 2 servings | Adapted from a recipe by Chef Terry Newkirk

2 boneless, skinless chicken breasts
  (7 ounces each), lightly pounded and
  tenderloin removed and reserved for
  another use
Salt and pepper

1 egg white, whipped until foamy
3 tablespoons sesame seeds
2 tablespoons butter
½ cup Dijon Mustard Sauce (*recipe follows*)

Season chicken with salt and pepper. Dip in egg white. Sprinkle both sides with sesame seeds.

Melt butter in a heavy skillet over medium-high heat. Sauté chicken until cooked through and moist, about 4 minutes per side, being careful not to burn. Serve on a pool of Dijon mustard sauce.

DIJON MUSTARD SAUCE

Yield: about 1 cup

Dijon is the capital of the Burgundy region of France and is one of the country's great wine-producing districts. The consumption of mustard in this area can be traced all the way back to 1336.

1 cup Béchamel Sauce (*recipe follows*)
2 tablespoons Dijon mustard

1 tablespoon white wine

Combine all ingredients and blend well.

BÉCHAMEL SAUCE

Yield: 1¼ cups

2 tablespoons unsalted butter
2 tablespoons all-purpose flour
¾ cup whole milk, scalded

¾ cup heavy cream
Salt and white pepper

In 1756, a Dijon mustard maker named Jean Naigeon substituted verjuice (green grape juice) for vinegar, thus changing mustard's typical flavor and revolutionizing the mustard world.

Sesame Chicken with
Dijon Mustard Sauce

Melt butter in a heavy saucepot. Blend in flour and cook slowly for 4 minutes, stirring constantly. Do not allow flour to darken.

Slowly add milk, beating briskly until blended. Add cream, salt, and pepper. Simmer 5 minutes. Strain.

Wild Mushroom Bruschetta

WILD MUSHROOM BRUSCHETTA

Yield: 12 servings | Recipe courtesy Chef Herbert C. Cade Jr.

Although historically gathered from forest floors, "wild" mushrooms sold in today's supermarkets are mostly cultivated.

1 baguette (French bread)

2 tablespoons olive oil

3 tablespoons minced onion

2 cloves garlic, minced

2 cups mixed wild mushrooms,
    stemmed and chopped

1 teaspoon dried basil

1 teaspoon dried thyme

½ teaspoon balsamic vinegar

Salt and pepper

Cut 12 ½-inch slices from the baguette. Toast baguette slices under broiler. Set aside.

Heat olive oil in a skillet. Add onion and sauté over medium heat until golden. Add garlic and cook 1 minute.

Add mushrooms, basil, thyme, vinegar, salt, and pepper. Cook over medium heat until mushrooms begin to wilt. To serve, spoon mushroom mixture on toasted baguette slices.

WILD MUSHROOMS:

Shitake, crimini, oyster, morels, etc.

CRAB CAKES

Yield: 4 servings | Adapted from a recipe by Sir Robin Hixson

1 pound fresh backfin crabmeat

2 hard-boiled eggs, finely grated

½ cup mayonnaise

1 tablespoon finely chopped fresh parsley

1 teaspoon prepared mustard

½ teaspoon salt

White pepper

Vegetable oil for deep-frying or sautéing

1 cup fine cracker crumbs

Lemon wedges (for garnish)

Sauce of your choice—remoulade,
    mustard, or cocktail sauce (optional)

Clean crab, removing all cartilage and bone. In a medium bowl, combine eggs, mayonnaise, parsley, mustard, salt, and pepper; mix well. Add crab and mix lightly. Cover and refrigerate at least 2 hours.

Heat oil to 340°F in a deep-fryer. Form mixture into 8 cakes. Coat crab cakes with cracker crumbs. Carefully place crab cakes in hot oil and deep-fry until golden brown, about 2 minutes. (Or, heat 3 tablespoons oil in a skillet over medium-high heat. Sauté crab cakes in hot oil for about 2 minutes per side.) Serve garnished with lemon or with a sauce, if desired.

VEGETABLE CREPES

Yield: 4 servings

3 tablespoons olive oil

2 cups peeled, seeded, and diced tomatoes

½ cup finely diced green bell pepper

¼ cup finely diced onion

¼ cup finely diced yellow squash

¼ cup finely diced zucchini

1 clove garlic, minced

2 teaspoons chopped green onions

2 teaspoons chopped fresh parsley

1 teaspoon dried basil

8 Savory Crepe Shells (*recipe follows*)

⅓ cup grated Swiss cheese

¼ cup grated Parmesan cheese

Preheat oven to 350°F. Heat olive oil in a skillet. Add tomatoes, bell pepper, onion, squash, zucchini, and garlic. Sauté until onion is wilted. Add green onions, parsley, and basil; simmer until moisture evaporates. Remove from heat.

Place crepe shells on a flat surface and spoon filling down the center of each crepe. Roll up and place on a baking sheet. Top with grated cheeses. Heat in oven until cheese melts.

SAVORY CREPE SHELLS

Yield: 14–16 shells

1 cup all-purpose flour

1 teaspoon double-acting baking powder

1 teaspoon salt

2 tablespoons melted butter

1 cup milk

⅓ cup minced fresh parsley or chives

Sift flour, baking powder, and salt into a mixing bowl. In a separate bowl, beat together butter and milk. Whisk in herbs. Make a well in dry ingredients and pour in the liquid ingredients; mix well. Cover and refrigerate 4 to 6 hours.

Oil a 5-inch skillet or crepe pan and place over medium heat. Pour in a small amount of batter, about 3 tablespoons, and tilt pan so batter coats the bottom of the pan. Cook over moderate heat until bottom of crepe is brown, then flip over and brown the other side. Remove crepe from pan and transfer to a plate. Repeat this process until all crepes have been cooked.

MINNESOTA WILD RICE SOUP

Yield: 8 servings | Adapted from a recipe by Chef Terry Newkirk

Wild rice is the official state grain of Minnesota, the only region in the United States where this aquatic grass plant is native. The seed of the wild rice plant was important to early Native Americans, who could store it indefinitely after curing. "Lake rice" refers to wild rice that grows naturally, while "paddy rice" is the name for cultivated rice.

¾ cup uncooked wild rice

3 cups water

2 tablespoons butter

2 cloves fresh garlic, chopped

1 carrot, finely diced

1 rib celery, finely diced

1 cup finely diced onion

½ cup sliced fresh mushrooms

¼ teaspoon white pepper

⅛ teaspoon black pepper

⅛ teaspoon granulated garlic

8 cups chicken stock

⅓ cup blond roux (*see page 24*)

⅓ cup heavy cream

2 tablespoons sherry

⅔ cup milk, heated

Chopped fresh parsley (for garnish)

Combine wild rice and water in a medium saucepan. Cover and simmer for 45 minutes, or until rice is tender.

Melt butter in a large soup pot. Add garlic, carrot, celery, onion, mushrooms, peppers, and granulated garlic. Sauté until onion is transparent.

Add stock and bring to boil, then reduce heat to a simmer. Cook 30 minutes.

Add roux, blending and whipping until mixture is smooth and thick.

Add wild rice, cream, and sherry. Return to a boil, then reduce heat and simmer 15 minutes.

Remove from heat. Add milk and adjust seasoning and consistency. To serve, ladle into bowls and garnish with parsley.

CRAWFISH PIE

Yield: 6 servings

3 tablespoons vegetable oil

2 cloves garlic, minced

1 rib celery, chopped

½ large onion, chopped

½ green bell pepper, chopped

1 whole bay leaf

¼ teaspoon dried basil

¼ teaspoon dried oregano

¼ teaspoon dried thyme

¼ teaspoon black pepper

Cayenne

1 tablespoon tomato paste

3 cups seafood stock

½ cup dark roux (*see page 24*)

1 pound crawfish tails, cleaned

½ cup chopped green onions

1 puff pastry sheet, 10" × 15", thawed
    if frozen

Egg wash (1 egg beaten with
    1 tablespoon water)

Lemon wedges (for garnish)

Heat oil in a heavy-bottomed saucepan. Add garlic, celery, onion, bell pepper, bay leaf, basil, oregano, thyme, black pepper, and cayenne. Sauté until onion is transparent. Add tomato paste and mix well.

Add stock and bring to a boil, then reduce heat and simmer 10 minutes.

Blend in roux and simmer until mixture thickens, approximately 20 minutes.

Add crawfish and green onions. Adjust taste and consistency.

Preheat oven to 375°F. Prepare pie tops by cutting circles of puff pastry ¼ inch smaller in diameter than plates. Remove bay leaf and spoon hot crawfish mixture into ovenproof soup plates. Top with pastry circles. Brush pastry with egg wash and prick with a sharp knife. Bake until golden brown, about 35 minutes. Garnish with lemon wedges.

KAHLÚA CREPES

Yield: 10 servings

10 Crepe Shells (*recipe follows*)

10 cups Mocha Cream Filling (*recipe follows*)

4 cups Kahlúa Butter Sauce (*recipe follows*)

10 long-stemmed fresh strawberries, cut into fans

Lay a crepe shell flat on a dessert plate. Using a pastry bag, pump a large line of mocha cream filling down the center of the crepe. Fold crepe in half and center it on the plate. Using a pastry bag with a star tip, decorate outside folded round edge of filled crepe with filling. Repeat process for remaining crepes.

Spoon warm Kahlúa Butter Sauce over crepes and garnish with strawberry fans.

CREPE SHELLS

Yield: 14 to 16 crepes

¾ cup all-purpose flour, sifted

2 tablespoons confectioners' sugar

1 teaspoon double-acting baking powder

½ teaspoon salt

2 eggs, beaten

⅔ cup milk

⅓ cup water

½ teaspoon vanilla extract

Combine flour, confectioners' sugar, baking powder, and salt. Sift together into a mixing bowl.

In a separate bowl, beat together eggs, milk, water, and vanilla.

Make a well in dry ingredients and pour in the liquid ingredients; mix well. Cover and refrigerate 4 to 6 hours.

Oil a 5-inch skillet or crepe pan and place over medium heat. Pour in a small amount of batter, about 3 tablespoons, and tilt pan so batter coats the bottom of the pan. Cook over moderate heat until bottom of crepe is brown, then flip over and brown the other side. Remove crepe from pan and transfer to a plate. Repeat this process until all crepes have been cooked.

NOTE:

This recipe contains raw egg yolks. There is a small chance of salmonella poisoning when consuming raw eggs.

MOCHA CREAM FILLING

Yield: 10 cups

½ cup Kahlúa liqueur
¼ cup instant coffee granules
4 egg yolks (*see Note*)

½ cup sugar
1 quart heavy cream

In a small bowl, combine Kahlúa and instant coffee granules; blend well.

In a mixing bowl, beat egg yolks on high speed of electric mixer for 15 seconds. Slowly add sugar and continue beating until mixture is thick and lemon-colored. Reduce mixer speed to medium and blend in Kahlúa mixture. Slowly add cream and beat on high speed of electric mixer until stiff peaks form.

KAHLÚA BUTTER SAUCE

Yield: 3 cups

1 cup (2 sticks) butter
2½ cups dark brown sugar (1 pound)

1 cup heavy cream
¼ cup Kahlúa liqueur

Melt butter in a medium saucepan. Add brown sugar and mix well.

Add cream and bring to a boil, then reduce heat to a low simmer. Cook until slightly thickened, about 2 minutes. Add Kahlúa and blend well. Remove from heat.

Black-Eyed Pea Salad, recipe on page 225

Coda

ON FEBRUARY 3, 2009, Harry Phillips, a business owner, licensed boat captain, and preservationist, leased the *Delta Queen* from Ambassadors International, Inc., with the promise to operate the boat as a "temporary" permanently moored hotel in Chattanooga, Tennessee. On June 5, 2009, the grand old lady received her first guests in her new setting. Ambassadors International has since declared Chapter 11 bankruptcy. In May 2011, TAC Cruises, an affiliate of Xanterra Holding Corporation, purchased the company's assets, including the *Delta Queen*, which is still operating as a boutique hotel in Chattanooga.

Efforts are still underway to persuade Congress to pass the SOLAS exemption so that the *Delta Queen* can sail overnight.

Shrimp Creole, recipe on page 161, photo by Ed Ball Jr.

Acknowledgments

MANY THANKS TO . . .

. . . the following institutions for access to their archives: The Clementine Paddleford Collection of the Richard L. D. and Marjorie J. Morse Department of Special Collections at Kansas State University, the California Historical Society of San Francisco, the Collection of the Public Library of Cincinnati and Hamilton County, the Jimmy Carter Library, the San Francisco Maritime National Historical Park, the California State Library at Sacramento, the Haggin Museum at Stockton, the Cincinnati Historical Society, the Missouri Historical Society, the Howard-Tilton Memorial Library at Tulane University, the Louisiana Secretary of State Office, The Historic New Orleans Collection, and the East Baton Rouge Parish Library;

. . . the *Delta King* Hotel, Vanessa Bloy of Majestic America Line, Scott Atthowe of Atthowe Fine Art, the *Louisville Courier-Journal,* Rick Rodgers, and Jeffrey Spear of Riverview Antiques;

. . . former crew members and employees for their firsthand insights: Joe Cornyn, Greg Abbott, Missy O'Neill, Tracey Smith, Rich Campbell, Paul Penta, Jim Reising, Keith Tinnin, Nadine Louviere, Bob Schad, Brandon Gipson, Darryl Reed, Pat Taylor, Mary Sward Charlton, Captain Donald Sanders, Captain Bob Reynolds, and especially Captain Clarke C. "Doc" Hawley;

. . . Chefs Gary Darling, Kathy Starr, Howie Velie, and Joe Cahn; former chief steward Sir Robin Hixson; Chefs Robert Harrington, Paul Wayland-Smith, Herbert C. Cade Jr.; and, above all, Terry Newkirk;

. . . the many, many passengers who shared their stories, menus, and photographs, and especially to the following: Laura Yorg, Bob Snyder, Barbara Hameister, Pat Traynor, David Dewey, Judy Patsch, and Jane Carey, with a great big thanks to JoAnn Schoen;

. . . historians who provided invaluable details: Bill Stritzel, Branwell Fanning, and Stan Garvey;

. . . Faun Fenderson and Ellen Sistrunk for testing recipes;

. . . Melinda Winans and Cheramie Sonnier for lending me their plates and bowls;

. . . and Susan Tucker of Newcomb College and Michael Mizell Nelson of the University of New Orleans for persuading me to write about food.

I am enormously grateful for Riverboat Dave's website at www.riverboatdaves.com, food historian Lynne Olver of www.foodtimeline.org, the posters on www.steamboats.org, and in particular to R. Dale Flick for pointing me in the right direction when I was lost;

. . . and finally, to my husband, Howard, for assuming the role of official taste-tester, for allowing me to neglect him, and, most of all, for his encouragement.

RECIPE CREDITS

All recipes received from chefs have been edited to conform to a consistent style, but the ingredients and preparation instructions have not been changed.

Chef Karea Anderson: *Mississippi Queen* Bread Pudding, Whiskey Sauce

Chef Herbert C. Cade Jr.: Baking-Powder Biscuits, Beignets, Buttermilk Pancakes, French Toast, New Orleans–Style Barbecue Shrimp, Tiramisu, Tiramisu Filling, Turtle Soup, Wild Mushroom Bruschetta

Chef Joe Cahn: Pralines

Chef Gary Darling: Eggs Crawkitty, Tasso Crawfish Hollandaise

Cincinnati Historical Society Library at Cincinnati Museum Center: Steamboat Mint Julep

The Cook Book of the United States Navy (1944; recipes identified by Joe Cornyn): Beef Chili Con Carne, Beef Goulash, Beef Stew, Cherry Roll, Cherry Sauce, Macaroni and Corn au Gratin with Bacon, Pork Chop Suey, Pot Roast of Beef (Braised Beef), Savory Brown Gravy

Brandon Gipson: Bloody Mary, Cape Cod, Iced Tea Julep, Mimosa, Salty Dog, Stoli Raspberry Cosmo

Dr. Robert J. Harrington: Fried Green Tomatoes with Remoulade Sauce, Roast Pork Loin with 3-Chile Jus

Sir Robin Hixson: Antipasto (Italian Salad), Black-Bottom Cheesecake, Crab Cakes,

Creamed Spinach, *Delta Queen*'s Famous Pepper-Dill Salad Dressing, Fruit with Honey Sauce, Missouri Blackberry Custard Pie, Popcorn Soup, Ratatouille, Steamboat Salad, Thanksgiving Turkey Dressing, Unbaked Pie Crust (10-inch)

Kansas State University, Clementine Paddleford Collection, Richard L. D. and Marjorie J. Morse Department of Special Collections (originally printed in *This Week* magazine, August 31, 1958): Blackberry Cobbler, Cornbread, Hush Puppies, Po-Boy Pudding

Manual for Army Cooks (1896): Pemmican

Newark (OH) Advocate (September 3, 1976): *Delta Queen*'s Roast Duckling, Orange–Green Onion Sauce, Regal Port Wine Sauce

Chef Terry Newkirk: Acadian Bisque, Apple Brown Betty, Beer and Cheese Soup, Butternut Squash Bisque, Cajun Crawfish and Pasta, Cajun Potato Salad, Calvados Sauce, Corn and Crab Bisque, Frog Legs Meunière, Lemon Crepes, Lemon Sauce, Marinade for Pork Tenderloin, Marinated Pork Tenderloin, Meunière Sauce, Minnesota Wild Rice Soup, Mocha Pecan Glaze, Muffuletta N'Awlins, Sesame Chicken, Sour Cream Raisin Pie, Speckled Trout Pecan, Steak Winona, Summertime Snowballs

From the *Delta Queen* recipe archives of Chef Terry Newkirk: Baby Back Ribs, Bananas Foster, Béchamel Sauce, Beer Batter, Beer Batter (for Brie), Beer Batter (for Shrimp), Beer-Battered Brie, Black Beans, Blackened Seasoning, Bourbon Sauce, Cajun Seasoning, Caviar Mousse, Ceasar Salad, Chicken and Andouille Gumbo, Chicken New Madrid, Chicken Pan Sauce, Chicken Velouté, Chili Dressing, Chilled Asparagus Salad with Raspberry Vinaigrette, Citrus and Watercress Salad, Cocktail Sauce, Coconut Beer-Battered Shrimp, Country Roast Chicken, Crawfish *en Croûte,* Crawfish Fritters, Crawfish Pie, Cream of Cauliflower Soup, Cream of Tomato Soup, Crepe Shells, *Delta Queen* Bread Pudding, Dijon Mustard Sauce, Garlic Toast, Gazpacho, Green Peppercorn Sauce, Ham, Cheese, and Red Bell Pepper Omelet, Honey Mustard Sauce, Italian Dressing, Jumbo Shrimp Cocktail, Kahlúa Butter Sauce, Kahlúa Crepes, Kentucky Chicken-Rice Chowder, Kiev Butter, Lighthouse Salad, Marinara Sauce, Marinated Mushrooms, Marinated Tenderloin, Mocha Cream Filling, Navy Bean Soup, Olive Salad, Oyster Po-Boy, Oyster Stew Dulac, Praline Sauce, Raspberry Sauce, Raspberry Vinaigrette, Red Beans and Rice, Roux (commercial recipe), Seafood Gumbo, Shrimp Creole, Shrimp Étouffée, Skillet Cornbread, Southern Chicken Pot Pie, Southern Fried Catfish, Southern-Style Fried Chicken, Spaghetti and Meatballs, Steak Diane, Steamboat Pudding, Steamed Lobster, Strawberry Pie, Strawberry Shortcake, Vegetable Crepes, Vegetable Soup

Old-Fashioned Holidays: Great Guest Chefs pamphlet by the Delta Queen Steamboat Company (1995): Gingerbread House and Cookie Ornaments, Royal Icing

Recipes from the Heartland pamphlet by the Delta Queen Steamboat Company (August 2001): Cheddar–Garlic Grits Spoon Bread, Crab and Asparagus Chowder, Roast Duck and Wild Rice Soup, Roast Duck Stock

Captain Bob Reynolds: Crème de Menthe Parfait

Chef Kathy Starr: Banana Pudding, Meringue, Southern Praline Pecan Pie, Sweet Potato Pie, Unbaked Pie Crusts (9-inch)

Chef Howie Velie: Black-Eyed Pea Salad, Buttermilk Ranch Dressing, Creole Tomato Sauce, Fancy Fried Chicken, Flash Sautéed Collards, Fried Catfish with Creole Tomato Sauce, Fried Chicken Salad, Lobster Baton Rouge, Low Country Shrimp Boil, Marinade for Fancy Fried Chicken, Mock Turtle Soup, Pimiento Cheese, Savannah Spice Blend, Smashed Potatoes

Chef Paul Wayland-Smith: Bayou Stuffed Catfish, Cajun Beurre Blanc Sauce, Corn and Potato Chowder, Cream of Five Onion Soup, Fried Green Tomatoes, Seasonal Fresh Berries in a Pastry Cup with Fresh Lemon Cream

Adapted by the author from *Delta Queen* archival recipes and from recipes submitted by various *Delta Queen* chefs: Mississippi Mud Pie, Remoulade Sauce

Contributed by the author: Calas, Roux (for home use), Stage Planks, and Yaka Mein

References

"About Wild Rice," Shoal Lake Wild Rice, Inc. www.canoewildrice.com/About-Wild-Rice.page (accessed November 22, 2011).

Arpy, Jim. *The Magnificent Mississippi.* Grinnell, IA: Sutherland Publishing, 1983.

Bates, Captain Nick. *Pinch of Salt: A Collection of Nautical Expressions and Other Stories.* Dobbs Ferry, NY: Sheridan House, 2006.

Bienvenu, Melissa. "The Final Turn." *Country Roads Magazine,* February 2008: 38–41.

"Birth of a Cocktail: History of the Bloody Mary," *Tabasco Pepper Fest.* www.tabasco.com/taste_tent/menu_planning/bloody_mary.cfm (accessed November 21, 2011).

Brown, Alan. *Haunted Places in the American South.* Jackson: University Press of Mississippi, 2002.

"The Coffee Trade and the Port of New Orleans." Louisiana Department of Culture, Recreation & Tourism website. www.crt.state.la.us/museum/online_exhibits/Coffee_Trade/ (accessed November 20, 2011).

Creecy, Col. James R. *Scenes in the South, and Other Miscellaneous Pieces.* Washington, D.C.: T. McGill, 1860.

Davidson, Alan. *The Oxford Companion to Food.* Oxford: Oxford University Press, 2006.

"*Delta Queen* to Be Back in Service." *Chillicothe (MO) Constitution Tribune.* May 18, 1982.

Dickens, Charles. *American Notes for General Circulation.* London: Chapman & Hall, 1842.

"Dijon Mustard," BurgundyToday.com. www.burgundytoday.com/gourmet-traveller/food/mustard.htm (accessed November 22, 2011).

Egerton, John. *Southern Food: At Home, on the Road, in History.* Chapel Hill: University of North Carolina Press, 1993.

Espy, G. Andrews. "The Greene Line." *Bulletin of the Historical and Philosophical Society of Ohio* 6 (April 1948): 50.

Fanning, Branwell. *The Wartime Adventures of the Delta Queen.* New Orleans: Delta Queen Steamboat Company, 1976.

Field, John. "Country Tub Thumping." *Hamburg (IA) Reporter*. August 26, 1982.

Fitzmorris, Tom. "Pascal's Manale," The New Orleans Menu website. April 17, 2011. www.nomenu .com (accessed November 21, 2011).

Fitzmorris, Tom. *Tom Fitzmorris's New Orleans Food: More Than 225 of the City's Best Recipes to Cook at Home*. New York: Stewart, Tabori & Chang, 2006.

"'Floating Palaces' for the Navy." *New York Times*. June 8, 1941.

Ford, Ashley. "Life on the Ohio: A Captain's View." *Queen City Heritage* 57 (Summer–Fall 1999): 26.

Garvey, Stan. *King & Queen of the River: The Legendary Paddle-Wheel Steamboats Delta King and Delta Queen*. Menlo Park, CA: River Heritage Press, 1995.

"Gingerbread House." *Old-Fashioned Holiday: Great Guest Chefs*. New Orleans: Delta Queen Steamboat Company, 1995. 34–35.

Greene, Letha C. *Long Live the Delta Queen*. New York: Hastings House, 1973.

Hamill, Sean D. "A Riverboat Could Be Cruising to the End of the Line." *New York Times*, October 25, 2007.

Hilliard, Sam Bowers. *Hog Meat and Hoecake: Food Supply in the Old South, 1840–1860*. Carbondale: Southern Illinois University Press, 1972.

Hing, Bill. "The Immigrant as Criminal: Punishing Dreamers." *Research & Seminars, U-Cal-Davis*, no. 4 (October 1998).

Historic Hotels: The Delta Queen. DVD. Produced by John McLean Media. Film Ideas, Inc., 2004.

Holian, Timothy J. *Over the Barrel: The Brewing History and Beer Culture of Cincinnati, 1800 to the Present*, vol. 1. St. Joseph, MO: Sudhaus Press, 2000.

Jones, Evan. *American Food: The Gastronomic Story*. New York: Vintage Books, 1981.

Keating, Bern. *The Legend of the Delta Queen*. New Orleans: Delta Queen Steamboat Company, 1986.

Kenney, William Howland. *Jazz on the River*. Chicago: University of Chicago Press, 2005.

"King and Queen of the Delta." *Pacific Marine Review* (July 1927): 320–24.

Koutsky, Kathryn Strand, and Linda Koutsky. *Minnesota Vacation Days: An Illustrated History*. St. Paul: Minnesota Historical Society, 2006.

Kuhl, Alice, ed. *Steam Cuisine—Taste of Tall Stacks '99*. Cincinnati: C. J. Krehbiel Co., 1999.

Lovegren, Sylvia. *Fashionable Food: Seven Decades of Food Fads*. Chicago: University of Chicago Press, 2005.

Lustig, Lillie S., S. Claire Sondheim, and Sarah Rensel. *The Southern Cook Book of Fine Old Recipes*. Reading, PA: Culinary Arts Press, 1935.

"Man Is Charged in Boat Slaying." *Charleston (VA) Gazette*. July 2, 1960.

"Mardi Gras Special Leaves Cincinnati Waterfront Dock." *Lima News*. February 20, 1949.

Mils, Mimi, and Tom Burkett. *The Legendary Delta Queen*, ed. Mary Pax. New Orleans: Delta Queen Steamboat Company, 1997.

"162 Years of Boating on *Delta Queen*: End of an Era?" *Pasadena (CA) Star-News*, March 18, 1973.

Moss, Robert F. "The Fried Green Tomato Swindle." August 19, 2007. www.robertfmoss.com/ 2007/08/fried-green-tomato-swindle.html (accessed November 27, 2011).

Olver, Lynne. The Food Timeline website. http://www.foodtimeline.org/index.html#about.

Park, Michael Y. "Happy Birthday, Bloody Mary!" The Epi-log. www.epicurious.com/articles-guides/blogs/editor/2008/12/happy-birthday.html (accessed November 21, 2011).

The Picayune's Creole Cook Book. 2nd ed. New Orleans: Picayune Publishing, 1901.

Price, Charlene C. "Foodservice Sales Reflect the Prosperous, Time-Pressed 1990s." *Food Marketing* (September–December 2000): 23.

Quick, Herbert. *Mississippi Steamboatin': A History of Steamboating on the Mississippi and Its Tributaries.* New York: H. Holt and Co., 1926.

Rayser, Dr. V. Fred. "Ghosts of the Mississippi River." *FATE Magazine.* October 1, 2000.

"River Mint." *Louisville Courier.* September 2, 1960.

Rodgers, Rick, and the Delta Queen Steamboat Co. *Mississippi Memories: Classic American Cooking from the Heartland to the Louisiana Bayou.* New York: Hearst Books, 1994.

Root, Waverley, and Richard de Rochemont. *Eating in America.* New York: Ecco Press, 1981.

Sellers, Jeremy. *Delta Queen* Offers Leisurely Ride on the Tombigbee River." *South Alabamian,* August 10, 2006.

Starr, Kathy. *The Soul of Southern Cooking.* Jackson: University Press of Mississippi, 1989.

Stevens, Patricia Bunning. *Rare Bits: Unusual Origins of Popular Recipes.* Athens: Ohio University Press, 1998.

Tassin, Myron, ed. *The Delta Queen: Last of the Paddlewheel Palaces.* 1973. Gretna, La.: Pelican Publishing, 2004.

Trollope, Frances. *Domestic Manners of the Americans,* 1832. www.gutenberg.org/catalog/world/readfile?fk_files=1476422 (accessed December 1, 2012).

Tucker, Susan, ed. *New Orleans Cuisine: Fourteen Signature Dishes and Their Histories.* Jackson: University Press of Mississippi, 2009.

Twain, Mark. "Food Quotes" at FoodReference.com. www.foodreference.com/html/qneworleans-food.html (accessed November 20, 2011).

Vasconcelos, Travis C. "The *Delta Queen* Calliope." *www.steamboats.org/whistle-calliope/ecaliope. html* (accessed November 23, 2011).

Way, Frederick, Jr. *The Saga of the Delta Queen.* Cincinnati: Young and Klein, Inc., 1951.

"Welcoming Ceremony Is Set on Monday for *Delta Queen.*" *Muscatine (IA) Journal,* October 1, 1971.

Wooten, James T. "Jazz Cruise Revives Glory of New Orleans." *New York Times,* December 8, 1972.

French Toast, recipe on page 247

General Index

Recipe Index